W9-AFQ-904

The Everyday Nation-State

THE
EVERYDAY
NATION-
STATE

◇◇◇◇◇◇◇◇◇◇◇◇◇◇◇◇◇◇◇◇◇◇◇◇◇◇◇

Community & Ethnicity
in Nineteenth-Century
Nicaragua • Justin Wolfe

The University of Nebraska Press
Lincoln and London

Publication of this volume was assisted by a grant from the School of Liberal Arts, Tulane University.

A slightly different version of chapter 4 was originally published as "Those That Live by the Work of Their Hands: Labour, Ethnicity, and Nation-State Formation in Nicaragua, 1850–1900," *Journal of Latin American Studies* 36 (2004): 57–83. Copyright © 2004 by Cambridge University Press. Reproduced with permission.

© 2007 by the Board of Regents of the University of Nebraska
All rights reserved
Manufactured in the United States of America
♾

Library of Congress Cataloging-in-Publication Data
Wolfe, Justin, 1968–
The everyday nation-state: community and ethnicity in nineteenth-century Nicaragua / Justin Wolfe.
p.   cm.
"A slightly different version of chapter 4 was originally published as "Those That Live by the Work of Their Hands: Labour, Ethnicity, and Nation-State Formation in Nicaragua, 1850–1900," Journal of Latin American Studies 36."
Includes bibliographical references and index.
ISBN 978-0-8032-4818-2 (cloth: alk. paper)
1. Nicaragua—Politics and government—1838–1909. 2. Nationalism—Nicaragua. 3. National state. 4. Ethnicity—Nicaragua. I. Title.
F1526.27.W65   2007
972.85′044—dc22
2007003291

Set in Adobe Garamond and Gill Sans by Bob Reitz.
Designed by Ashley Johnston.

Contents

Illustrations

Figures

Maps

Tables

Acknowledgments

Seneca once said that no good thing is pleasant without friends to share it. Researching and writing this book was pleasant indeed, and it is a joy to thank the many friends who helped me along the way. At the University of California, Los Angeles, I was encouraged, guided, and challenged at every step by fellow travelers of many stripes. The late E. Bradford Burns, José Moya, Mary Yeager, and James Lockhart all taught me how to be a historian. So too did Jeffrey Gould (Indiana University), whose generosity and fellowship in a time of need are treasured gifts. They have all left an imprint on me and on this book, and it is better for their efforts. Many other colleagues did the same and I thank them all, but some are due special remembrance, for without the particular kindnesses of Eric Schantz, Cathy Komisaruk, Omar Valerio-Jiménez, Kristen McCleary, and Tom Mertes, I would have never completed this project. None of us would have survived UCLA very long without the wisdom and boundless heart of Beebee Bernstein. And finally, I would not have begun this journey without Steve Volk, who first taught me the history of Latin America at Oberlin College and who remains ever a friend and inspiration.

My research in Nicaragua and Guatemala was made possible by a number of institutions that provided financial support, facilities for research, and professional collegiality. I am grateful for funding from the Institute of International Education Fulbright Program and the UCLA Latin American Center. Completion of the book was aided by summer research support from Tulane University, especially through the Georges Lurcy Fund, Newcomb College, and the Roger Thayer Stone Center for Latin American Studies. In Nicaragua, the Instituto de Historia de Nicaragua y Centro América and its director,

Margarita Vannini, supported my work at every step. Ana Rosa Morales and Eliazar Morales made working in the Archivo de la Municipalidad y de la Prefectura de Granada a pleasure. Dieter Stadler and the Casa de los Tres Mundos have always provided me a haven and home away from home. I must also thank the staff of the Registro Público of Granada for putting up with a researcher in the midst of their functioning public office. A special debt is owed to Dr. Hector Mena Guerrero, who was generous with his time and without whom I would not have discovered Granada's notarial archive. In Guatemala, the Archivo General de Centro América and its staff made my time there a breeze.

In my travels and travails I have been fortunate to share the intellectual and personal camaraderie of people who made my work worthwhile and improved it and me along the way. In Nicaragua these include Margarita Vannini, Frances Kinloch Tijerino, Miguel Angel Herrera Cuarezma, Dieter Stadler, Alvaro Rivas, Fernando Lopez, and Johannes Kranz. Maricela Kauffman and Galio Gurdián have always been there with good food, good conversation, and a room with a view. These friends, along with Michel Gobat, Aldo Lauria-Santiago, Jeff Gould, Lowell Gudmundson, Julie Charlip, Virginia Garrard-Burnett, and Elizabeth Dore, remind me why I am a Central Americanist. My life in New Orleans would not be what it is without my colleagues in both the History Department and the Stone Center for Latin American Studies at Tulane University.

A number of scholars and friends have read various stages of this work over the years and helped me improve it in innumerable ways. I am particularly indebted to Julie Charlip, Elizabeth Dore, Michel Gobat, Galio Gurdián, Daniel Hurewitz, Aldo Lauria-Santiago, Tom Luongo, Marc McLeod, Marline Otte, Pablo Piccato, Steven Pierce, Michael Snodgrass, Edith Wolfe, Elliott Young, and the anonymous readers of University of Nebraska Press. This book also benefited from the care and attention it received at the University of Nebraska Press. The excitement and aplomb of Elizabeth Demers, who originally championed this project, carried over to Heather Lundine. In shepherding it to completion, she, along with Sabrina Stellrecht, have been a joy to work with. Jonathan Lawrence's copyediting was wonderfully thoughtful and careful. I deeply appreciated everyone's advice, even if I did not always heed it.

Nonacademic families must wonder why their children pursue the seeming insanity of this career. Thankfully, mine has given me its unstinting support and love. My mother and stepfather, Helaine and Lew Randerson, and my father, Michael Wolfe, read my work, listened to my ideas, cheered my progress, and provided safe harbor from the storms of life. If we got to choose our families, I would choose them. I did get to choose Edie—and thankfully she chose me, too. She is my best friend and my true love, and everything is so much more pleasant when shared with her.

The Everyday Nation-State

Introduction

Civil war broke out once more among Nicaragua's elites in 1854, the latest in a series that had marked the period since Nicaragua gained its independence from Spain in 1821. Hoping to acquire an advantage this time around, the Liberals of León contracted with American military adventurer William Walker. Walker and his men entered Nicaragua in 1856 and defeated the Conservatives of Granada but then turned upon their Liberal allies and conquered the entire country. He reinstituted slavery, which had been abolished in 1825, began to confiscate properties, and held a sham election to claim the presidency. In the end, he hoped to claim dominion over all of Central America. The Conservatives and Liberals regrouped and united, and with the help of military forces from their Central American neighbors they carried on a successful but devastating two-year campaign to expel Walker. The so-called National War (Guerra Nacional) and Walker's scorched-earth retreat in 1857 left Nicaragua in ruins. As the country's elites attempted to understand how and why they had arrived at such a moment in their history, they questioned the sources of their disunity, their position in an emerging world of nation-states, and their relationship to their fellow Nicaraguans.

Decades of political and cultural fragmentation had followed Nicaraguan independence in 1821. Regional *caudillos* (regional strongmen) and relatively autonomous towns dominated the political landscape in a country of city-states; the occasional, transitory "state" proved feeble at the most basic tasks of coercion and taxation.

Rural communities, especially indigenous ones, remained in many ways worlds apart from the few institutional structures that did exist—not that these communities were closed to the world around them; rather, they tended to retain significant cultural and political autonomy. Civil war and rebellion were commonplace, frustrating attempts to overcome the often petty differences that separated elites from one another.

After independence, liberal ideals of citizenship and nation pervaded elite discourse, but such ideals rarely led to action. Elites of all stripes advocated a liberal project of modernity that heralded an increasingly secular, interventionist state, a growing export economy, an ample labor supply, and expanded private landholding.[1] In the first decades after independence, notions of a Nicaraguan nation seemed too fluid and gossamer to overcome the elites' divergent social and political desires or to engage Nicaragua's local communities. Although initially there had been fairly significant subaltern support for Walker's invasion, the war to oust Walker did not so much spur the elites to reconceptualize the nation as to foreground it in their political imagination. There was no transfiguration of elite identity or epiphany of brotherhood. Rather, the elites came to see the nation as the umbrella under which liberalism could be conceptualized as a shared project.

The National War forced Nicaragua's elites to confront the consequences of their failure to construct a viable polity. In broadsheets and newspapers, speeches and correspondence, both Liberals and Conservatives argued that overcoming their bloody history required building the country anew as a nation-state: strong, unified, activist, sovereign, and inclusive. This vision of the nation-state entailed profound transformations in the political, economic, social, and cultural underpinnings of society. By the end of the nineteenth century, and despite a legacy of internal conflict, Nicaragua had undergone seemingly alchemical changes.

The size and scope of the state, military, and police (previously ramshackle structures barely worthy of the term "institution") expanded, increasingly impinging upon people's daily lives. The national infrastructure developed, with new roads, railroads, telegraphs, and ports propelling changes in both the internal and external economies. The state curbed the autonomy of the Roman Catholic Church, taking from it responsibility for education and social welfare. Land-tenure patterns shifted from mostly communal toward private landholding. Smallholding expanded, but so too did the land-poor laboring population. These shifts, in turn, eroded the institutional bases of indigenous communities and identity, and, in some areas, appeared to disrupt it completely. Finally, the elision of Nicaragua's multiple ethnic identities allowed for the nation to be defined as explicitly non-indigenous (ladino) and only implicitly mixed (mestizo).

How can we account for such startling changes? How did the project take root when just a decade earlier it was so vehemently despised that throngs took up machetes and sticks to attack its advocates and agents? Put another way, what is it that leads people to see a state as their State, to see themselves as its sovereign subjects? The answer is found not so much in the coercive imposition of elite ideology as in the construction of a nation-state that made this ideology appear, if not commonsensical and natural, then at least legitimate. Throughout the nineteenth century, Nicaragua was a fundamentally agrarian, multiethnic society. A project of liberal modernity meant to upend such a world, and, inevitably, land, labor, and ethnic identity became the flash points of struggle and negotiation. As such, my study concentrates on these core arenas, tracing out their material and discursive changes, at once distinct and intertwined. The analysis relies on a wide range of newly available archival sources to explore the state's negotiation with local communities to legitimize the nation-state. Through this process the state created localized forms of state institutions that enmeshed the liberal project within the everyday life of the community.

Colony, Nation, and Place

Although Nicaragua shone like a bright gem to Spanish conquistadores during the first decades of conquest, by the mid-sixteenth century

Map 1. The kingdom of Guatemala in colonial Central America

it settled into the quiet, almost hermetic existence typical of peripheral colonies in the emerging Spanish empire. The initial economy
relied on Indian slavery and mining, but these had been exhausted by
the mid-sixteenth century. Indian slavery was extinguished by 1550,
but not before as many as half a million Indians had been shipped
in bondage to Panama and Peru. Nicaragua's Indian population collapsed even further from European-borne diseases, so that by 1581
more than 90 percent of the original indigenous population had disappeared.[2] Once the Spaniards' easy money-making opportunities
had disappeared, they were left with agriculture; but without large
Indian populations to work the fields, the local economy became almost entirely subsistence in nature. While in Peru small *encomiendas*

4

(royal grants of Indian labor and tribute) to prominent Spaniards, encompassed thousands of Indians, in Nicaragua large ones were limited to a few hundred people. Mining and small-scale merchants remained throughout the sixteenth century, but British pirates made these activities costly and only intermittently remunerative. Furthermore, the establishment of the kingdom of Guatemala and its *audiencia* (regional court of appeals) in 1570 directed limited imperial resources away from Nicaragua and solidified its position as a marginal colony (see map 1).

Although the western part of Nicaragua was fairly quickly pacified, the eastern half was never more than nominally under Spanish control during the colonial period.[3] The semi-sedentary indigenous groups of the eastern hinterlands resisted the Spanish throughout the colonial period. While this area remained a terra incognita for the Spanish, the British began engaging the indigenous, and later African, inhabitants. This created a series of problems for the Spanish. First, the British planted a stake in the mainland Americas from which to contest Spanish hegemony. Second, it began a period of cultural connections with the British that exacerbated indigenous antipathy toward the Spanish and, in the long run, produced a more Anglicized regional identity. Third, it brought into question "Nicaragua" as a coherent territory. Although the British were temporarily forced to abandon Nicaragua from 1783 to 1816, and eventually gave up technical control of the Caribbean coast region in 1860 with the signing of the Treaty of Managua, none of these situations changed significantly and the newly independent state of Nicaragua would not gain effective control of the region until 1894.

Even within the sphere of Spanish control, political and economic rivalry separated the two main centers of population, León and Granada.[4] Although Granada was founded first, in 1524, León was designated as the province's colonial capital. Neither city, however, exercised enough economic power to overwhelm the other and compel its undivided loyalty. These problems were exacerbated by the Bourbon reforms, which inclined Granada to seek greater independence from León, and León to tighten its grip over the entire province. Perhaps not surprisingly, then, it was in Granada that the first rumblings for independence were heard in response to Spain's crisis of power during the Napoleonic Wars and the Cortes of Cádiz. Even the seeming fait accompli of independence that arrived with the news of Mexico's secession from Spain in 1821 did nothing to ameliorate these divisions. In fact, while León voted to join Guatemala and Mexico, Granada declared independence on its own and organized a separate government.

Nicaragua emerged from the economic doldrums of the seventeenth century thanks to investments in cattle, cacao, and cochineal and indigo dye production. Cacao and cattle had been staples of Nicaragua's local isthmian economy, feeding, in particular, a far wealthier Guatemalan market. A boom in chocolate consumption in Europe, however, opened up new opportunities, and Nicaraguan producers expanded to take them. Similarly, the growth of European textile production propelled investment in indigo and cochineal production. While Nicaragua never produced on the scale of neighboring El Salvador, it experienced economic growth unseen in more than a century. The Bourbon reforms in the latter half of the eighteenth century reduced local costs and expanded access to markets. For the first time since the 1500s, Spaniards began immigrating to Nicaragua, introducing new families and wealth unassociated with the descendants of the original wave of colonizers. Indeed, many of the families most associated with wealth and power in Nicaragua today arrived with this new tide of migrants. Despite this boom, the sparse population of Central America's largest province meant that land was plentiful and labor difficult to attract. As in much of Latin America, the diminished state authority that attended independence exacerbated this situation.

The indigenous population of Nicaragua has been estimated to have exceeded half a million at the time of the Spanish encounter. Indian slavery and European-borne disease, however, reduced their numbers by more than 90 percent by the end of the seventeenth century.[5] A census taken in Nicaragua in 1776 claimed a total population of 103,943, of which approximately 45 percent were listed as Indians.[6] Nicaragua held limited attraction to Spaniards for most of the colonial period, leading them to compose a mere 5 percent of the population in 1776. The remaining 50 percent of the population consisted of ladinos (two-thirds mulattoes and one-third mestizos). For the most part, Indians lived in small rural towns or dispersed hamlets and worked in agricultural labor (their own or forced). Spaniards tended to live in León and Granada, although important populations could be found in Rivas and Estelí. They favored large-scale agriculture, commercial endeavors and the professions. The ladino population grew steadily throughout the seventeenth and eighteenth centuries, coming to labor in every sector of society, but most especially as artisans and petty merchants.[7] The growing ladino population, especially in more rural areas, began to challenge indigenous communities for local resources and power and set the stage for conflict after independence when Crown protection of distinct Indian rights and authorities ceased.

While independence emerged in the throes of colonialist ideologies, it hardly culminated in the establishment of a Nicaraguan national identity. Rather, it opened a power vacuum. Wealthy Spaniards and ladinos responded with violent power struggles, while poor ladinos and Indians reacted by retreating from state authority. Moreover, what colonial authorities had long considered stultifying problems for Nicaragua simply worsened. In particular, the rivalry between Granada and León intensified to new levels of bloodletting barbarity, and the eastern half of the region pulled farther away from western control and closer to the British. In this context, the idea of a Nicaraguan nation found fairly unyielding ground in which to take root (see map 2).

Traditionally, nineteenth-century Nicaraguan history is divided into three periods: the years of anarchy from independence in 1821 to 1857, the Conservative Thirty Years from 1858 to 1893, and the Liberal Revolution from 1893 to 1909. In such a narrative, the defin-

Map 2. Nicaragua showing nineteenth-century departmental divisions

ing moments belong to the elite, and the history is of their marking. Nicaragua's subaltern communities might well be part of the nation, but they were to have no constitutive role in its formation. Their part was set, their character defined. The majority of Nicaraguans, however, proved a poor match to this dichotomy; and rather than serve as props in the elites' unfolding narrative of nation, they sought to transform that narrative and their places within it. Although the initial impulse for nation-state formation derives from political elites, the fundamental restructuring of collective identity implied in the process requires a historicizing of the fundamental—though generally disclaimed—role that subalterns play in the process. This is not a top-down process in which elites impose the nation upon the subaltern or fool them with an exoteric "romantic culture," but one in which elites and subalterns negotiate the meaning of the state and national identity from unbalanced power positions. Outright coercion may be used to create and maintain the state, but its protracted use inevitably leads to a denial of the state's legitimacy and to the increased salience of non-national collective social identities. Given the conceptually inclusive nature of national citizenship, traditional mechanisms for ordering and controlling society often prove inadequate for or contradictory to the elites' discourse of nationalism.

Following the National War, a national constituent assembly met to hammer out a new constitution. From its enactment in 1858 this document served unaltered until 1893, when José Santos Zelaya headed a coup that overthrew the government of Roberto Sacasa and began a period of dictatorship that would last until 1909. Zelaya was a committed Liberal in the mold of Guatemalans Justo Rufino Barrios and Manuel Estrada Cabrera, and the constitution he and his compatriots crafted reflected some of the key features that distinguished Liberals from Conservatives. Most notable among these were the abandonment of Catholicism as the official religion, complete religious tolerance, and the abolition of the death penalty.[8] The constitution also appeared to offer a wider manhood suffrage than previously provided, prohibited debt imprisonment, and freed municipalities from executive power oversight. As will become clear in the ensuing chapters, however, most of these changes were only marginally new or just briefly enacted. In 1896 the constitution was revised with hundreds of new provisions, including the reestablishment of incarceration for debts and of executive regulation over municipal government.[9] Zelaya's greatest innovations were dictatorial rule, a more persistent pursuit of Central American union, and a new regional and political balance of power.

Throughout the second half of the nineteenth century, state authority was organized and executed at three distinct levels: national, prefectural, and municipal.[10] Local townspeople who had the right to vote annually elected the mayor (*alcalde*) and municipal council (*regidores*). A number of others, mostly local policing and judicial officials, were also elected at this time. Prefects, chosen by the president (or his designate), had responsibility for the monitoring of municipal officials and had veto power over municipal decrees and taxation. Moreover, municipal conflicts were frequently resolved through prefectural authority. Prefectural authority was subordinate to executive authority. Officials whose jurisdiction went beyond a single municipality, such as agricultural agents, were named by prefects or the president. The president was elected every four years through a popular representative system in which citizens voted for electors who then voted for president. In an effort to promote national unity and institutional stability, each elector voted for two different candidates, one of whom had to be from outside the elector's home prefecture (also known as a department).[11] Despite the executive's apparent monopoly on authority, especially through his naming of prefects and their management of municipal governments, municipalities often contested state authority and frequently met with success.

At the municipal level this power structure was complicated by the numerous indigenous communities that dotted the prefectures of Nicaragua. Although few of these communities owned lands by the 1860s, most retained access to it through *ejidos* (municipal commons) and *cofradías* (lay religious brotherhoods). They also often possessed a coffer (*caja de comunidad*) that provided capital for community needs, be they festivities or the hiring of a lawyer. In addition to these resources, many indigenous communities could rely on their parish priests as mediators with state officials, whether municipal or national. Even more important, however, were indigenous leaders and elders who maintained community political structures and rallied behind community history and "customs and uses" in struggles with municipal, prefectural, and national authorities. Conflict between ladinos and indigenous communities frequently turned on the contested authority of constitutional alcaldes (as municipal mayors were

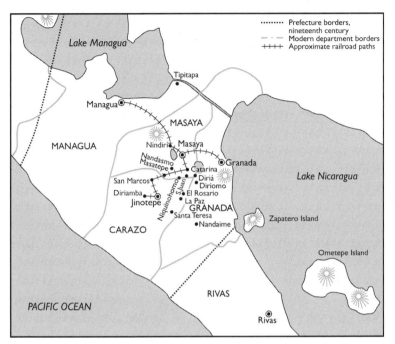

Map 3. The prefecture of Granada

generally called) and indigenous ones. Although ladino authorities often decried the toleration of these pre-republican forms, it was not until 1906 that the Zelaya government even attempted to abolish the communities—an effort that failed.[12]

My research focuses on the prefecture of Granada, politically and economically the most important region of Nicaragua for most of the nineteenth century. For most of the second half of the nineteenth century it encompassed the modern departments of Granada, Masaya, and Carazo, and about 20 percent of the country's population (see map 3). This region possessed considerable geographic, agricultural, demographic, and ethnic diversity. Towns ranged from as few as five hundred inhabitants to as many as fifteen thousand, from almost completely indigenous to completely ladino and mixes of the two. Cattle, coffee, sugar, and subsistence crops were all cultivated, although crops varied by region of the prefecture. This diversity serves as an asset in our analysis as we explore how the politics of nation-state formation played out in everyday experience. Elite-centered analyses tend to ignore such distinctions as epiphenomenal to the macropolitical practices that are equated with nationalism.[13]

The study of ethnicity and ethnic relations offers a useful starting point for thinking about nations and national identity. All collective social identities are premised on a group's relationship to collective "Others" and the construction of difference between them in historically specific circumstances.[14] With ethnic relations, these divisions structure social, economic, and cultural inequality, defining the relative positions of groups within a larger society.[15] As such, ethnicity creates "we-them" relations where difference signifies one's relative social position and where the discourse and experience of ethnicity can differ depending on that position. Nonetheless, while such ethnic relations—and the consciousness of them—develop historically, they can become hegemonic, taking on the appearance of being natural, given attributes that define and structure individual and community life.[16]

The persistent salience of ethnicity is enmeshed with the relations it describes. This suggests both the difficulty of understanding how and why ethnicity breaks down and how central such a question is to the study of nation-state formation. The answer may lie in the complex process through which ethnicity both ceases to be meaningful for the maintenance of structures of inequality and no longer "provide[s] the terms of communal action."[17] The implications are instructive, for they link elite nationalist ideologies with local social, cultural, and political changes. On the one hand, the nation must be inclusive to such a degree as to potentially upend the idea that ethnic difference is entirely incompatible with the nation itself. On the other hand, the modern liberal project that the nation legitimates portends a restructuring of social and economic patterns and institutions so as to undermine the established foundations of ethnic affinity and action.

Benedict Anderson's study of the genesis and diffusion of the nation is by now deeply embedded in the academic (and to some extent popular) imagination.[18] The idea that the nation is a cultural construct meets little resistance outside ultranationalist circles. An enormous literature has worn deep ruts in the paths trod by Anderson and others, such as Eric Hobsbawm and Ernst Gellner.[19] But where these and their followers have shown the power of the national idea, they have failed to detail how these imaginings gained their power in the first place. Anderson, for example, sees states choosing vernacular languages, the advent of the print revolution, and the crisis of certainty engendered by the Enlightenment as the central factors. Even if these were preconditions (and of this I am not convinced), they reveal nothing of the process by which conceptions of identity shift to enact the nation as the ultimate sociopolitical identity. Charles Tilly, by contrast, argues that nationalism emerged as states were forced into "bargaining with their subject populations over the yielding of conscripts, war materials and taxes."[20] Neither author, however, provides a methodology for examining the processes by which such identities are created.

Since the 1990s there has been a great deal of exciting and innovative scholarship on the emergence of national identities, subaltern culture and politics, and struggles over ethnicity, but we have hardly begun to understand the links between local and national politics or the daily struggles over authority, identity, and legitimacy that underpin the rise of nation-states.[21] It is the formation of this everyday nation-state that is at the heart of this book. I argue that we should conceive the nation as a continuous process of struggle over the legitimacy of the state and the meaning of popular sovereignty. Nation is not the sum of particular nationalist practices and ideologies; rather, it is the ceaseless, often mundane playing out of their entanglements. It is neither a program of state planning nor simply the expression of ethnic aspirations for state power, although both may well be nationalistic. These are, rather, manifestations of the process of nation-state formation. Understood in these terms, nation is not dependent on the European Enlightenment (although its political manifestations certainly served this development); nor, by any means, is a literate bourgeoisie necessary.[22]

Nationalists tend to cast the nation as both ancient and eternal, but it arises out of an explicitly constructed ideology, promoted by elites as they confront other states in the world.[23] Their success depends on the degree to which the idea of nation ceases to be openly contested, transforming people's frame of social identity so that its primary political reference is the national state rather than their local, frequently autonomous communities.[24] In some ways, such was already suggested in Eugen Weber's classic *Peasants into Frenchmen*, but Weber's analysis is too enmeshed in modernization theory and imagines this process as the spread of centralized, urban authority and ideology onto peripheral, rural inhabitants. Once Paris decided to incorporate the peasant hinterlands, it simply required the right tools (railroads, mass education, etc.) to carry out the task. Peasants could resist, but they would be overcome and certainly could not change what it meant to be French.[25] By contrast, my approach in this study explores more deeply the complexities and anxieties of the everyday intrusions of the state and how local communities met such challenges through resistance, engagement, and negotiation.[26]

In nineteenth-century Latin America, the nation-states through which elites sought to organize society were new, while the identities they confronted were older and generally more well established. This was not an issue of the "traditional" confronted with the "modern," but rather of the postcolonial state's efforts "to gain control over both the material and semantic practices through which their would-be subjects produce and reproduce the very bases of their existence."[27] Nationalist efforts to refashion social identity, however, cannot simply try to replace or deny non-national identities. Rather, as Clifford Geertz has suggested, the nation-state works to delegitimize other forms of social identity in their relation to the state, "by neutralizing the apparatus of the state in relationship to them, and by channeling discontent arising out of their dislocation into properly political rather than parapolitical forms of expression."[28] Inclusion and dissolution.

To become the dominant mode of sociopolitical identification, the nation-state must proffer a new social identity that elides differences within society through an inherently populist discourse. As Tom Nairn explains, "Although sometimes hostile to democracy, nationalist movements have been invariably populist in outlook and sought to induct lower classes into political life."[29] There is, however, a problem with such a conceptualization. Both Nairn and Anderson deny a constitutive role for the "lower classes" in the formation of the nation-state; no such role is necessary for them, because the national identity is already formed—the "invention" of the middle class or elite.[30]

Recent studies of nationalism in Latin America convincingly demonstrate the inadequacy of this stance.[31] Since membership is conceptually open to everyone, traditional mechanisms for ordering and controlling society often prove inadequate or contradictory to the elites' discourse of nationalism. As Florencia Mallon argues, "Within such a broad vision there [is] much room for disagreement; thus, in any particular case, nationalism [will] become a series of competing discourses in constant formation and negotiation, bounded by particular regional histories of power relations."[32] To understand nation-state formation, then, is to attempt to articulate and analyze these competing discourses and their relationship to the material world of everyday life.[33] The chapters that follow take up this challenge to understand nation-state formation in Nicaragua in the nineteenth century.

Organization of the Text

Understanding this process necessitates an examination of elite ideologies of state and nation in the wake of Nicaragua's independence from Spain. Chapter 1 focuses on the development of these ideologies in the 1830s and 1840s in the face of local and international forces. While many doubted Nicaragua's viability outside a larger Central American union, intense localism and aversion to Guatemalan hegemony provided countervailing forces. Yet Nicaraguan elites, unable to see the nation beyond their brotherhood of class, promoted a project of liberal state formation that generated violence and antipathy in local communities that had long maintained autonomy from colonial state authorities. Although the Liberals and Conservatives evolved a common nationalist language descended from a discourse of patriarchalism, it would take the threats of British and U.S. intervention, and subjugation by U.S. filibuster William Walker, to convince them that their state project would fail without the popular support engendered by a more inclusive nationalism.

Chapter 2 examines the formation of the national state through an analysis of the state's most critical core functions: taxation and coercion.[34] Contrary to earlier assessments of the post-Walker period as one of stagnation, the national state mushroomed in size and scope, with a focus on public works and education on par with that of Costa Rica. At the same time, the chapter explores how local community constructions of identity and politics mediated and constrained the grasp of the national state. Although policy might be formulated in the capital, it succeeded or failed at the local level of adjudication and enforcement.

Chapters 3, 4, and 5 explore the fundamental pillars of Nicaraguan life: land, labor, and ethnicity. Elite nationalism idealized the productive farmer as citizen, excluding the lamentable laborer from such political rights. But such neat divisions butted up against the complicated and often contradictory relationship between the historically ascribed "laboring nature" of indigenous peoples and their equally historical claim to landholding by dint of indigenous community access to communal lands. Moreover, as community political strategies shifted toward an engagement with, rather than a rejection of, the nation-state, community authority (whether indigenous or non-indigenous) waned in the face of national law and institutions.

Chapter 3 traces the efforts to transform Nicaraguan land tenure along liberal lines, pushing to convert communal landholdings into private ones. Although this is generally viewed as the triumph of large landholders, the reality is more complicated. Despite a boom in coffee production beginning in the 1880s, there was no mass land expropriation or creation of a huge landless population. Instead, a new and impressive class of market-oriented smallholders emerged, one that came to identify the state rather than the local community as the legitimate arbiter of land claims. Throughout the colonial period and much of the nineteenth century, land had been divided between communal peasant holdings and large estates. While such holdings continued to exist at the end of the nineteenth century, they were joined by small and medium-size farms whose owners felt invested in national citizenship and who came to dominate local politics. What had been a fairly bifurcated society developed into one of more complex stratification in which social and economic striving found cultural and political expression in the nation-state.

Chapter 4 analyzes the development of the state's institutional apparatus for controlling labor and labor relations. Since the colonial period, elites had defined peasants as laboring people whose subsistence lands allowed for rudimentary consumption. After independence, however, local communities employed both the law and nationalist liberalism to try to reinscribe the meaning of the peasantry. Peasants had a long history of producing surpluses for the market, and with the rise of the coffee economy even minimal holdings could produce a surplus that lifted them out of "laborer" status under the law. Those without access to communal or private lands, however, found themselves dependent on wage labor. Such strategies valued law over community membership, undermining community political organizing.

Chapter 5 analyzes the changing meaning of ethnic identities and the declining autonomy of local communities during the nineteenth century. The project of liberal modernity was expected to sweep away the colonial divisions among peoples of indigenous, European, and African descent, and part of this process was an effort to refuse to recognize such explicit divisions. While European and mixed-race peoples may have accepted this transition to a homogeneous national identity, others balked at such transformations. Beginning in the late 1840s, Nicaraguan leaders came face-to-face with politicized ethnicity as they had never before known it, with widespread indigenous uprisings, Miskitu rejection of Nicaraguan sovereignty, and British reassertion of their protectorate over the Mosquito Coast. Until recently, however, Nicaraguan historiography has relegated indigenous communities to a few episodes of cataclysmic violence and narrated their experiences as uniformly disastrous. Yet, analyzing everyday conflicts within local communities in the post–National War era makes evident that indigenous peoples struggled for their place in the nation. Even in the face of historical racism, however, social and economic environment played a key role in shaping their experiences and determining their relationships with ladinos. In communities with burgeoning coffee economies and significant indigenous populations, such as Diriamba and Diriomo, ladinos fought to delegitimize indigenous authority and identity in order to wrest control of land, labor, and local politics. By contrast, in places dominated by indigenous people but with fewer export agriculture opportunities, such as Catarina and San Juan de Oriente, indigenous communities became the leaders of the municipal government. While some indigenous communities appeared to have disintegrated by the end of the nineteenth century, others carried on amid the more militarized state apparatus of the Zelaya dictatorship, seeking new means to survive within the nation. With the military incorporation of the Mosquitia in 1894, indigenous communities increasingly sublimated their struggles within a national idiom as people of the Atlantic coast emerged as a seemingly unassimilable "Other," against which inclusion in the nation could be measured.

ONE

Brothers and Others
Elite Conceptions of Nation and State

At the moment when Central America broke free of Spanish dominion in 1821, neither nation nor state existed in what is today Nicaragua. Such was the strength of localist passion and enmity that the
province's two main cities, Granada and León, could not agree on a
policy in pursuit of independence. While Granada voted to sever its
ties to Spain but affirm them with Guatemala, León sought freedom
from both. Nicaragua existed on paper, of course—both juridically
and cartographically—but that did not ensure its viability. The region's potential for an interoceanic canal undoubtedly provided vital building blocks of territorial integrity and identity, but even this
could not constrain the numerous local identities that threatened
to divide the territory.[1] The violence that ensued, however, should
not be understood as the "anarchy" of traditional historiography but
rather as the very foundation of Nicaraguan state formation. Despite
the apparent political differences that drove various factions of the
elite into one bloodbath after another, the elites shared the basic out-
lines of a project of liberal modernity. By the late 1840s, when Liberals and Conservatives briefly joined together to crush popular rebellions that were threatening them throughout the country, the basic
elite ideologies of the state and nation had formed. However, it was
not until the National War (Guerra Nacional), fought between 1855
and 1857, that Nicaragua's elites unified behind these ideologies.

While violent struggles for independence enveloped much of

Latin America, Central America received the news without fanfare, severing its ties to Spain with the simple stroke of a pen.[2] The disappearance of Spanish dominion, however, left an immense power vacuum, and as local elites rushed to fill the void, the isthmus erupted in thunderous violence. In the years immediately following Central American independence, "Nicaragua" was not high on the list of potential political identities. León, Granada, Central America, and even, momentarily, Agustín de Iturbide's Mexican empire seemed more viable.[3] The province of Nicaragua easily became the provinces of León and Granada, each with its own government. In 1825, amid this war and uncertainty, the province of Nicoya seceded from Nicaragua and joined Costa Rica.[4] Finally, the ability of even a united Nicaragua to control the Atlantic coast region was as elusive as it had been during the colonial period. These were not promising signs for Nicaraguan nation-state formation.

Despite this evidence, most studies of post-independence Nicaragua succumb to a belief in Nicaragua's a priori existence as a nation at independence.[5] There is a common recognition within Nicaraguan historiography of violent localism (especially between León and Granada) and the total absence of a central state, yet the inevitability of the Nicaraguan nation-state is equally fundamental to this literature.[6] After all, the argument goes, Nicaragua exists. Many scholars have transformed localist struggles into mere signs of Nicaragua's failures on the path toward its true destiny. Alberto Lanuza typifies this attitude when he writes that Nicaraguan instability can be traced to "a colonial past that had made, according to Sarmiento's bon mots, 'of every village a sovereign State.'"[7] True enough, but in Lanuza's argument we must assume an already-existing Nicaragua that found its sovereignty compromised by Spanish colonialism.[8] Similarly, José Coronel Urtecho implies in the title of an influential essay that these years are an "epoch of anarchy," a stage through which Nicaragua would pass on its way to becoming a modern nation-state. This is not to dismiss these scholars' perceptive investigations of Nicaragua's colonial past but rather to contest their teleological approach to nation.

Much of this stance derives from a belief that states exist, at root, to promote progress and development within society. Coronel Urtecho, for example, conceives of the state's true function as "impel[ing] . . . the development of the country." This is critical to his interpretation of state formation in Nicaragua: the failure of Nicaraguan elites to grasp this conception of state, as opposed to the Costa Ricans' success in doing so, explains their divergent histories.[9] Humberto Belli likewise laments elite backwardness in perceiving the state as "a strategically important resource" for "distributing privileges, reward, commercial monopolies and posts." Mired in "semi-feudal Hispanic values," Nicaraguan elites could not conceive of a broader "society" and refused to submit to state authority.[10] Despite their reliance on diverse theoretical models, the leading analysts of the early nineteenth century all arrive at the conclusion that Nicaragua's unhealthy years of "anarchy"—whatever their source—led to the birth of a deformed state. Nicaragua's colonial history greatly influenced its post-independence developments, but in their focus on understanding the origins of the state's deformity, these studies fail to develop a historicized account of state formation.

If, instead, we take the state as the locus of monopolized coercion and resource extraction, the years following independence take on a different cast.[11] Our focus shifts from assessing the inability of Nicaraguans to create a viable state to an analysis that views the post-independence conflicts as *part of* the process of state formation. It is in these struggles that the meaning and structure of the state developed, a state that greatly resembled its Central American neighbors.

This chapter is divided into four main sections. The first examines the post-independence struggles with state formation, reassessing their importance and meaning. The second and third examine how two important proto-nationalist discourses developed out of the early struggles for state formation to inform the process of post–National War nation-state formation. The first discourse, which I call "patriarchal nationalism," borrowed the neo-Aristotelian scholasticism of the Roman Catholic Church as a means of constructing elite unity in the nineteenth century. The second discourse located Nicaragua within the system of world states, functioning to interpret Nicaragua's position within it. The chapter's final section focuses on how the National War served to solidify this emerging elite nation-state ideology into the basis for a radical restructuring of Nicaraguan society according to the terms of that ideology.

When Anarchy Is State Making

The historiography of nineteenth-century Nicaragua is overwhelmed by references to what has come to be called the "epoch of anarchy," a period of violent political struggle that followed Nicaragua's independence from Spain. Despite a general recognition of two distinct types of instability, caudillism on the one hand and social anarchy on the other, the events of these years and their meaning are frequently lumped together as a nearly incessant anarchy. Faced with the assertion that civil war and rebellion bloodied twenty-five of the thirty-seven years between 1821 and 1857 and that twenty-five men jostled for control of the government in the twenty-nine years between 1825 and 1854, other conclusions find little space in which to maneuver.[12]

Yet these figures are both crude and misleading. Why should a simple counting of events suffice to define the severity or importance of the rebellions and civil war that took place after independence? In the evidence so frequently cited above, each uprising, no matter how short-lived or regionally based, comes to define the year it occurred in as "anarchy." The issue of the Nicaraguan presidency is even more suspect. First, until after the National War, the term of office was just two years, ensuring at least fifteen presidents over the twenty-nine years. Second, Nicaragua's constitutions required the president to cede power to the head of the Congress when he took the helm of the army. Should we count these as moments of instability? Hardly. The chief of state's ability to relinquish power and retrieve it subsequently serves, if anything, as evidence of institutional stability.

Compared to Mexico during the same period, Nicaragua might be considered quite stable.[13]

This characterization of the post-independence years, however, chains us to a concept that simultaneously legitimates centralized state power and obscures its development. The terms "anarchy" and "disorder" peppered elite discourse during these years, of course, but without forming a coherent construction of the period's history. It is, instead, after the National War that these years are forged into a "period" of anarchy that has served since as a touchstone against which to measure contemporary stability.[14]

To some extent this traditional interpretation derives from the earliest works of Nicaraguan history. Despite ranging across the ideological spectrum, Nicaragua's first historians—Tomás Ayón (conservative), Jerónimo Pérez (moderate), and José Dolores Gámez (liberal)—saw the first decades following independence in much the same way. Not surprisingly, they tended to level more criticism at those of different political stripes, but in general they laid blame for Nicaragua's early years of caudillo battling at the feet of all involved.

In the decades following the National War, Pérez published numerous articles on the history of Nicaragua, including biographies of many of its major political figures.[15] More parable than history, each tract provided a dash of civics mixed with a healthy dose of caution against "the overflow of evil passions." Pérez's assessment of the failure of Nicaragua's leaders to pursue "real," ideologically based partisan politics following independence drips with cynicism: "At the beginning of our revolutions, we adopted names . . . that were expressive of ideas, although at base they were not professed; later . . . each party became recognized by the name of its caudillo, which demonstrates quite well that the factions have not been, nor are they, more than groups or circles that stand in place of their respective leaders."[16] Pérez's contemporaries and subsequent generations have echoed these sentiments.[17] No amount of bloodletting seemed sufficient to remove the bad humors from Nicaraguan politics.

However, such a conclusion confuses cause and effect. From the perspective of the post–National War "oligarchic pact," Pérez could look back and claim that "both [parties] profess the same principles and the same beliefs, and that the unfortunate dissensions that have decimated the Nicaraguan family have been for petty party interests, for personal profit and not for the good of humanity."[18] But what Pérez saw as petty interests merely reflected the actual political possibilities of a country in which the state barely existed. As Miles Wortman explains: "Centralized government did not exist in Nicaragua. As if Bourbon rule had never occurred, local authorities dominated their areas, with landed families controlling the political situation. Vestiges of the Bourbons remained: some government titles, some local jurisdiction, and the names of some uncollectible taxes. But in Nicaragua, Bourbon centralization did not survive."[19] Certainly this lack of institutional solidity militated against the type of partisan political struggles Pérez valued. But to succumb to the depoliticization that Pérez advocates is to imbibe the nationalist mythology that he, his contemporaries, and his successors were constructing.

The collapse of meaningful centralized authority after independence enabled the hundreds of small towns and villages in Nicaragua to enjoy greater autonomy from the main cities. At the same time, it allowed local caudillos and regional (often family-based) political networks to imagine taking the reins of state power, a situation that often led to war.[20] Although rural communities tried to keep state-centered politics at arm's length, they could not entirely avoid the violence these politics invoked. This is not to say that the majority of Nicaraguan society was inward-looking and avoided contact with outsiders or entirely feared outside institutions and people. There was, in fact, an active market culture and extensive contacts in towns along the more populous Pacific coastal areas. Rather, to the extent that rural communities could regulate their contact with the rest of society, they did so to the best of their advantage.[21] Where a political relationship existed between members of the elite and the rest of society, it tended to form along lines of caudillo patronage.[22] The correspondence between local caudillos and local autonomy gave these ties a vitality that militated against the extension of centralized state power.

Although several popular rebellions occurred between 1821 and 1854, none had the impact or ferocity of those that took place between 1845 and 1849. These uprisings came in response to the first serious efforts at state making, at building institutions that went beyond the more restricted realm of caudillo politics. These efforts antagonized the majority of Nicaraguans who lived outside the elites' "evil passions." The new state struck directly at local social, economic, cultural, and political structures, causing widespread rancor. Popular rebellions erupted throughout the country, plunging elites into terror and forcing them into closer alliance than had ever before occurred. Both the origins of these popular rebellions and elites' responses proved vital to the subsequent process of nation-state formation. Unfortunately, this critical period in Nicaraguan history has been relatively neglected.

Until recently, these uprisings have generally been viewed as banditry and barbarism against legitimate authority.[23] Even scholars taking a social-historical approach tend to focus on the rebellions as responses to social and economic transformations divorced from state-making efforts. This reflects, in some ways, an acceptance of elites' use of the term "anarchy" as disorder and trespasses on the social order, distanced from the issue of state formation. E. Bradford Burns notes how elite discourse during this time referred to bandits and barbarians as pre-political in the sense argued by Hobsbawm. Why should we not view popular revolt as coherently anti-state—in other words, anarchic—rather than just random gestures of anger at the swirling changing world around them? In essence, the pre-political stance argues for a static, peaceful world that explodes when pressurized by the outside world. The forms and determinants of local politics are dismissed as nonexistent or unable to encompass the outside world. Yet, as the rebellions in Nicaragua between 1845 and 1849 indicate, the relationship of specific types of changes to rebellion exists.

I want to suggest that we focus, instead, on the relationship between state formation and what we might term "social anarchy." This is an effort to see the conflicts between elites and the population at large not merely as resulting from social transformations (which undoubtedly were occurring) but as responses to state formation.[24] State institutions do not exist isolated from society, since their very existence is premised on the idea that they serve to coerce, extract from, and adjudicate for the population subject to them.

While head of the government from 1845 to 1847, José León Sandoval tried to create new state institutions and to reinforce the few that already existed. A good indication of the nascent nature of state formation at this time is Sandoval's creation of the first real, functioning governmental ministries: War, Treasury, and Foreign Relations. It took elites more than twenty years from independence to formalize the structures that form the core of every state. Sandoval's policies, however, went beyond the symbolic. He contracted with José Trinidad Muñoz to form a professional army, and he created new taxes, especially through the monopolization of *aguardiente* (cane alcohol) production and distribution.[25] Furthermore, to grasp better the entire territory under the state's control and hoping to evaluate economic and social development throughout the country, Sandoval's government began gathering census and other statistical information.[26]

The newly expanding state generated immense pressure and resistance. Sporadic but frequently sustained opposition by the rural poor sprang up throughout the country. While it would be an overstatement to say that these uprisings represented a unified voice of discontent, they all attacked the same enemy. The tentacles of the state invaded the lives of rural communities, and the poor responded by trying to sever them.

The invasive nature of the state's expansion is evident in the widespread rebellions against it. The revolt of Indians in Matagalpa between 1845 and 1847 hardly seems surprising, since they lived at the frontier of state control and had a limited history of political and social integration with the rest of the country.[27] But the uprisings also extended deep into the heart of the longest-established cities and towns, where state authority was strongest. In June 1845 some seventy men rampaged through Managua. In March 1846 a small band attacked the hacienda of a senator and aguardiente contract recipient, killing him. In February 1847 a group of ladinos attacked Nindirí and Masaya, freeing prisoners from the local jail and expressing a particular wrath toward the local distributor of aguardiente.[28] While many similar episodes occurred, these are representative of the diversity and geographic spread of the unrest.

Perhaps most significant is the fact that the traditional distinctions maintained by patron-client relationships seemed to break down. Liberals and Conservatives were attacked indiscriminately, the apparent logic of old political relationships broken. This response, however, makes sense given that the new political logic employed in these efforts at state formation muted the legitimacy of traditional political networks. Importantly, the popular response helped to bring about the first real post-independence unity among wealthy Liberals and Conservatives. Temporarily putting aside old enmities and suspicions, they joined forces to crush the popular revolts. Although the unity would not last, it provided a historical touchstone to call upon in constructing a more lasting elite unity during the National War. At the same time, it both expressed what they saw as the limits of popular responses to their policies and inculcated the need to negotiate change in order to avoid the physically and materially costly results of forced transformations.

Patriarchal Nationalism and the Construction of Elite Unity

The new day of Central American independence had scarcely dawned when Nicaraguan elites began to struggle over control of the would-be state. In the first decade, in fact, the actual form of the state remained up in the air. Would Nicaragua end up as part of a larger state, such as the Central American Federation, or would it be split into smaller units, such as León and Granada? Even if a form could be decided upon, questions over who would rule and how the wealth and power of the state would be distributed remained unanswered.

Despite their debates, which were at times ferociously violent, elites agreed substantially on what role the state should have in society. They saw Nicaragua's future as a nation-state and understood that the state's effective extension into people's daily lives was central to the nation-state's formation. Between 1826 and 1893, Nicaraguan leaders of various political stripes enacted four different constitutions. These varied in openness of franchise, divisions and relations of governmental powers, degree of religious tolerance, and civil rights and responsibilities, yet they all also envisioned Nicaragua as a democratic republic and enshrined the preservation of liberty, equality, and security as fundamental tasks of the state.[29] Nonetheless, from the 1820s to the 1850s, political violence often discouraged the effective resolution of these political debates. This fact was hardly lost on some. José Guerrero, at the opening of the 1847 constituent assembly, expressed his sense of the debate's impotency: "We cannot say, absolutely, that our institutions have been bad. If we haven't managed to construct them, how can we judge them accurately?"[30]

Although warring subsided briefly in the 1830s and allowed for modest institutional developments, Liberal attachment to Central American union limited official expressions of Nicaraguan nationalism. In 1829, upon taking power in Guatemala, Liberal Francisco Morazán ordered Honduran general Dionisio Herrera to enter Nicaragua and put an end to the worst inter-elite violence since independence. While Herrera's campaign of pacification brought a modicum of peace and tranquillity to Nicaragua, it also assured Liberal control of the region. While many of León's Liberals certainly favored the Central American Federation for ideological reasons, these ties also provided them with the political and military might to exercise control over the rest of the country. For Liberals to have eschewed Central American union—with Guatemala in the lead—meant reigniting old rivalries that threatened to divide the country again. As such, Nicaraguan Liberals vitiated the articulation of a meaningful nationalist discourse until the eve of Nicaragua's secession from the Central American Federation in 1838.[31]

The exception to Leonese reticence was José Núñez. In 1834, upon taking power as supreme director, Núñez spoke mournfully of recent rebellions in Granada, Segovia, and Rivas and the violence the state mustered to put them down. In his lament he offered up a view of Nicaragua's future that formed the foundational bedrock of elite nationalist discourse: "That Nicaragua be a family of brothers."[32] It is hardly surprising, then, that this Liberal sought Nicaraguan secession from the Central American Federation. When Núñez returned to power in 1837, following the assassination of José Zepeda, it was to the "State of whom I am a son." Upon receiving the Nicaraguan Congress's approval of his momentous decision, Núñez offered the following advice to these "favored sons of the fatherland": "Sacrifice to her [Nicaragua] your last efforts, and make it so that your names will be immortalized in the *history of Nicaragua*."[33] Although "history" is frequently cited in elite discourse prior to this, it was used as history with a capital *H*, the history of all time. Here, perhaps for the first time, we see the nationalization of history in elite discourse.

Unlike his Liberal predecessors and his immediate successors, Núñez invoked the well-developed conception of the patriarchal family—honed during the colonial era—to express what I have termed "patriarchal nationalism," a seemingly all-encompassing discourse on national membership, rights, and responsibilities. Nicaraguans were "sons" of the fatherland and "brothers" to one another. "Honor" provided a set of rules and roles for all members of the family—men, women, and children—that served to guide the actions of citizens and the state.[34]

Although political conditions had only recently allowed the expression of patriarchal nationalism, its roots extended far into the colonial era. Spanish Creoles had long construed "family" as encapsulating a particular set of social relations that they expressed as the most desirable foundation for Nicaraguan society. From at least the fourteenth century forward, the doctrine of the Roman Catholic Church promoted a patriarchal organization of society from the basic family unit to the state.[35] Moreover, the scholastic basis of colonial Spanish education inculcated the patriarchal theory of political organization in Aristotle's *Politics* as a defense of the monarchy.[36]

Given its colonial roots, the discourse appealed to Conservatives. Moreover, Conservatives such as José León Sandoval and Fruto Chamorro drew out this thread, explicitly establishing the link between the church and patriarchal nationalism. Sandoval's argument for Christianity's miraculous earthly powers is emblematic: "[It] serves as a brake on functionaries, sanctions equality, guarantees patriotism, establishes the union of associates, and through this makes us great and strong; and in a word, the Christian religion, as a celebrated publicist says, 'which seems only to produce happiness for the other life, also does so for this one.'"[37] Liberals such as Núñez, on the other hand, elided the relationship to religion. But with the rise of social anarchy in the mid-1840s these differences proved unimportant, because patriarchal nationalism functioned to unite Liberals and Conservatives around the goal of state formation.

Despite its broad resonance among elites, patriarchal nationalism proved problematic to extend more broadly and inclusively. Nicaragua's wealthy landlords and merchants were generally unprepared to recognize the majority of their fellow countrymen as "brothers." The problem was not one of equality in the strictest sense, since the discourse promised no such thing. There were always younger and older brothers, poorer and richer brothers. However, just as the prodigal son, despite his sins, could return, fully accepted, to his family, so all of the nation's "brothers" were intrinsically deserving of the same rights. Each brother was entitled to co-determine the fate of the family. Such an idea was unacceptable and inconceivable to this sliver of society in the 1840s (if not later); when Núñez pleaded before the legislative assembly "that Nicaragua be a family of brothers," he was scanning the faces of his would-be brothers.

Although the discourse of patriarchal nationalism found a ready audience among Nicaragua's wealthy citizens, one question remained vexing: Who's the father? The answer, as Sandoval explained in a speech, should be obvious: "The Government is your father."[38] All of Nicaragua's nineteenth-century constitutions also embraced such a vision, claiming a unitary sovereignty embedded in the state. Typical is the declaration in the 1858 Constitution that "sovereignty resides inherently in the nation: no part of it nor any individual can take its functions upon itself."[39] But old ways die hard. The personalism that had until then dominated and would continue to dominate Nicaraguan politics vied with this more inclusive conception of patriarchal nationalism. Responding to complaints in the legislature that his reaction to rebellions against his administration had been excessively brutal, the very same Sandoval unapologetically insisted that the Nicaraguan family needed a strong patriarch—in this case, himself—to impose social order and uphold its honor, both internally and externally.[40] Here, Sandoval uses patriarchal nationalism as a defense for authoritarian governance; clearly, "Supreme Director" aptly described the role of the head of state.

Patriarchal nationalism provided a means of uniting Liberals and Conservatives in the project of state formation, but not necessarily the threads to bind them together. The two Liberal administrations that followed Núñez's, for example, showed themselves to be the exceptions to patriarchal nationalism's ubiquity within elite discourse. Both administrations were inclined to rejoin, in some form, the Central American Federation. Unable to commit fully to a Nicaraguan nation and continuing to flirt with a Central American one, neither administration could (or necessarily wanted to) articulate a meaningful and convincing nationalist discourse.[41] During the years of social anarchy between 1845 and 1849, however, elites turned to patriarchal nationalism in united defense of themselves and their socioeconomic position against the rest of Nicaraguan society, a society that felt threatened by efforts at state formation. Once the crisis had ended, however, old enmities resurfaced, fraying the newly woven fabric.

The Ambivalence of Foreign Relations

The period of Central American independence was an extremely confusing time. In the 1820s the pace of change was staggering and difficult to control or understand. Leaders from the former colonies struggled to imagine new futures for themselves. What form would their government take? What territorial boundaries would they control? Who would be friends and who enemies? The former colonies were forced to play a constant game of hurry up and wait. News traveled slowly between the Americas and Europe, but when it eventually arrived, the changes were frequently monumental, requiring quick decision making.

Immediately following independence, Father José Antonio Chamorro, a Nicaraguan, offered his support for Agustín de Iturbide's Plan de Iguala. Although Chamorro believed that "the Guatemalan [independence plan] is infinitely better," he felt it was unrealistic compared to the Mexican plan. Mexico, after all, was much stronger, being "infinitely superior in wealth and arms to Guatemala," and could contend more successfully with what Chamorro referred to as the "Anglo-American threat." Even if Chamorro had considered his personal political identity to be Nicaraguan, he had no illusions about Nicaragua's viability in the jittery post-independence years.[42]

It is not surprising, given these circumstances, that Nicaraguans remained under the thumb of Guatemala until 1838. This is not to say that some Nicaraguans did not favor Central American union—many did—but rather that most also chafed under Guatemalan efforts to control Central American resources and monopolize regional political power. This situation had changed little since the colonial period, but Nicaraguan internal divisions remained deep enough to derail serious attempts to counter Guatemalan political and military hegemony.[43] The greater stability of the 1830s, however, enabled more sober reflection on the costs of membership in the Central American Federation, leading to its collapse in 1838. By then, as Ralph Lee Woodward argues, "Despite Conservatives sympathies [with Rafael

Carrera's Guatemala], it is doubtful that these two states [Nicaragua and Costa Rica] would again have accepted the political hegemony of Guatemala without bitter resistance."[44] Certainly the notion of union held a powerful sway over some of nineteenth-century Nicaragua's most powerful men, but during the second half of the nineteenth century they never abandoned local politics and local identity in favor of their dreams. Even so active and partisan a unionist as Liberal Máximo Jerez never forsook his native Nicaragua. Though often forced to live in exile in other parts of the isthmus, he always returned to Nicaragua.[45] Moreover, whatever the continuing interest in union, there is scant evidence of its resonance among popular sectors of post–National War Nicaragua. As the conflicts and struggles examined in chapters 3–5 attest, individuals and communities often called upon "nation," "fatherland," and "the Nicaraguan constitution" as sources of legitimacy for their claims, but never upon "union." Even the most propitious opportunity for unionism since 1824, led by Nicaragua's own president José Santos Zelaya, collapsed with ease. Notably, the key figures of twentieth-century unionism, such as Salvador Mendieta, saw the failures of nineteenth-century union arising from its failure to resonate with the everyday lives of Central Americans.[46]

Out of these experiences and those to come, the discourse of patriarchal nationalism that developed went hand in hand with reflections upon the nature of the world system of states and Nicaragua's place within that system. Just prior to the outbreak of rebellions that would spread through Nicaragua between 1845 and 1849, Blas Antonio Sáenz called for the Nicaraguan legislature to establish "a national union that would give us international respectability, internal security, credit and universal amity."[47] The first (and the majority) of these benefits bespeak an understanding of Nicaragua's place in the world, benefits that accrue to survival in a world of unequals.

This emphasis on world politics reflected far more than a reactive instinct for survival, which, in fact, seemed a rather weak trait in early-nineteenth-century Nicaragua. Rather, Nicaraguans proactively pursued foreign relations in order to fulfill the long-held dream of an interoceanic canal across the territory.[48] Nature had endowed Nicaragua with "brilliant circumstances," foretelling its future as the "chosen portion" of the world.[49] But nature needed a helping hand to transform Nicaragua into the emporium of the world, and neither the state nor local merchants and landowners—even under the best of circumstances—could offer sufficient monetary or technical support on their own. Treaties and contracts would have to be negotiated and signed with foreign businessmen and governments if the canal was to materialize. As with guano in Peru, Nicaragua's potentially unique situation brought with it pressures and possibilities that had never before been experienced.[50]

Once the social anarchy of the late 1840s had begun, then-president José León Sandoval worried over its geopolitical consequences. Given the importance ascribed to the canal, it is hardly surprising that Sandoval placed alongside disruption to trade and fears for the safety of elite landholders the loss "of the very honor of the State in the outside world."[51] Without honor, unable, as it were, to maintain the sanctity of its own house, the world could rightly question the useful existence of Nicaragua. Honor, in essence, stood as shorthand for Nicaragua's sovereignty, a marker of state health; without it the sickly state would be picked for devourment by stronger states. Weaker specimens could survive, but at the price of diminished capacity to define their position and identity within the world system of states.

Where Sandoval spoke in the vague but clearly understandable term of "honor," his successor, José Guerrero, voiced the urgency of his time much more explicitly. Watching the war between the United States and Mexico (1846–48) from not safe enough a distance, Guerrero issued a wake-up call to Nicaragua's warring factions: "We must not allow the spirit of party and localism that has born fruit in the tears and grief of our people to a drag upon us, nor can we dream that we possess the perfection and intelligence necessary to constitute ourselves at the level of other countries. Consider the disgrace in which the great Republic of Mexico—richer, more enlightened and more powerful than all of Central America—finds itself: we see it subjugated, its national honor insulted, and prisoner to a foreign power, *all due to internal divisions.*"[52] The El Salvadoran newspaper *Amigo del Pueblo* had already sounded the alarm of British imperial expansion as early as 1844.[53] Unfortunately, these calls proved prescient. Within months of Guerrero's warning, Great Britain had taken control of the Atlantic coast port of San Juan del Norte and forced Nicaragua to swallow a bitter pill: the recognition of much of the coast as a British protectorate.[54]

The Nicaraguan government often refused even to acknowledge the British protectorate. The Nicaraguans claimed sovereignty over the entirety of what is modern-day Nicaragua through the legal principle of *uti possidetis juris,* which aimed to establish territorial dominion over colonial claims, even if such claims were never fully occupied or explored.[55] The coast was recognized by Nicaragua's constitutions, and in the colonial period the Spanish crown had considered the territory and its peoples Spanish subjects.[56] To recognize claims by the British, then, would admit the possibility that British engagements on the coast were anything but the illegal actions of a superior military force.[57] Still, Nicaraguan opinion on the subject was not unanimous. According to Mario Rodríguez, in 1849, Nicaragua's minister plenipotentiary in Great Britain, Francisco Castellón, "was willing to sign a treaty with the British recognizing San Juan del Norte as English," while Minister of Foreign Relations Sebastián Salinas adamantly rejected such an option.[58]

The coast, especially the port of San Juan del Norte, provided vital economic resources to the Nicaraguan state. Figures from 1841 to 1853 indicate that the value of imports through San Juan del Norte varied between $150,000 and $500,000 per year.[59] This considerable source of tax revenue impelled Nicaraguan authorities to attempt to control the port city. According to Robert Naylor, after the death of the Mosquito King Robert Charles Frederick in 1842, "British authority at the mouth of the San Juan River ranged from negligible to nonexistent and depended solely on the presence of a British warship from Jamaica."[60] Despite this and the apparent ambivalency of British Colonial Office officials toward the costs of controlling the region, the Nicaraguan government exercised only the slimmest authority over the region.[61]

José Guerrero believed that in the world of international relations Nicaragua walked a fine line between "fear and hope." The ideas of British and German Enlightenment thinkers on interstate relations and the rules of warfare may have dotted the landscape of Nicaraguan thought, but theory was never confused with practice.[62] Guerrero hoped not just for the canal but for Nicaragua to be treated as an equal member in the world of states. At the same time, he feared that the canal would turn Nicaragua into the historical battlefield for the world's remaining imperial powers.

Guerrero may well have underestimated the repercussions of such foreign engagements, for while the establishment of the first trans-isthmian route across Nicaragua in 1851 quickly proved to be profitable, it also highlighted the international and domestic weakness of the Nicaraguan state. Although imagined as an eventual canal route, it started out as a mixed steamship-overland route when Nicaragua contracted with American financier Cornelius Vanderbilt in 1849 to establish the Accessory Transit Company. Vanderbilt used Americans for most of the company's administrative jobs, but he hired Nicaraguans for much of the hard labor and provisioning. Yet, the company provided more than employment. According to Miguel Angel Herrera, it also allowed local peasant communities to maneuver for greater autonomy by using its political and economic power to limit government interference in the lives of its workers and others along the transit route.[63] The seriousness of Vanderbilt's power, however, became most evident when the U.S. warship *Cyane* bombarded and then briefly occupied Greytown in 1854.[64] While this event had more to do with U.S.-British relations, it suggested the willingness of the United States to use military force in support of U.S. capital and the potential for future clashes around any canal route.

The National War and the
Consolidation of Elite Ideology

Threats to Nicaraguan sovereignty in the 1840s had planted the seeds of national unity among elites, but they remained dormant; the lessons learned seemed forgotten as the civil war of 1854 broke out. The Liberals, in fact, contracted with U.S. military adventurer William Walker to aid their side in the fighting. To their great dismay, they quickly learned that Walker's interests lay beyond their party disputes as he attempted to subjugate the country. He declared himself president, reinstated slavery, and confiscated the property of his enemies. Although in the American South Walker's mission was sold as the annexation of Nicaragua to the United States as a slave state, his interests lay more in establishing dictatorial control over a united Central America.[65]

William Walker was the most infamous figure of nineteenth-century filibustering, the private military adventuring that filled the American public imagination with living icons of "Manifest Destiny." As Robert May notes, "Filibustering provided the nation [United States] with heroes, martyrs, and villains."[66] For countries like Nicaragua, filibustering proved equally complicated. In 1849 Nicaragua began turning to the United States as a counterweight to increased British aggression against Nicaraguan sovereignty. Newly assigned U.S. chargé d'affaires E. George Squier met with widespread acclaim when in July of that year he proclaimed in a public address in León, "The American Continent belongs to the Americans, and is sacred to Republican Freedom."[67] Nicaragua had already been in treaty negotiations with the United States with Squier's predecessor, but this pro-American enthusiasm reflected more than geopolitical strategy. José Guerrero's horror at the U.S. invasion of Mexico in 1846 appeared not forgotten but rather forgiven by 1850, when a Leonese newspaper blamed Mexico's "misfortunes" on its own "erroneous conduct."[68] As Frances Kinloch Tijerino has noted, Nicaraguan elites heralded the United States, like the idea of the canal, as a symbol of the cosmopolitan civilization.[69] For much of Nicaragua's population, William Walker initially embodied this heroic notion of American civilization.[70] As Walker dashed so many dreams of "Republican Freedom," however, his villainy unified Nicaraguans like no previous experience.[71]

The war to oust Walker brought together an odd and unlikely coalition of forces. Although Walker initially counted on the support of Vanderbilt's Accessory Transit Company, once Walker felt himself in control of Nicaragua he turned against Vanderbilt and revoked the company's charter. Vanderbilt took his revenge by providing men, financing, and arms to bring Walker to heel. Moreover, just as so many Nicaraguan Liberals and Conservatives overcame their differences to fight against Walker, so too did Guatemalans, Costa Ricans, Hondurans, and El Salvadorans. This coalition army, led especially by the Costa Ricans and supported by Vanderbilt, proved vital to defeating Walker and his army and forcing their retreat from Nicaragua. Any hopes that this show of Central American unity would resuscitate the union, however, were quashed by Nicaragua's 1858 Constitution, which proclaimed the country "sovereign, free and independent" and relegated the unionist ideal to the last of the document's articles.[72]

Soaked with Nicaraguan blood, the seeds of political unity began to blossom and bear fruit. Liberals and Conservatives began to unite to defeat their new, common enemy. Drawing on the discourse of patriarchal nationalism, Liberals extended an olive branch that asked Conservatives to push aside questions of blame: "We must only contract ourselves to the great object of the salvation of the Fatherland [*patria*], and for this, set aside *all small questions, all family dissension.*"[73] The Conservatives responded favorably, asserting themselves "disposed to set aside all idea of party in order to unite the forces of all Nicaraguans against the enemy of our nationality."[74] Building a united front against outsiders demanded reining in ideological differences.

Within three months, the two sides, "united with bonds of fraternity," came to an agreement, frequently referred to as the "oligarchic pact."[75] In the scope of its consensus and application the pact provided a base for the consolidation of elite nation-state ideology. Critical to the pact's success was its sweeping political amnesty. If reconciliation was to be a new chapter in Nicaraguan history, there had to be a radical break between considerations of the past and the present. Indeed, the only history of this period written in the nineteenth century makes just such a break.[76] Thus, while in the first volume of his history of the Revolution of 1854 and the National War, Jerónimo Pérez laid blame for the Walker affair at the feet of the Liberals, in the second volume he focused on the development of a unified elite that, through "rationality," had come to understand that they belonged to "one family."[77]

The framework of elite unity was continually strengthened along two mutually reinforcing fronts. First, Liberals and Conservatives proclaimed a new era of Nicaraguan history, where the distance of time allowed for dispassionate analysis of past mistakes. A newspaper article in 1866, for example, argued that in the past, "ambition" to rule had provoked divisions within Nicaragua, not meaningful party differences. The author, in fact, argued that the classic ideological stances of Liberals and Conservatives—reduced in the article to "liberty" and "order"—should be integrated into a single national goal.[78] The lesson was clear: in the past, Nicaraguans suffered from tunnel vision, looking at the same national goals but through separate, single lenses; by bringing the two views together, they gained a new, binocular vision, one that added depth and perspective previously unavailable to them.[79]

Second, to cement the new historical moment that followed the National War, Liberals and Conservatives proclaimed the ahistorical association of Nicaraguan "brotherhood," the national thread that was to unite the family, despite its differences. Strongly representative of this discourse was President Fernando Guzmán's inaugural address in 1867. Short on specific policies, the address hammered at the evils of "party colors," the petty differences that were "the principal cause of our misfortunes, the origin of our evils, that black political intolerance that poisons the air of the Fatherland [*patria*] and declares the dissident brother to be an irreconcilable enemy."[80] Like the early discourse of Nicaraguan patriarchal nationalism, the post–National War discourse addressed elites, not the general public.[81]

The degree to which differing Liberal and Conservative views melded following the National War remains debatable; how elites acted upon their views, however, did change significantly. Scholars have frequently dismissed this period as one of little change, when Liberals remained powerless and discredited because of their complicity with Walker while the Granada-based Conservative oligarchy impeded real political and economic progress.[82] The relative peace enjoyed by Nicaraguans for the rest of the nineteenth century should not be underestimated. The few elite "revolutions" prior to José Santos Zelaya's coup in 1893—most notably in 1869, 1876, and 1884—fizzled like old firecrackers. And when they failed, the architects usually just faced exile until the next administration invited them to return, while minor participants were given amnesty immediately. Jerónimo Pérez did not exaggerate when he commented on the new era of civility among elites: "Only after the bloody struggle of 1854 did the word *death* to the political enemy ring with horror in the ears."[83] Liberals and Conservatives appeared to achieve a new kind of political culture, a consensus that was ruptured by the Zelaya dictatorship and later exacerbated by the U.S. intervention in Nicaragua from 1912 to 1933.[84]

But transforming Nicaragua into a viable nation-state required wealthy Nicaraguans to move beyond their own unification. They had to transform society so that the state became integral to—yet barely visible in—peoples' everyday lives. Discursively, at least, they promoted an ideology of universal membership and rights within society. But rights had to be balanced against responsibilities, with the state mediating between the two through a framework of authority and justice. Property ownership and labor were understood as the twin foundations of national life and progress. All of these ideas were to be promoted and furthered through education (the most important source of "progress"), cultural homogenization, and respect for the state.[85]

On the surface these propositions read like a positivist laundry list. As Ralph Lee Woodward notes, "positivists claimed credit for reforming outmoded political institutions, for bringing about the industrial revolution, for beginning the process of mass popular education, for destroying the traditional power of the Church, for giving the military professional status, for reforming penal codes, for expanding national frontiers, for modernizing the cities, for introducing immigration of both men and ideas and, thus, fomenting the material welfare of the continent."[86] Woodward cites Guatemalan Justo Rufino Barrios as one of the best examples of "a liberal dictatorship that accepted the Comtean idea of an elite to run the society."[87] Yet, it is unclear how much influence positivism actually had in Nicaragua. While Máximo Jerez, the avatar of Nicaraguan Liberalism, was an avowed positivist, no group like Mexico's Científicos emerged in Nicaragua.[88] The term itself appeared rarely in Nicaraguan intellectual circles, which, if anything, tended more toward Krausism.[89] Moreover, the everyday politics of land, labor, and local authority reveal that positivism was far from unanimously endorsed by members of the elite, be they mayors, judges, prefects, or government ministers. Whatever sociocratic impulses may have run through intellectuals and politicians in nineteenth-century Nicaragua, the decades after the National War saw the expression of a far more inclusive liberalism than was found in Guatemala or Mexico or Brazil.[90] While it is clear that local autonomy declined over the length of the nineteenth century, so too is it evident that political participation and access in the national state grew over that same period.

In debates over national unity and the formation of a viable state, elites tended to employ a discourse centered on metaphors of the patriarchal family. But while they considered patriarchal nationalism appropriate for themselves, it lacked broader applicability. First, elites tended to conceive of honor and the ideal of the patriarchal family as exclusive to themselves. At the close of Latin America's colonial period, as Ann Twinam has argued, "Social and racial tension increased, as members of the elite who rationalized their place in the hierarchy by their honor, and their honor by their whiteness and legitimacy, now felt increasingly challenged from below."[91] Others might claim honor, but elites often refused to acknowledge it.[92] Second, while patriarchal nationalism did not necessarily imply equality but rather the intimate and structured relationship of the patriarchal family, it could be interpreted as a more radically equal brotherhood. Still, even as its use waned, the discourse persisted. Since the colonial period, government officials liked to construe their role as "father" over the filial subjects, and subaltern communities often acknowledged this hierarchy when they sought adjudication from the state.

Although patriarchal nationalism did not entirely disappear, elites turned to what I term "corporeal nationalism." Where the former borrowed the metaphors of family, the latter relied on metaphors of the body and "scientific" conceptions of its structures and functioning. In this discourse Nicaragua is a body, with Nicaraguans the cells that compose it. The discourse of the body that predominated in nineteenth-century Europe and the Americas provided rich material for the description of society. Microscopic studies of the human body—from as early as the seventeenth century—revealed a seeming uniformity of the body's most basic building blocks despite the macroscopically distinct appearance of the body's parts, that is, unique (individual) bodies created from manifestly similar components.

By the mid-nineteenth century the body was fully conceived as a system or machine built of interdependent parts—and these composed of individual cells—where the proper functioning and survival of the body depended upon the successful integration and coordination of the body's subsystems. Bodies changed progressively, from undeveloped, unproductive forms incapable of self-sufficiency into mature, reproductive forms capable of surviving on their own. A deep understanding of the detailed mechanics of human physiology mattered little in constructing broadly metaphorical correlations between the institutions and infrastructure of society and the seeming

functions and structures of the body.[93] The power of this discourse
stemmed from how humans narrate the experiences of their own
bodies and from centuries of cultural management of the body. That
injury—say a burn on the arm or a gash on the leg—could be understood as harmful to the whole body transferred easily to a conception
of society as organism. This discourse certainly was consonant with
the era's positivist thinking, even as it relied on a narrower language
of human biology. Moreover, the positivist scientific justification of
hierarchy would have also meant that a *brazo* (an arm, but also used
to mean laborer)[94] did not have the worth of a *jefe* (head, or chief).
The discourse also retained the paternalistic qualities of patriarchal
nationalism through the now "scientific" perception that those individuals who were believed to be physically or mentally abnormal
("physical or moral defects," as the 1883 census called them) or psy-
chologically immature (such as women and children) lacked their
own independent sense of citizen-self.

Conclusion

In the first decades of independence from Spain, Nicaragua struggled
to exist as both a sovereign state and a political identity. With the
disintegration of the Central American Federation, however, Nicaraguans found themselves having to grapple more seriously with the
organization of the Nicaraguan state. Such a task required a modicum of unity, something elites could not seem to muster until the late
1840s when a series of mass uprisings and renewed British interest in
the Atlantic coast. Out of that experience they developed a discourse
of patriarchal nationalism that provided the seeds of national unity,
but they could not overcome weak institutions or meaningfully include the country's resistant subaltern communities.

The National War against Walker provided the necessary catalyst to the process of nation-state formation. The idea of nation was
hardly new, but its inclusiveness would be. After the war, elites built
upon the discourse of patriarchal nationalism developed in the 1840s,

continually reinforcing its message. Through this discourse and that of positivist-influenced corporeal nationalism, the elite sought to legitimize the state and its actions. How effective they would be, however, remained to be seen. The task at hand, after all, was the transformation of Nicaraguan society, building intrusive state institutions, and limiting the power of local communities. The process would prove complicated, involving social, cultural, economic, and political struggles at the national, regional, and local levels.

TWO

Death and Taxes
Building the National State

The devastation of the National War tainted the joy of defeating William Walker and his forces. In his 1857 inaugural address, President Tomás Martínez stood witness to the horror: "Our fields lie bleached with the ashes of our dead; our cities lie in ruins."[1] Nicaragua would rebuild, but painful memories of the National War would linger for decades to come. The war had taught Liberals and Conservatives two interrelated lessons that would be critical in the history of Nicaraguan nation-state formation: first, deep internal divisions among elites and between elites and the rest of Nicaraguan society threatened Nicaraguan sovereignty; second, Nicaragua needed a strong state in order to defend itself against other states and to quell internal divisions when they arose.

Nicaraguan elites overcame the initial obstacle to nation-state formation when they united to defeat Walker. Their ability to put aside their differences marked a profound change. As they worked assiduously to maintain their cohesion, they turned to a much more difficult problem: transforming the relationship of the state to municipalities and indigenous communities. Throughout the rest of the nineteenth century, but especially in the 1860s and 1870s, government officials at the national and prefectural level carefully (and sometimes warily) approached these local communities. Memories of the social anarchy of the late 1840s left a deep imprint on the elite psyche; wholesale top-down structural changes of the type tried by the Sandoval and Guerrero administrations were considered ill-advised.

Understanding the formation of the nation-state in a country like Nicaragua, which had a limited and anemic state until after the late 1850s, requires an examination of the development of the state's core institutions. In providing that analysis, this chapter is divided into four main parts. The first two focus on how the state was financed and on the state's coercive powers—the two areas most fundamental to any state's survival. The final two sections analyze different facets of the state's efforts to transform the meaning and practices of social control and social organization. In all of these cases, success or failure depended on the relationships developed between the state and local communities.

Financing the State

Until the late 1840s, Nicaraguan state finances relied entirely on legacies of the colonial taxation system.[2] These sources of income, including the colonial import tariff (*tarifa de aforo*), a kind of sales tax called the *alcabala*, and others, continued well into the late nineteenth century, although they diminished in importance or were transformed and modernized. Between 1858 and 1900 the Nicaraguan state grew phenomenally, with revenue and expenditures growing an average of approximately 8 percent per year.[3] Growth fluctuated over this period, of course, tending to rise and fall with the vagaries of the external economy and internal crises. The fluctuations in revenue tended to be greater, since the Nicaraguan state had little power over the world economy. Expenditure, on the other hand, tended to be slightly more conservative than revenue generation, and the state could smooth out spending through the use of loans and other measures (see table 1).

In the first decades following the National War, government officials looked more inwardly for taxation. The three largest internally generated sources of revenue—the aguardiente and tobacco monopolies and the tax on cattle slaughter—accounted for far more than any other source. Customs revenue expanded steadily and more rapidly over the second half of the nineteenth century than any other tax,

Table 1. Total state revenue and expenditures, 1858–1900 (four-year averages)

	Revenue		Expenditure	
	Value (pesos)	Growth (%)	Value (pesos)	Growth (%)
1858–1860*	338,222	—	349,712	—
1861–1864	481,853	42	472,345	35
1865–1868	675,729	40	688,473	46
1869–1872	772,463	14	765,526	11
1873–1876	1,084,167	40	1,084,167	42
1877–1880	1,244,817	15	1,247,278	15
1881–1884	1,599,379	28	1,680,320	35
1885–1888	1,532,245	-4	2,004,209	19
1889–1892	2,566,244	67	2,594,666	29
1893–1896	2,998,003	17	2,811,895	8
1897–1900	4,690,774	56	4,647,436	65

Source: Calculated from Nicaragua, Ministerio de Hacienda Pública, *Memoria* (1878) and *Memoria* (1903).
*Because data are unavailable for 1857, this data point is a three-year average.

averaging growth of 10 percent per year. Booming coffee production fueled the appetite for imports, leading customs revenue to overtake the aguardiente monopoly in the mid-1870s. Import tariffs formed a mainstay for most nineteenth-century Latin American treasuries, and Nicaragua was no exception (see figure 1).

Each municipality administered the tax on cattle slaughter within its territorial jurisdiction, with a surcharge going to local coffers. Although the value of the surcharge was locally determined as part of the annual *plan de arbitrios* (local budget and regulations), it was subject to ratification by the prefect. In the late 1860s the tax averaged 2.90 pesos per head, of which .40 pesos went to the municipality.[4] For the most part, the slaughter tax grew impressively, averaging nearly 16 percent per year. Given the weakness of the state in the first decades after the National War, it is not surprising that the state placed the task on the shoulders of the municipalities. Their share of the tax served as an incentive to collect it.

Whereas the tax burden of the aguardiente and tobacco monopolies fell most heavily on the Nicaraguan poor (for whom the consumption of these goods was a part of daily life), the tax on cattle

Figure 1. Sources of state revenue, 1858–1900 (four-year averages)

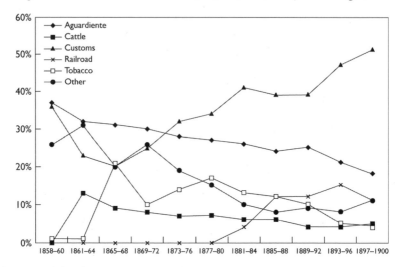

Source: Calculated from Nicaragua, Ministerio de Hacienda Pública, *Memoria* (1878) and *Memoria* (1903).

slaughter primarily hit the larger cattle producers. In his 1874 analysis of Nicaragua's economic potential, Pablo Lévy first argued that the power of the cattle producers, which he called "the richest families, and by consequence the most influential," diminished this potentially significant tax.[5] In fact, he estimated that nearly half of the cattle slaughtered each year went unaccounted for and untaxed.[6]

Numerous authors have repeated Lévy's claims, echoing the sentiment that Conservative cattle-ranching families were one of the main impediments to national progress.[7] That the tax on slaughter provided an incentive for illegal slaughter is obvious. Although many cattle were slaughtered in Nicaragua for local sale of their beef and export of their hides, it should be remembered that the majority of cattle were exported on the hoof to other parts of Central America. The lack of border facilities for monitoring overland trade makes it difficult to do more than guess at the number of cattle exported during the nineteenth century.[8] In any event, the focus on evasion of the slaughter tax as a sign of the retrograde nature of cattle ranchers fits more neatly into the prejudicial constructions of Liberal historiography than into actual analysis.

Although tobacco had been a lucrative product for many years, it was not until 1863 that the legislature authorized the government to reorganize its taxation. The result was an 1864 decree that gave the state a monopoly on the buying and selling of tobacco and manufactured tobacco products.[9] Previously, tobacco had been handled exclusively by the English merchants Thomas Manning, Jonas Glenton, and Walter Bridge, who received the tobacco monopoly from the Nicaraguan government in exchange for various loans.[10]

In preparation for implementing the tobacco monopoly, the state enacted an 1862 decree that required tobacco growers to register themselves at regional Ministry of Treasury offices, indicating the amount of tobacco they intended to grow and paying a tax on that amount. Throughout the growing cycle, inspectors in each department were to visit each of the growers to count their plants in an effort to ensure compliance with the law.[11] The decree's effectiveness is questionable, but perhaps more importantly, the decree facilitated the implementation of the tobacco monopoly two years later by providing the state with the names and approximate plantation size of growers.

The tobacco monopoly proved a fairly rich source of income for the state, providing between 1865 and 1892 a share of state revenue between 10 and 21 percent. To run its new establishment, the state created administrative offices in Rivas, Masaya, Managua, Chinandega, Juigalpa, León, and Matagalpa.[12] The position of inspector general was also created to oversee the details of both the tobacco and gunpowder monopolies. Despite the difficult institutional setup required, including storage and production facilities, guards, and officials, the monopoly was immediately profitable.[13] Nonetheless, its contribution to the state treasury proved distressingly inconsistent. The state found it difficult to react to market signals; the tobacco growers did not.

The history of the aguardiente monopoly dates back to 1845, when then minister of treasury Fruto Chamorro, in an attempt to control drinking and fund the state treasury, laid out the decrees for the collection of taxes on aguardiente and consecration of regional monopolies for its production and distribution. The monopolies raised prices, and the state used the means at its disposal to seek out and eradicate illegal production. These combined efforts provoked widespread public rebellion among both Indians and ladinos, who suffered disproportionately from this form of taxation.[14]

According to E. Bradford Burns, "By 1852, the [aguardiente] tax provided more income than any other source, well over one-third of total government revenue or $109,161 pesos for a budget of $296,373."[15] This trend continued nearly uninterrupted through 1874, when tariffs paid in cash overtook all other sources of income. Although the aguardiente monopoly required constant vigilance to fight contraband and tax evasion, revenue rose steadily, providing the necessary resources for a growing state and military which in turn helped collect these taxes. This growth, however, was clearly at the expense of the peasantry, the primary consumers of aguardiente.

The national government also mandated another significant form of taxation, one that is generally overlooked because the state never actually saw or accounted for a single peso of this tax: local works projects. Although municipalities elected their own officials and were nominally independent, they answered directly to their respective regional prefects, who in turn were responsible to and named by the national government. Consequently, although the municipality planned and administered local taxation, it did so within the bounds of prefectural prescription. Complaints of unfairly levied local taxes were not uncommon, and, importantly, relief from prefects was not unknown.

Although the state's taxation fell regressively upon Nicaragua's poorer, rural communities, its forms tended to mask themselves compared to those of the municipality. While the state owned the monopolies on aguardiente and tobacco (both products of local consumption), taxed the slaughter of cattle, and taxed the importation of consumer products that might end up in a local merchant's storefront, these all presented themselves as optional or avoidable taxes. One need not smoke tobacco, drink aguardiente, or buy a new cooking pot. When times were hard, such purchases could all be put off. Moreover, these items could also be obtained illegally: contraband tobacco and aguardiente and clandestine slaughter of cattle constantly stymied Treasury officials.

The municipality's local taxes and public works requirements, however, proved less escapable. Although the state may have bemoaned the threat of contraband to its fiscal well-being, one can also look at contraband as a release valve that made state policy less onerous. Each year every municipality created a plan de arbitrios that outlined all local regulations, public works requirements, and taxation. Each plan required prefectural approval and was frequently returned for modifications. The state wanted to avoid rebellions caused by overzealous local officials. This created tension between the state and municipalities, because, at least until the early 1880s, the state's development projects—its efforts at "progress"—focused on national issues: a railroad to connect Corinto to León, a telegraph line from Managua to Chontales, and national secondary schools in León and Granada.[16] Local construction of roads, churches, and schools had to be funded at the municipal level.

Local taxation also highlighted class stratification and ethnic difference within the community, since wealthier, usually ladino, townspeople could avoid labor drafts through cash payments. Commonly, for example, all men between eighteen and fifty would be required to provide two days of labor per month to maintain and fix local roads. One could avoid this work, however, by paying 50 centavos per day of the labor requirement, the equivalent of a day laborer's wage. Although the majority of a town's inhabitants could not afford such expense, over time work on public projects came to be associated with Indians, who found themselves increasingly poor and unable to avoid it. Thus, for example, when the Indians of Diriamba complained that the tax requirements placed upon them were too heavy and that they faced the harassment of the ladino alcalde, government minister Buenaventura Selva acted quickly. In a brief note that began "Urgent!" he ordered the abrogation of Diriamba's plan de arbitrios and the drafting of a new, fairer one.[17] A decade later the government minister again intervened in Diriamba because the town's plan was unfair to the "proletariat," placing the onus of public works upon their shoulders while permitting a very small "propertied class" to escape such work.[18]

Of course, a significant distinction was drawn between projects viewed to be of community importance and those that were not. The indigenous community of Masatepe complained that the ladino community did not provide funds for the maintenance and improvement of the parish church, whereas the Indians did. Their complaint, however, was not the cost they had assumed but rather the ladinos' lack of proper religious spirit. Conversely, they decried the cost, both monetarily and in labor, that the indigenous community had been forced to endure for the public water project, since they received almost no benefit from it. Water became more easily available for the ladinos who lived in the town center, but the Indians still had to trudge a significant distance to gather their water.[19]

In all cases, however, the success of these works projects derived in great part from the fact that they were locally organized and managed. Each community had a far greater understanding of its own possibilities and limitations than the state ever could, a reality made plain in the 1881 Matagalpa rebellions. Although it was far from the sole reason for these uprising, the "compulsory and underpaid labor for building the telegraph from Managua" was cited as a primary factor.[20] Whereas projects such as road and church repair could be imbued with a local character, the telegraph could not. Especially in the more frontier regions such as Matagalpa, it simply represented the state's unwanted invasion.

Tools of Coercion

In the aftermath of the National War, which had left Nicaragua deeply scarred both emotionally and physically, state officials concentrated less on healing wounds than on simple self-preservation. In the 1860s and 1870s, spending on the military and police consumed the majority of the state's funds. As memories of the war faded and social and economic concerns reemerged as the state's vital interests, however, spending on coercion declined and state institutions began to extend slowly into Nicaraguan rural communities and people's everyday lives.

The ramshackle, undisciplined armies that sprouted up across Nicaragua periodically in the decades following independence often seemed more a threat to nation-state formation than a foundation for it. Finally, after decades of disregard and missteps, the state sought to regularize and professionalize the army.[21] Driven by not wholly unwarranted fear of foreign intervention, the state emphasized the military in its discourse and spending in the 1860s.[22]

In his annual report in 1860, the minister of government claimed that the state had turned over a new leaf on martial preparedness and organization. Where Nicaragua's elites had in the past "created nothing but disorder and repugnance for the military profession," the new government understood that the military was "the most important [branch of state] for all nations, especially for ours which lives and will live threatened by foreign intervention."[23] Tension existed between those inclined to coercion and those determined to effect social and economic transformation, but the state's weakness and the fear produced by the National War favored the generals over the scientists.[24] Indeed, spending on coercion between 1858 and 1860 occupied an average of 45 percent of the state's annual budget, a level never again reached during the nineteenth century. The military remained prominent, but with the exception of temporary spikes at the outbreak of war, coercion's share of the budget declined to an average of 23.5 percent between 1860 and 1900 (see table 2).

Table 2. Spending on coercion, absolute and relative to total spending, 1858–1900 (four-year averages)

	Absolute spending (pesos)	Growth (%)	Relative spending (pesos)
1858–1860*	157,096	—	45
1861–1864	112,075	-29	24
1865–1868	160,822	44	23
1869–1872	218,603	36	29
1873–1876	364,617	67	34
1877–1880	223,834	-39	18
1881–1884	190,850	-15	11
1885–1888	409,267	114	20
1889–1892	410,092	0	16
1893–1896	614,695	50	22
1897–1900	1,777,172	189	38

Source: Calculated from Nicaragua, Ministerio de Hacienda Pública, *Memoria* (1878) and *Memoria* (1903).
*Because data are unavailable for 1857, this data point is a three-year average.

Although the military grew over the rest of the century, it never
approach the ten-thousand-man army envisioned in the military
code.[25] To some extent this highlighted the lack of need for such an
extensive force in Nicaragua, but it also indicated the problems the
state had in recruiting and filling its battalions. In 1863 the minister
of war reported that the days of "horror" long associated with recruitment of soldiers were gone, as "day after day they [people] see
the exactitude with which soldiers are paid and the punctuality with
which their military service is completed."[26] Nonetheless, recruitment remained difficult. Arturo Cruz argues that until the rise of the
Zelaya dictatorship, the succession of post-1858 governments "wished
to keep the army weak."[27] While this may have been the case, the
coercive potential of Nicaragua's police and military forces should
not be underestimated.

The state's viability depended on its ability to call upon military
forces, as the so-called Revolution of 1869 revealed. In that year,
Tomás Martínez and Máximo Jerez, who had been thrown together
in the binary presidency of 1857 but who otherwise seemed sworn
enemies, joined together in an effort to overthrow the government

of Fernando Guzmán. Although the uprising was defeated, the costs brought on a fiscal crisis that made it impossible for the state to pay the salaries of its soldiers.[28] In a plea to the "good men" of the country's leading cities, Minister of War Anselmo Rivas exclaimed, "we cannot resolve to see dying of hunger the soldiers that guard the public tranquillity."[29] By reapportioning the state's spending, money was found to pay for the soldiers. Rivas defended these expenditures in terms that bespoke a belief that the state's survival depended on its ability to maintain control of the reins of coercion: "True, this system of garrisons is very expensive; but the government believes that the larger social interests which it is duty bound to care for and which would be put in danger by a lack of such safety measures advantageously compensates for these costs."[30] If Rivas's request ruffled any feathers, they were soon smoothed by the economy's resurgence and the subsequent boom in revenue.

Whereas funding the military simply required a commitment of resources or occasionally shifting money from one project to another, recruitment proved a much more difficult operation. To facilitate the process, the state had the municipalities take a census of men between eighteen and sixty, listing marital status and occupation.[31] From these lists officials created a two-part system: each town maintained the first part, which consisted of lists of those eligible for service and the timing of their duty rotation; the garrisons maintained the second part, which listed the contingent's members, their rank, town of origin, and similar information.[32]

Historically, military duty had fallen lightly, if at all, upon the shoulders of Indians.[33] Considered unaccustomed to the rigors of military service, they were shunned in favor of men of African descent.[34] Nonetheless, with independence, Indians were increasingly asked to take on these responsibilities, although the extent to which they did so remains unclear.[35] Part of the problem derives from the ambiguity involved in the use of the term *Indian*. Who were these "Indians"? Were these self-identified "indígenas" from the numerous indigenous communities throughout the country, or simply ladino peasants, who, by occupation, residence, and phenotype, were called "indios" by the elites who wrote about them?

That the poor have made up the ranks of the military in all times is not in doubt. Pablo Lévy reported as much from his visit to Nicaragua in the late 1860s: "The injustice [of recruitment] is limited, in general, to those who do not wear shoes, that is to say, the poor. When rich or simply well-off youths consent to serve, they do so solely as officers."[36] Burns, however, because of his conflation of Indians with peasants, assumes that Indians made up the majority of the military at all times.[37] Common among accounts from the nineteenth century, however, are references to a contingent of archers here or there, heroic "noble savages" battling for the cause of national sovereignty despite their implied primitiveness.[38] Although these accounts form the basis of analyses of indigenous military participation, they offer little that is useful for understanding the determinants and particulars of such participation. Did indigenous communities participate because they felt threatened by one faction or another? Were they siding with their ideological kin? Or were they responding to existing patron-client relations? While both the reasons for and the extent of participation remain debatable, the growing importance of Indian recruits following the National War and their resistance to this shift suggests that prior to then participation was limited and not desired.[39]

By the late 1860s, as state institutions began to expand in earnest, complex interrelationships among the state, municipalities, and indigenous communities began to change. What had been relationships of occasion and convenience became regular and necessary. Although it remained possible to evade the state's grasp in many areas of life, doing so became increasingly difficult. Running to the hills when the tax collector came for his yearly appraisal simply no longer sufficed. Avoiding conscription into the army or forced public works labor required either drastic steps, such as moving self and family to the frontier regions or organizing collective action. The latter, although sometimes effective, implied an attempt to negotiate the fulfillment of the state's obligations rather than to negate them.

Faced with these changes and the growing predominance of Indians in the military, the indigenous community of Diriomo wrote to the prefect of Granada in 1868 to seek exemption from military service. Perhaps reflecting the historical relationship of Indians to the state, and to the military in particular, the prefect initially showed a willingness to entertain the possibility. Minister of War Bernabé Portocarrero, however, expressed the constraints of the new state in denying the Diriomeños' request.[40] Portocarrero confided to the prefect that the government was having serious difficulties filling the battalions that already existed and could not afford to limit its choice of recruits so drastically.[41]

More significantly, Portocarrero felt that such an exemption would strain the relationship between Indians and ladinos, leading ladinos to complain that Indians received preferential treatment and thereby alienating the state's most important ally in the process of nation-state formation. Like ships passing in the night, the distinct positions—that of the indigenous community and that of the state—brooked no compromise and afforded no point of intersection. The Diriomeños sought not engagement with the state, but withdrawal from it. Consequently, the indigenous community made no effort to contest the abstract "fairness" of political theory with the concrete reality of discrimination faced by Indians.

Rather than give up or negotiate with the state, the Diriomeños—with the help of their parish priest—looked to the external power historically most involved in their daily lives: the church. They wrote to Manuel Ulloa y Calvo, the bishop of León (Nicaragua's highest-ranking religious official), and he agreed to take up their cause. He received cordial treatment from the state, which agreed to reexamine the issues more fully. In the end, however, the decision remained the same.[42]

What might have been a straightforward case in other circumstances became complicated by the indigenous community's search for support from the church and the church's decision to offer it.[43] Although the nature and structure of relations between the church and the indigenous community remain poorly understood, these relations formed a significant axis of power in Nicaraguan indigenous society. What is clear, however, is that the state's apparent deference to the church's highest official disintegrated into the repudiation of the church's authority in matters of state policy. The church maintained sway over spiritual issues (although this, too, would face threat), but terrestrial intervention was to be the sole dominion of the state.

The transformation of the military was dramatic, as a long, multifaceted complaint by the alcaldes indígenas of Masatepe in 1880 highlights. No longer focusing on transfiguring the relationship between the indigenous community and the military, the alcaldes promoted the fulfillment of the state's obligations within its own national discourse. Planted firmly in the assertion that they "have always remained faithful to the government and friends to the cause of order," the community's leaders attacked the failure of ladinos in the town to maintain this standard and bemoaned the unjust treatment nonetheless accorded to the community's members. Despite ladino "treachery," which went "to the extreme that many of them engrossed the ranks of the bandit filibusters [of William Walker] . . . only the unhappy Indian is forced to go to all of the military posts and guard posts of the country."[44]

The Indian community's attack simultaneously positioned its members as ideal Nicaraguans while casting Masatepe's ladinos as traitors in the mold of Padre Agustín Vijil, willing to sell their own country in the name of power. Although Vijil was hardly the only member of the elite to have welcomed Walker's arrival, his open support and service as Walker's envoy and minister plenipotentiary to the United States branded him as the archetypal traitor.[45] The response of Ramón Navarro, the municipal secretary of Masatepe, sparked with anger but failed to flame. Although unable to deny that some ladinos in the town had joined Walker's troops, Navarro asserted that the actions of individual ladinos could not be fairly ascribed to all of ladino society.[46] He reflected the typical response of an essentialized racism: ladinos were individuals with agency and choices, while Indians were a group whose actions and ideas were culturally fixed. It was this type of discrimination that informed the indigenous community's complaint. Yet Navarro simply asserted that if Indians outnumbered ladinos among the military's ranks, this merely reflected the racial breakdown of Masatepe. The military governor of Granada, however, reported that Indians formed not simply the majority but the entirety of the Masatepan contingent.[47]

After spending on its coercive forces had grown slowly and steadily for about two decades, the state began to limit its spending in this area. Not only did spending decline in the late 1870s, but the ratio of coercive spending to total spending dropped even more. The military's budget began to rise again in the late 1880s, but it took off explosively during the regime of José Santos Zelaya. After the military's share of total state spending had dropped to an average of less than 18 percent between 1877 and 1896, it jumped to 38 percent between 1897 and 1900 (see table 2).

Spending, however, simply reflected the transformations that Zelaya attempted to work upon Nicaraguan society. In his analysis of the Zelaya regime, Benjamin Teplitz emphasizes the dictator's militarization of Nicaraguan society. Jerónimo Pérez, who had lived through the devastation of William Walker and who served in the first postwar government, believed that the National War heralded a new age in Nicaragua. "Only after the bloody struggle of 1854, did the word death to the political enemy ring with horror in the ears," he argued.[48] Zelaya, part of the new generation of leaders who were either too young to remember the war against Walker or had not experienced it firsthand, did not seem to take these words to heart. Teplitz notes that in just one coup attempt an estimated two thousand people died.[49] This level of violence simply did not occur in any of the inter-elite struggles that occurred between 1858 and Zelaya's rise to power in 1893.

The Criminalization of Everyday Life

In 1845 the state embarked on a process of restructuring acceptable forms of everyday life practices by asserting ownership of or control over resources that had previously belonged to individuals. Although the exertion of control extended to diverse areas, two efforts in particular—the creation of the state aguardiente monopoly and the establishment of vagrancy laws—stand out for their fiscal importance and contrasting success. In the first case, the state reinstated its control over the production and distribution of aguardiente, a practice of leisure and consumption as much as of production. Aguardiente had been a colonial monopoly, but it was abolished in 1811 after the monopoly was blamed for inciting rebellion.[50] In the second case, those who happily lived off the fruits of the land were now labeled as "vagrants," as if by letting their labor power lie fallow they had forfeited the right to control it. Both of these policies highlighted the highly contested and contradictory relationship between domination and negotiation. Officials experimented with different methods of achieving these policies, because the nature of the state's task—the criminalization of everyday life—depended on the state's ability to balance the use of arbitrary police authority and mediation with local communities. As Terry Eagleton has argued, "Authority lives in a kind of ceaseless self-undoing, as coercion and consent reinforce yet undermine one another in a cat-and-mouse game."[51]

Aguardiente

Despite serving as an important source of state revenue throughout the nineteenth century, the aguardiente monopoly suffered constantly from problems with contraband. The number of laws enacted to combat contraband serves as an excellent index of the state's ineffectiveness. Some of the laws were poorly written, while others failed to encompass fully the state of the problem they sought to rectify. In the 1840s state officials employed a discourse of health and community well-being in their justification for monopolizing aguardiente production. Drunkenness was identified as "the most dangerous vice, exalting the imagination of drunks, disposing them to crime, and is precisely why we must dictate measures that moderate the use of liquors."[52] But how could the state moderate the consumption of alcohol when its revenue stream was so dependent on that consumption? Unable to bend logic to such a geometry, officials began to turn less to a moral justification and more to an economic one.

Although aguardiente production continued outside the state's purview, many home brewers initially sought to avoid clandestine production or altercations with the police by simply switching to *chicha fuerte*, an alcohol made from fermented corn. The effect on the treasury was immediately noticeable and brought on the control, if not illegalization, of chicha and all other strong alcoholic beverages not sanctioned for production by the state. All infractions received the same punishment meted out for illegal aguardiente producers. Indigenous communities, which used chicha during festivals, retained the right to production, but only for such occasions and subject to inspection by local authorities.[53]

Trial and error solved such problems, but achieving the right mix of threat and enforcement proved more vexing. Initially, illegal aguardiente production was fined with thirty days of public service for both men and women. Local judges and Treasury employees faced stiff penalties (a 25-peso fine and firing, respectively) if they failed to enforce the law actively.[54] Given the turbulence of the ensuing decade, it is hardly surprising that the first revisions to these laws were not made until 1858.

From the National War until the aguardiente monopoly was abolished, it seemed as if each administration tried its hand at stamping out contraband. Initially, however, the state lacked the means to handle defiance of its policies. As contraband spread, especially in the country's frontier regions, the state struggled with its own weakness, seeming to grasp helplessly for "the most appropriate means [of eradication]," one that could "interest one and all Nicaraguans in vigilance and persecution of contraband." Since there was no popular desire to control aguardiente production, new legislation tried to generate such interest by providing a financial incentive. For turning in your contrabandista neighbor you would receive two-thirds of the potential fine, starting at just over 6 pesos and paid half in hard currency and half in bonds.[55]

States may learn to use the carrot, but they never forget the stick. From the punishment of public works labor imposed in 1846, the Nicaraguan state moved in 1858 to punishing illegal producers with ten to thirty days' imprisonment (or 5 to 15 pesos) for the first offense. A second conviction meant twenty to sixty days in jail, while a third meant two to three months in the prison of the Castillo Viejo fort.[56] Within two decades, the law meted out this harsh punishment to first-time offenders. This initial two months in the Castillo Viejo was now to be followed by a cumulative two-month ,addition for each subsequent conviction.[57]

While the "considerable disequilibrium in fiscal rents" attributed to contraband certainly irked the Treasury, it nonetheless enjoyed handsome profits from the monopoly throughout its existence.[58] However, the ubiquity of contraband production proved symptomatic of a far more serious condition: the recalcitrant behavior of local officials charged with enforcement of contraband laws. Indeed, laws punishing the lack of official enforcement accompanied nearly every law established to persecute illegal production.[59]

Statements by the mayor of Diriá in 1887 evidence the failure of the state's policy. Responding to complaints of contraband production, the mayor indicated that "even though aguardiente is distributed on the street, he will not take any measures against the contrabandistas." The government minister reacted coldly and ordered the prefect of Granada to express the state's displeasure with such defiance and "if despite your excitation, they [local officials] show themselves weak, you will employ upon them the coercive measures that the penal regulations and other laws establish for such cases."[60] If the prefect made any effort to carry out these commands, it is unclear how immediate or effective his actions were. Six months after the mayor of Diriá's flagrant disregard of the law, contraband was still being produced and sold "in an almost public manner" throughout the prefecture of Granada, reflecting a generalized lack of enforcement by authorities charged with the task.[61] Nonetheless, the threat of such insubordination and the concomitant drop in state income it implied could not go unanswered. Reports of lax enforcement appeared to cease following a reform of the "Reglamento de Contrabando" the following year, and income from the aguardiente monopoly rose dramatically. Perhaps investments made in policing in the mid-1880s, which had more than doubled the average spending on coercion compared to the early 1880s, were beginning to show results.

The state's failure to find a ready solution to contraband production led it to punitive responses that illuminated how ill-prepared the state was for the unintended consequences of its policies. In criminalizing an aspect of everyday behavior, the state, with the stroke of a pen, turned law-abiding citizens into criminals. Since criminal conviction abrogated the rights of citizenship and home brewing was so ubiquitous, the very act threatened to subvert the inclusiveness of the nation-state. Given alcohol's commonplace use in Nicaragua for both leisure and ritual, it is hardly surprising that the state made little effort to alter the cultural significance of alcohol and its consumption within society. Still, as the effectiveness of policing increased, the courts and prisons were confronted with the mass of criminals that the aguardiente monopoly had created. The administration of President Joaquín Zavala was so worried by the rapidly growing population in the prison at the Castillo Viejo that in 1882 judges were ordered to halt sending new criminals there.[62] Greater spending could be budgeted to prison construction, but Nicaragua was not yet ready to be a carceral society.

The pervasiveness of home aguardiente production was exacerbated by the fact that women were the most common producers. Not only did the criminalization of aguardiente production create a whole new class of criminals in Nicaraguan society, but it threw a large number of women into that group. Although it was never believed that women were incapable of crime, nineteenth-century gender discourse and their lack of legal personhood tended to create them more as victims, not victimizers.[63] Until the 1870s, laws regarding contraband punished men and women equally. Indeed, the laws specifically explained that these punishments were "for men and women," suggesting how male gendered the law implicitly was. Since women had no legal stature of their own, they were not subjects of the law, although they were subject to it.[64]

As the punishments became increasingly harsh, the implication that men and women were equally capable of criminal behavior threatened the prevailing gender discourse. The resolution, interestingly, was to reorient both the punishment and the understanding of the crime for women. Instead of being sent to the prison at the Castillo Viejo, starting in the 1870s women were sent to either the Hospital of León or the Hospital of Granada.[65] In so doing, female *contrabandistas* were transformed from criminals into patients. Their deviant behavior became an illness requiring medical attention rather than a crime subject to incarceration. Women, like children, the mentally ill, and the "physically or morally deformed,"[66] lacked the complete control over their minds and bodies necessary for full participation in the nation-state. This apparent aberration could be cured, according to one observer, if "the criminal [woman] finds proper occupations for her rehabilitation and improvement of habits in a constant dedication to the practice of charity, that sublime virtue that would transform a lost woman into a sister of charity."[67] Although this law was abrogated a year later in response to complaints from the hospital staffs, the new law still segregated women and men. Instead of hospitalization, these homebrewers were now to be placed in the homes of responsible citizens who were to guide them to ensure they repaid their crimes through labor on public works projects.[68] In both cases, these women were constructed as wretches who had slipped from the ideals of female honor. The solution to this problem was not to be found in a reappraisal of nineteenth-century gender discourse and the relationship of women to the law, but in a process that transformed their "crime" into an acceptably female expression.[69]

Vagrancy

Following the National War, the state also began to reorganize its role in controlling and distributing labor to meet both public and private demands. Although "not laboring" had been criminalized as early as 1845 in the first of Nicaragua's "vagrancy" laws, it was not until the stability of the postwar period that the state could begin to enforce these laws. Any adult man who could not provide the means of subsistence for himself and his family was classified as a day laborer (*jornalero*). To be so labeled yet without gainful employment meant the threat of impressment into public works labor or to contract with an employer (agricultural or artisanal) through an agricultural judge.

Until the coffee production boom in the 1880s, enforcement of vagrancy laws appears to have been relatively lax. In fact, the level of enforcement showed no lack of effort, but rather a lack of institutional stability, reach, and coordination. A law from 1858, for example, ordered police to destroy the property of those who lived far outside the center of a town if their holdings were insufficient for their needs—that is, if they were jornaleros.[70] These laws tended to attack those who lived outside broader community structures: those who had fled the centers of community life for the outskirts.

Although local officials—from mayors to policemen to judges— made individual efforts to enforce these laws, their failure to work in concert limited their effectiveness. Moreover, ambiguities over the chain of authority and the value or fairness of some laws exacerbated the situation. Between the late 1850s and the mid-1880s it was common for government ministers to complain that "outsiders [*hombres forasteros*] with no known office or profession are found [everywhere], thefts occurring with frequency."[71] More importantly, this situation was attributable to the failure of local officials to carry out their duties.[72] These efforts were complicated in the 1860s and 1870s by power struggles between officials charged with carrying out state policies. Officials at the municipal and canton level, for example, often fought over jurisdiction, ignoring each other's requests and orders, even if legally charged with such duties. At the same time, those with greater power and jurisdictional reach, such as agricultural judges, frequently questioned the authority and fairness of their peers.[73]

As the state extended its control over everyday aspects of local social and political administration, it was aided by the increasingly parallel interests of local and national elites. The control and discipline of labor remained difficult, but the struggles between state officials played a decreasing role in the situation. Laborers demonstrated tremendous mobility throughout the century and became increasingly evasive as the state mounted greater coercive pressure upon them. The state's efforts to eradicate contraband aguardiente production failed in great part because local state officials disagreed with the policy and refused to enforce it. With vagrancy, on the other hand, the state's policy found almost universal acceptance among local officials, but until at least the late 1880s they lacked the means to implement it.

The Institutionalization of Social Control

Although taxation and coercion necessarily form the basis of all states, they are insufficient for the construction of a functioning nation-state. The Roman Catholic Church had long played an important role in the formation of local identities, but increasingly the state viewed the church as a potential threat. Over the rest of the nineteenth century, the separation between church and state grew as the state tried to transform local social organization. As the church's power diminished, the state took greater interest in structuring mechanisms of social control and education in an effort to legitimate itself.

The relationship of the church to nineteenth-century Nicaraguan society is little studied; relations between the church and the state are almost as poorly understood.[74] Prior to the National War, these two relationships can be described (in an admittedly cursory way) as deep and limited, respectively. While the Bourbon reforms may have had little lasting impact on Nicaraguan society, the church's role in creating and maintaining social organization and control was never in doubt.[75]

The church showed the strains of internal division during the struggle for independence. Although the leadership supported the royalists, numerous priests supported independence.[76] Even after the empire had been overthrown, memories of the church's ambiguous position rankled many in the new state. By 1825, however, the leadership of the church had changed hands, with Nicaraguan son José Desiderio de la Quadra taking the helm. To the extent possible, Quadra kept the church away from the storms that battered the rest of the country between independence and his death in 1849. Given the rapid leadership turnover during the early struggles for state formation, overly close ties would have proved problematic. From then until the National War, church-state relations began to turn rocky, but these took a backseat to the civil strife that began to engulf the country.[77]

Church-state relations changed dramatically following the National War. The reasons are manifold and, not least, included the state's increased role in everyday social organization and control, an area previously dominated by the church. However, a single event seems to have stood as the clarion call for this changing relationship: the treason of Padre Agustín Vijil.[78] Long an admirer of the United States, Vijil generously embraced Walker and his efforts, becoming his minister plenipotentiary to Washington in 1856.[79] In his history of the National War, Jerónimo Pérez focused Vijil's actions through the prism of nationalism. As if to underscore how universally Vijil's "sin" was understood, Pérez quoted the archbishop of Baltimore, who apparently asked upon meeting Vijil, "Is it possible that a Catholic priest could come to this country to work against his own religion and against his own Fatherland?"[80] That Vijil, a member of the church hierarchy, could betray Nicaragua for Walker cast doubt on the church's role in the process of nation-state formation and began the process of separation that would be enshrined in the 1893 Constitution. Although some have argued that the 1858 Constitution's proclamation that Nicaragua is a "Catholic country" exemplified the Conservative nature of the state prior to José Santos Zelaya's 1893 coup, evidence for such a view is limited.[81]

The church remained an important part of society. Moreover, the state could not immediately have taken over the church's nonreligious tasks. In 1860 the bishop of Nicaragua, Bernardo Piñol y Aycinena, stopped in several Nicaraguan towns during a trip to Guatemala. A letter from Government Minister Jerónimo Pérez to local prefects on the eve of the bishop's trip plainly indicated the government's position in relation to the church: "The harmony of the powers [*Potestades*] is seen as a great good for the state, and it [the state] desires that you and all of your subaltern authorities make demonstrations conducive to proving the favorable sentiment that animates them toward the Chief of the Church of Nicaragua."[82] Nonetheless, new legislation and executive decrees began chipping away at the church's authority and autonomy.

Just two years after the bishop's return from Guatemala, the state ratified the Concordat of 1862, which established a broad decree regulating the church. The tithe and monastic orders—two important sources of income—were abolished. More importantly, all church officials were required to pledge allegiance to the state. Finally, the state appropriated review of appointments and the right of censorship.[83] Although not without precedent within the Catholic world, these changes might have been achieved more smoothly in Nicaragua because of the church's relative poverty and weakness.[84] The struggle over corporate lands so violent in Mexico and Guatemala, for example, has no counterpart in Nicaragua. Nonetheless, once accepted by the church, these conditions for continued favor within the state permanently altered the relationship between the two.

Despite the accommodation achieved between the diocese and the state, church-state relations showed frequent strain at the parish level. Especially in the 1860s and 1870s, parish priests generally found their most ardent supporters and most generous contributors among the indigenous populations of the municipalities to which they ministered. Not uncommonly, these same priests found themselves confronting the state, be it at the municipal, prefectural, or national level, in parallel with the indigenous communities they served.[85]

When the rebellion of 1869 broke out in León, a number of parish priests left their flocks to join the call to revolution. Angered by a seeming return to the treasonous example of Padre Vijil, Minister of State Teodoro Delgadillo acted aggressively, calling upon mayors in every town to gather information "about the public and private conduct of priests during normal times, and about the practices executed by them in the most recent revolution."[86] Delgadillo appeared to overstep the boundaries of the state's legitimate authority, and in less than a week he retreated from this position, explaining that the government only sought investigation of those priests who had abandoned their parishes during the rebellion, which he claimed to have evidence for in Jinotepe, Masatepe, Masaya, and Nindirí, and that it should not be misconstrued as a witch-hunt again priests in general.[87] Nonetheless, church-state relations had taken a turn for the worse.

When Vicente Quadra assumed the presidency two years later, the scars left by the priests' flirtation with politics had yet to fade. In a public speech following his election in 1871, Quadra affirmed his constitutional duty to protect the Roman Catholic Church but declared with undisguised anger, "I will never permit them [the ecclesiastic authorities] to treat the prerogative of the republic's laws and civil authority with impunity."[88] His directness helped to right the teetering relationship, leading to a decade of quiet and stability between church and state.

In 1881, however, the connections between Jesuit missionaries and the rebelling indigenous communities in Matagalpa once again unsettled the relationship.[89] Following the outbreak of violence, the state began to investigate the Jesuits and limit their movements.

Over the course of a single week it forced all Jesuits to return to the capital city of whatever department they resided in, eventually requiring them to gather in Granada.[90] Rumors that the Jesuits might be expelled spread rapidly, and numerous protests—generally led by women—broke out.[91] The leading members of the Granadino elite counseled against expulsion, but in the end President Zavala decided to force their exit.[92]

The potential repercussions of such a move were intense. Indeed, a second Indian uprising in Matagalpa in August 1881 appeared to be fomented by both the expulsion order and the increasing secularization of Nicaraguan society.[93] Elite opposition to these same measures also surfaced in the support by dissident Conservative factions for riots in León. The so-called Olanchanos (Conservatives rooted in León and Chinandega) and Iglesieros (an ultramontane faction headed by Granadino Manuel Urbina) worked together politically and conspiratorially to check what they saw as increasingly anti-Catholic cosmopolitanism in Nicaragua.[94] When they could not sway the 1884 presidential election from the atheist Adán Cárdenas, they plotted his overthrow, but these plans were foiled, with numerous participants jailed or exiled.[95] Unlike in the first years after independence, when more liberal challenges to the social and cultural status quo of the colonial period seemed to engender unending civil war, the state's vigor now secured Nicaragua to the path of liberal modernity.

After these crises in the early 1880s, church-state relations remained relatively stable until 1893 when José Santos Zelaya took power in a coup. Under Zelaya a new constitution established the explicit secularization of the state and curtailed much of the church's means of income.[96] Faced with such an attack, the church began actively to oppose state policies and officials, both in individual parishes and at the highest levels of leadership.[97] In 1894, for example, a newspaper called *La Unión Católica* began to be published. Vehemently anti-Liberal, the paper sought funding from parish priests throughout the country.[98] For at least the next decade, church and state would struggle against each other.

The separation that Zelaya imposed, however, merely sealed a division evidenced by the fact that a decade earlier an openly atheist candidate won election to the presidency. In his inaugural address, Adán Cárdenas clarified his position:

> Whatever my opinions in philosophical matters and my ideas about the political convenience of an official church, I recognize and will respect the constitutional principle that assures the state's protection of the worship of the Roman Catholic religion. I take the opportunity to make this declaration, not to satisfy the feigned scruples of people who unfortunately have taken unfair advantage of religious sentiment in this country, *making use of it as a factional weapon*, but to provide peace of mind for those sincere Catholics who had felt threatened by my rise to power.[99]

Caught between his desire for a secular state and the constitution's explicit claim that "Nicaragua is a Roman Apostolic Catholic country," Cárdenas took a middle road. The state's role may have been to proactively promote a Catholic society, but now that role was reconceived as reactive, simply protecting Catholic religious practice when threatened in any way.

The growing distance between church and state mirrored an increase in state activity in areas previously controlled by the church. One of the most important of these involved the collection and maintenance of statistics about the population. Although the Sandoval administration had initiated the gathering of social and economic data in 1845, these efforts paled in comparison to the onslaught of census taking that occurred following the National War.[100]

Demographic censuses served initially to establish membership in a municipality and the necessity to pay taxes and accept other community responsibilities. Escaping from such counting was difficult except for those in the farthest outskirts of most towns. Even the largest towns in the prefecture of Granada, such as Diriamba and Jinotepe, numbered just a few thousand. Moreover, since direct taxes went straight to the municipalities, it was in their interest to collect them as vigorously as possible.[101] At times, however, such lists calculated individual capital endowments to determine those with sufficient means to pay for specific social institutions (e.g., the Hospital of Granada) and the occasional forced loan.[102] Not surprisingly, these latter efforts met with resistance from community members who felt the taxes excessive.[103]

While census lists facilitated local taxation, determining a community's size also established its juridical status within the state. As a town rose each rung in status, first from village to town and finally to city, its relationship to the state and the communities around it changed. Initially an area may have formed part of the outskirts of a town to which it paid taxes and under whose local laws and governance it existed. As these communities grew, however, their members often began to question the use to which their taxes were being put. The indigenous community of Masatepe, for example, lived across a river from the main center of the town, a river that ran furiously during the rainy season. The indigenous community's children could not normally cross the river by themselves during these months, and consequently they questioned the municipality's plan to convert the town's parish church into a local public school since their children would fail to benefit from it. If Masatepe's leaders felt a public school would be beneficial, the community asked, why not build it on the other side of the river, where their young children could make use of it?[104] Achieving even "village" status would have allowed the barrio the Indians lived in to make such decisions themselves as well as allowed them to collect their own taxes and use them for local development. At the same time, each new village created a new locus of local power tied to the state.[105]

Although government officials portrayed census taking as beneficial both to local communities and to the state as a whole, local officials were often remiss in carrying out their duty.[106] The actual task of collecting the data may have been time consuming, and in smaller towns it might have seemed senseless to repeat the task every year. Moreover, since the state lacked the resources to enforce a uniform census, the results varied from town to town. El Rosario's 1867 census listed all men and women by name, with age, marital status, number of children, and occupation. Jinotepe's 1858 census, on the other hand, listed men and women in family groups, but without an indication of the number of children, and with the addition of capital estimates for all male heads of household.[107]

Unsatisfied with the haphazard nature of these data, the state created an office of statistics to reorganize and standardize its data collection.[108] The earliest and most significant efforts of this office were two censuses, one demographic, the other agricultural. For both, uniformly printed forms were distributed to each municipality. Even these forms, however, allowed for a certain amount of local caprice.[109] Nonetheless, these censuses took the collection of statistics to new heights. The demographic census added legitimacy of birth, race, education, right to vote, religion, country of birth, vaccination, and physical and moral defects to the categories of data previously gathered. The agricultural census attempted to quantify land value, size, usage, production, and ownership.

Despite the growing distance between church and state in Nicaragua, for the first two decades following the National War the state continued to rely on parish priests to collect and calculate monthly demographic movements. From these data officials loosely calculated patterns of internal migration and attempted to anticipate infrastructural and social development needs. As the institutional apparatus of the state grew and expanded, however, it simultaneously developed the means to carry out such organizationally intensive tasks as secular birth, death, and marriage registries, and confronted the need to eschew those who felt there existed any authority higher than the state's.

At the canton level, officials maintained lists of men eligible for voting.[110] The 1858 Constitution limited voting to adult men with at least 100 pesos in wealth. While this certainly limited suffrage, it was hardly an exceptional policy, similar to those in many European countries until the mid- to late nineteenth century. The voting rolls were updated yearly to accommodate the economic fluctuations that added men of recently acquired means while removing those whose wealth had slipped below the threshold or whose personal actions deprived them of the right to vote.

To what extent, however, was suffrage available and exercised in nineteenth-century Nicaragua? The available documentation on these issues in the municipal archive of Granada, at least, is voluminous and varied, consequently limiting the possibility of an adequate analysis here and begging future research. Rather than investigate these distinct but related issues, however, scholars have tended to deny their importance out of hand. In one of his reports to his superiors at the State Department toward the end of the nineteenth century, U.S. minister in Managua H. H. Leavitt expressed the not entirely surprising view that "By name Nicaragua holds the position of a Republic and her people free, which to us is the meaning of Republic, but she differs as widely as the Imperial Government of Russia to the United States."[111] That scholars have often unflinchingly reiterated this view leads to the continued relegation of a crucial aspect of the inclusive discourse of the nation-state outside of analysis. Implicit in such a view, moreover, is a belief that the only elections of note are those at the national level. The regularity and fastidiousness of the state's voting lists is, significantly, exceeded by the complaints, letters, investigations, and reports on elections and voting rights.[112]

As with other social work performed by the church, education had not, historically, been within the state's sphere of activity. In fact, until 1877, when the state declared primary education "free and obligatory," the organization and funding of primary education had been left to parents and individual municipalities. Given the unstable and contested nature of the state between 1821 and 1858, such an arrangement is not surprising. Indeed, the instability of post-independence years throughout Latin America led to similar situations through the region.[113] Moreover, European thought had nibbled away at the scholastic foundations of Central American education, and a more thorough pedagogical overhaul in Nicaragua only began in the late 1870s with the arrival of six freethinking professors from Spain.[114] Nearly every discussion of educational reform, from the earliest, in 1831, focused on the need to emphasize the sciences and practical arts, but the curriculum never seemed to change.[115]

In the wake of the war against William Walker, the discussion of education turned not just on technical reforms but on the role of education in forging national citizens. Nicaragua needed "citizens more than inhabitants," and education would produce them.[116] Indeed, in a discussion of the state's failure to promote agricultural production and achieve "progress" in general in 1860, one commentator expressed the feeling that law, in and of itself, was insufficient to produce the desired results. An agricultural law would help, "but in no way will it root out the sickness we deplore; only education of the masses will work this wonder."[117]

In 1860 the Ministry of Government reported that "public teaching . . . is not well conceptualized."[118] By this it meant that the relationship of education to the state was weakly defined and therefore not capable of producing results significantly different from those of the past. The very nature of the state's relationship to education had to change if it was to change the way education functioned in Nicaragua. As state officials increasingly saw the importance of education for developing national citizens, they sought to reform education and exert more control over the ways in which municipalities carried out the education project. However, until the state was willing and able to spend money toward that end, education would remain outside its control.

Historically, the state had relied on church-run and other private schools. Local authorities and local taxes financed the public schools. Serious problems stymied this approach, however. Since money was gathered and administered locally, fraud beyond the state's control was common.[119] Indeed, records of mortgages in Granada from the 1840s indicate that the local Board of Education (Dirección de Instrucción Pública) was one of the most important sources of credit.

Given that it could gather—in 1871, at least—somewhere on the order of 200,000 pesos, such uses are hardly surprising. Funding that was meant for monthly disbursements could be made productive over the course of a year by lending it out at 18 to 24 percent a year—according to the going rate. Unfortunately, to whom such distributions went and with what efficiency they were canceled appears to have been problematic.

The state's lack of attention to education enabled a profusion of community-driven approaches to schooling. Each town produced its own teachers and intellectuals, who tended to teach what was considered necessary to preserve the status quo within that community. Minimal teaching of reading, writing, and moral doctrine provided the means for maintaining the levels of social differentiation that already existed in these communities. The Ministry of Government's push for educational progress and attendant pedagogical notions were nowhere to be found here, since they were felt to serve no purpose—except, perhaps, to disrupt the community's equilibrium. In one case, after a school inspector visited the barrio of Jalteva in Granada, he recommended that the local teacher be replaced because of his incompetence in the areas of instruction that the state wished to promote. The parents in the community, however, believed that the teacher provided the instruction that the children of the community needed and should therefore remain.[120]

As the state's relationships with towns and local authorities increased, its ability to take control of education grew. Spending increased, and education became a significant priority from a budgetary perspective. The number of schools and pupils enrolled grew dramatically over the second half of the nineteenth century. Based on his travels in Nicaragua, Pablo Lévy reported that in 1872 barely forty-five hundred students received education in the 101 schools throughout the country. By the end of the nineteenth century the state boasted more than three times as many schools, teaching almost five times as many students.[121] Education might not have received the financial attention that elites claimed to desire, but neither was it

Table 3. Spending on education, absolute and relative to total spending, 1858–1900 (four-year averages)

	Absolute spending (pesos)	Growth (%)	Relative spending (pesos)
1858–1860*	0	—	0
1861–1864	953	—	0
1865–1868	845	11	0
1869–1872	878	5	0
1873–1876	4,148	372	0
1877–1880	55,608	1,241	4
1881–1884	124,720	124	7
1885–1888	133,863	7	7
1889–1892	211,848	58	8
1893–1896	67,392	-68	2
1897–1900	337,142	400	7

Source: Calculated from Nicaragua, Ministerio de Hacienda Pública, *Memoria* (1878) and *Memoria* (1903).
*Because data are unavailable for 1857, this data point is a three-year average.

ignored. The state's spending on education in the years immediately following the National War barely registered on the account books, averaging between 1 and 2 percent of total spending. It rose steadily, however, and by the early 1880s it averaged around 8 percent of total spending, a figure that placed Nicaragua on par with Costa Rica and significantly above the rest of the isthmus (see table 3). Per capita enrollment figures reveal a significant expansion in primary education: in 1872 primary education was limited to just over 16 Nicaraguans for every 1,000 in the population, while by 1897 access had tripled to over 50 Nicaraguans per 1,000. Nicaragua provided significantly better access to education than Guatemala and lagged only slightly behind Costa Rica.[122]

Now more firmly in control of education, the government began producing textbooks and curricula that would ensure the production of a certain kind of student, those who would not only be good citizens but would also inculcate their education into their children, friends, and neighbors. Scholarships were provided for a limited number of poor students—usually one from each town in the country—to attend secondary school in León or Granada, with the understanding that upon completing their studies they would return to the homes and educate the youth—especially the poor—of their communities. This newly elevated class of petty bureaucrats was expected to advance the ideal of the nation and the grasp of the state in the most distant reaches of Nicaragua. The precise form of this education remained hotly debated. While Liberals championed modern, scientific education, ultramontane Catholics claimed that this inculcated Freemasonry and secularization.[123] As one commentator in the 1880s wrote in a barely veiled allusion to León and Granada, "The Doric spirit [of Sparta] was hard, austere, friend of rules and order; the Ionic spirit [of Athens], on the contrary was light, subtle, sparkling, independent, fond of beauty, friend of freedom, even to toleration. Consequently, the education system was different in the two cities, although they shared the common goal of forming citizens such that the individual disappeared before the personality of the State."[124] Although political and philosophical differences might advance distinct educational styles, they aimed for the same end.

Conclusion

The Nicaraguan state grew at a remarkable pace following the National War. The stability of postwar intra-elite relations facilitated more effective tax collection and the expansion of the state's coercive forces, which, in turn, provided the means to assert dominion over aspects of social control and organization long entrusted to the church. Revenue and coercive powers sustained the state's existence, but as the experiences of the 1840s rebellions and the National War made clear, the creation of Nicaraguan "citizens" would be fundamental to the process of nation-state formation. Fermín Ferrer, who served as perfect of the Departamento Oriental (roughly what became the prefectures of Granada and Chontales), argued in 1850 that those "not under the immediate inspection of public functionaries bring harm to the state."[125] But this was a difficult proposition, because such "immediate inspection" brought on popular rebellion in the first place.

Expansion of the state demanded intimacy with people's everyday lives, the kind that the church had established over hundreds of years of negotiation in local communities. Bishops could make great pronouncements, but parish priests were charged with implementation. The formation of the nation-state, too, demanded an engagement with local officials and the negotiation of social organization and social control. There was no lack of ideas about building Nicaragua into a modern liberal nation-state, but efforts at changing the structure and functioning of the state in local communities illuminated the instrumental role these same communities would have to play. Municipalities and local state officials did not have to perceive a benefit from state policies or institutions in order to implement them, but it helped. More significantly, as the case of Nicaragua's failed attempt to eradicate contraband aguardiente shows, if the state's efforts appeared detrimental to local society, they would likely fail.

THREE

The Wealth of the Country
Land, Community, and Ethnicity

A decade after the National War, six prominent, wealthy Nicaraguans—merchants, landlords, and politicians all—coauthored a report, ostensibly as part of the state's discussion of potential immigration policies. Their contribution, however, focused less on specific immigration policies, which they considered a futile effort, than on what they saw as the fundamental driving force of both the economy and the state. Rather than promote immigration, they prescribed the following salve for the Nicaraguan body politic: "to improve the current condition of our society . . . we must procure the increase in public wealth by means of agriculture." Far from thinking themselves alone in this assessment, they claimed it was the opinion "of the majority of the nation" and "founded upon reasons that need no enunciation."[1] Defining "agriculture," however, remained a hotly debated topic. Nicaragua's mostly rural peasant communities, which had long participated in both subsistence and market production, envisioned themselves as vital participants in the country's agriculture. Landlords and merchants, in contrast, tended to define it more narrowly as export-oriented production, equating their more limited interests with those of the larger society. In some ways this had always been the case, and it was certainly visible in the more oligarchic imaginings of pre–National War patriarchal nationalism. According to this new vision, however, improving society required restructuring Nicaragua's land tenure system to encourage market-oriented production.

80

Few deny that the structure of land tenure was transformed during the second half of the nineteenth century, but the nature, process, and outcome of this change remain fiercely debated.[2] Until recently, the dominant interpretation in Nicaraguan historiography, offered most forcefully by Jaime Wheelock Román, argued that in the late nineteenth century, coffee growers amassed enormous landholdings through the mass expropriation of communal lands from Indians and mestizo peasants and *baldíos* (nationally owned lands). This led, in turn, to the creation of a Nicaraguan society stratified between the mass of proletarianized workers and a mix of coffee elites and the traditional oligarchy.[3] More recent interpretations based in more extensive empirical research, however, show that Wheelock Román's work oversimplifies the diverse and complicated social and economic relations that existed during the nineteenth century. While significant differences remain among this new generation of scholars, all of them emphasize the importance of smallholders in the transformation of the Nicaraguan economy.[4]

In this chapter I examine the transformations in land tenure and the resulting conflicts in order to understand the everyday relationships among land, community, state, and nation. The rise of a smallholding class—or rural petty bourgeoisie—within the nineteenth-century Nicaraguan economy, I will argue, is at the heart of the process of nation-state formation. The chapter is divided thematically—and somewhat chronologically—into three sections. The first looks at the shift in elite economic ideology, from the idealization of trade to that of agriculture, and the efforts of the state to transform society to meet the new ideology.

The second section focuses on the relationship of communal lands to conceptualizations of community identity while analyzing the parallel changes in communal landholding patterns and the relationships among indigenous communities, municipalities, and the state. Until the late 1870s, communal landholding dominated in Nicaragua, and municipalities and local community structures formed the center of daily life. The state, weak and still reeling from the Na-

81

tional War, sought over the next two decades to strengthen its base of revenue, expand its structures of control and coercion, and slowly extend its influence over local communities. Although the state began to build the juridical foundation upon which land tenure could be transformed, it avoided, as much as possible, actually enmeshing itself in struggles over land, trying not to upset the precarious peace achieved after the National War.

The third section examines the dramatic rise of private property ownership beginning in the late 1870s. Although communal landholding continued to be important in many areas, private landholding became the dominant pattern, leading to profound changes in the social structures of rural society. A new class of smallholders arose with ever-growing ties to the state and to the national and international economies. At the same time, increasing numbers of people found themselves forced to labor without hope of acquiring enough land to provide for their own subsistence. Throughout, government officials directed their efforts toward solidifying state institutions related to the control and use of land and strengthening the links between individuals and local communities and these institutions.

My analysis relies on a number of sources, including court cases, notarial records, correspondence, agricultural censuses, public land registry books, and newspapers. Since much of this chapter discusses the changing relationships of local communities to the state, most of the analysis is at the local community or national level. The enormous amount of data collected from the land registry, however, does not here permit a full analysis of the individual towns that made up the prefecture of Granada. Instead, I have chosen to aggregate the data along the departmental lines that developed by the end of the nineteenth century: what had been the prefecture of Granada became the departments of Carazo, Granada, and Masaya. Broadly speaking of these departments in economic terms, we can say that from 1850 to 1900 Carazo and Granada had the most in common, with Masaya frequently the outlier to their dominant position in prefect-wide changes. Carazo and Granada were considerably more market-oriented than Masaya. Similarly, private landholding took hold sooner in Carazo and Granada than in Masaya.

Aggregation has its shortcomings. The contingent historical experiences of each town or city and its geographic and ethnic diversity led to distinctly different paths that an aggregate analysis cannot always reveal. The town of Niquinohomo, for example, with its growing coffee economy, appeared more like the towns of Carazo than those of Masaya, the department to which it belonged. Neither La Paz nor El Rosario, on the other hand, had suitable lands for coffee cultivation, and consequently they developed more like towns in Masaya than others in their department of Carazo. Similar logic would place Santa Teresa in Granada rather than Carazo and Diriá in Masaya rather than Granada. Because most of the towns that tend to lie outside the aggregate picture of their departments are small, their statistical influence is limited. Therefore, despite the existence of ill-fitting pieces, an overall aggregate analysis remains useful.

Throughout this chapter, landholdings are grouped by size into five categories to help illuminate economic and social stratification: minifundio (less than 10 manzanas), small (10–49 manzanas), medium (50–199 manzanas), large (200–499 manzanas), and latifundio (500 or more manzanas).[5] These divisions follow those suggested by Julie Charlip in her study of the development of Nicaraguan coffee production.[6] Minifundios were small enough to be worked by an average family, but often they were too small to support the family's subsistence. Smallholdings normally required extra labor, depending on the crops grown and the intensity of their harvest. While in some cases this meant hiring outsiders, many families also engaged in reciprocal work arrangements with extended family and neighbors. Toward the upper limit of smallholdings and into medium- and large-size holdings, labor requirements would grow beyond community networks and include the use of hired laborers. Latifundia were relatively uncommon, and most were survivals from the colonial period when landholdings tended to be either extensive, such as the large tracts used mostly for cattle ranches, or minifundio-size holdings, held largely as ejidos.[7] Indeed, what emerged so prominently and importantly in the second half of the nineteenth-century were the small- and medium-size landholdings made possible by independence and promoted by the state.

Elite Ideologies of Economy, State, and Society

From the end of the eighteenth century through the middle of the nineteenth, the words "progress" and "agriculture" rarely appeared on the same page in Nicaraguan writings. Although some scholars view this as stemming from a cultural deficiency, a more satisfying explanation can be found in Nicaragua's colonial experiences. Throughout this period Nicaraguan landlords and merchants had been diligent entrepreneurs, continually searching for those export products that would make them both wealthier and more competitive within the Spanish empire, and hence make their home less of a backwater region.[8] Some elite families successfully rode the waves of boom and bust, planting and replanting as necessary in an attempt to diversify their interests and reduce their risk. Stepping back from the *patria chica*, however, reveals a general pattern of experimentation and failure marching in lockstep. Agriculture could hardly be expected to form the foundation of meaningful, sustainable progress.

The motor of Nicaraguan society and economy was to be found in two words: "commerce" and "canal." In the dizzyingly fast-paced years following independence from Spain, Nicaraguans dreamed that their small country could become a new Constantinople, the crossroads of the world. The world would come to Nicaragua, bringing trade, production, and civilization. Inaugural addresses, government reports, and newspaper articles echoed with the mantra "our geographic position," as if sufficient repetition would actually lead to the canal's construction.[9]

Competition among Great Britain, France, and the United States over the potential canal site initially fired elite hopes, but the quest for equal partners led to unwelcome advances; "Manifest Destiny" seemed incompatible with Nicaragua's "destiny." In 1847, less than a year before the United States annexed nearly half of Mexico's territory, Nicaragua's president, José Guerrero, worried aloud about the consequences of "the great Mexican Republic, richer, more enlightened and more powerful than all of Central America . . . [becoming] prisoner to a foreign power."[10] As if to fulfill this prophecy, the British took control of the Atlantic coast port of San Juan del Norte just three months later, forcing Guerrero to sign a treaty recognizing Britain's protectorate status over the area.[11] Guerrero impotently lamented that "in the current century it is not force but reason that must regulate the conduct of nations," but Nicaragua had learned its first lesson in the functioning of the world state-system: reason is a feeble weapon in power politics.[12]

Concerns over foreign domination soon faded before the shimmering promise of the gold rush. The American drive westward initially flowed through Panama, but Nicaragua quickly mounted a considerable challenge. Although people had crossed through Nicaragua before 1851, American financier Cornelius Vanderbilt made the Nicaragua route more attractive when he inaugurated his system of steamship and overland travel known as the Accessory Transit Company.[13] The route proved almost immediately profitable, and Vanderbilt hoped soon to convert it into a canal route.[14] For Nicaraguans, too, the transit trade brought impressive change. Americans dominated the transisthmian trade, often pushing aside regional merchants, artisans, and tradesmen, but as tens of thousands of gold rushers began to flood across the country, Nicaraguan exports and ancillary services grew, and with them Nicaraguan spirits.

So well regarded had the American face of the transit route become that when William Walker first landed in Nicaragua in June 1855, he and his men found themselves welcomed by a wide array of urban elites and rural communities.[15] Although Walker's initial support came from the Liberals who had contracted his services, his control of Nicaragua rested on a foundation that was far broader than is often acknowledged. As Michel Gobat argues, "Walker so easily consolidated his political authority only because he was aided by elites throughout the country."[16] To these, Walker added the popular muscle of local caudillos like José María Valle, alias Chelón. Walker faced resistance, of course, especially among Granadino Conservatives; however, it was insufficient to shake his grip on power. Wider opinion on Walker finally began to sour in July 1856 as he took the presidency of Nicaragua in a fraudulent election, began confiscations of elite properties, and started work toward his ultimate goal of controlling all of Central America.

Faced with possible loss of sovereignty, Liberals and Conservatives finally set aside their differences to fight against Walker.[17] The war against Walker and his forces produced the most propitious conditions for nation-state construction in Nicaragua's post-independence history. Unlike in the late 1840s, when Liberals and Conservatives found common cause in crushing Nicaraguan popular movements that threatened their political and economic power, they united in defense of national sovereignty and against the threats of foreign intervention. Moreover, the fighting, outbreaks of disease, and Walker's eventual scorched-earth retreat led to intense social and economic dislocation for many Nicaraguans. The confluence of these two opened the door for profound social transformations; however, the experiences of the 1840s and of Walker's initial broad support highlighted patriarchal nationalism's failure to develop the kind of cohesion such changes required. Overcoming these challenges demanded a new vision of the nation, one that was more inclusive and inward-looking.

Until the mid-1850s, Nicaragua's future seemed driven by a vision of the country as an international commercial center. Looking for alternate destinies after the war against Walker, Nicaraguans began to turn inward toward the opportunities afforded by agricultural development. In the aftermath of the war, U.S. efforts to secure the Nicaraguan transit route were foiled first by Nicaraguan anti-Americanism and, later, by the U.S. Civil War. The canal certainly remained a vital goal, but Nicaragua faced a conundrum: how to encourage the necessary foreign investment, technology, and engineering without opening itself to unwanted foreign interference or intervention.[18] Even more than a decade after the closing of Vanderbilt's transit route, Nicaraguans still looked fondly to its economic and cultural influence. As one newspaper reported in June 1868, "The moral influence of rubbing shoulders with foreigners has contributed considerably in awakening our spirit of enterprise."[19] Such cheer might have been muted by the newspaper's simultaneous translation and serialization of Walker's *The War in Nicaragua*.[20] Agriculture did not replace the canal, but rather denoted a shift in the balance of state policy and discourse. More significant, however, was the fact that by paying greater attention to agriculture, the state focused on transforming the foundation of Nicaraguans' everyday lives.

The failure of Nicaragua's commercial aspirations stood in stark contrast to Costa Rica's success with coffee exports and the concomitant growth in state revenue.[21] Costa Rica, after all, had contributed far more soldiers and firepower toward defeating William Walker.[22] Perhaps in emulation of Costa Rica's success, an important part of Nicaragua's reconstruction following the National War involved decrees promoting export crops—most notably coffee, but also sugar, indigo, and cotton—through import tariff rebates, military service exemption, and other incentives.[23] Nicaraguans were clearly enamored of coffee's potential (and would continue to be throughout the century), but it was evident that monocultural production posed dangers for the economy. As the minister of development and public works noted in 1867, many Nicaraguans invested in cotton production in the early 1860s only to go bankrupt when the boom prices brought on by the U.S. Civil War collapsed with the war's end.[24] Moreover, sugar (mostly consumed internally in aguardiente production), tobacco, and cattle all fed vibrant domestic and Central American regional markets that had shown greater consistency of demand between the seventeenth and nineteenth century than had export products like cacao, indigo, and cochineal. Even when coffee became the dominant export crop, Nicaragua still produced significant quantities of other crops, and coffee never rose above 50 percent of the value of total Nicaraguan exports.[25]

Despite these early efforts, Pablo Lévy's study of Nicaragua lamented the lack of progress in Nicaraguan agriculture, blaming the cattle ranching oligarchy's narrow attitudes and field of vision for what he saw as the state's retrograde agricultural policies. While this oligarchy remained in power, its policies would continue to strangle Nicaragua's economy. What should have been expanding fields of sugar, tobacco, and coffee, Lévy argued, were instead trampled by cattle because there were no laws requiring cattle ranches to put up fences.[26]

Lévy's book grew out of his travels in the late 1860s, soon after the failure of U.S. Civil War–inspired cotton plantations in Nicaragua. While cattle remained a profitable and generally stable product, other export crops had proved themselves the subjects of dramatic boom-and-bust cycles. Had Lévy visited Nicaragua in the late 1870s and 1880s, he would undoubtedly have been significantly more enthusiastic about the state's efforts.

Unfortunately, scholars of Nicaragua have frequently brandished Lévy's description of the Nicaraguan economy and state policy to bolster the claim that a conservative, backward Nicaragua remained stagnant, awaiting transformation through its belated "Liberal revolution." The specific moment in time when Lévy wrote balloons until it becomes a thin film of "fact" extending from the 1850s to 1893, when José Santos Zelaya took power. Jaime Biderman's discussion of these years is exemplary in this respect:

> Though the traditional landed oligarchy, whose orientation was essentially towards extensive cattle haciendas and merchant activities, did facilitate land concentration and labor recruitment through various laws, it didn't go far enough, and didn't specifically provide incentives for the expansion of coffee cultivation. In other Central American countries, the coffee boom was well underway by the 1870s and the new wealth and power of the

coffee "bourgeoisie" was translated into control of the State, which meant among other things "liberal" laws facilitating the private appropriation of church, indigenous and public land, more attention to the creation of a labor market or "peonaje," specific incentives to stimulate coffee cultivation and foreign immigration, as well as the provision of infrastructure.[27]

Besides too narrowly conceiving of the Nicaraguan economy and society, Biderman's assertions find little support in the available evidence. Beyond the numerous incentives to produce export crops, the state invested in significant infrastructural developments, such as ports, roads, and railroads. In fact, by 1887 Nicaragua had self-financed a rail system covering ninety-four miles and offering the lowest freight costs in Central America.[28] Such institutional support is hardly surprising, since most members of these governments— be they supposed "Liberal coffee growers" or "Conservative cattle ranchers"—held economically well-diversified investments.[29] Robert Williams found that six of Nicaragua's eight president from 1857 to 1893 were involved in various aspects of production, processing, and exporting of coffee alone.[30] A more thorough analysis of senators, ministers, and prefects would undoubtedly reflect the same economic diversification.

It is, of course, difficult to determine direct correlations between state incentives and actual production. Nonetheless, Nicaragua's previously moribund economy clearly flourished in the second half of the nineteenth century.[31] Although from 1850 to 1857 wars worked to stifle both exports and the economy as a whole, the relative peace of subsequent decades enabled Nicaragua's economy to recover, displaying impressive, if uneven, growth (see table 4). From 1856 to 1875 Nicaragua posted an average yearly growth rate for exports of 6.5 percent; during the same period, imports grew somewhat more slowly, at an average of 4.6 percent per year. By the 1880s, Nicaraguan elites must have felt they had arrived. The economy chugged along, with more consistent growth in exports. From 1876 to 1895 exports grew at

Table 4. Nicaraguan exports and imports, 1856–1900 (five-year averages)

	Exports (pesos)	Imports (pesos)
1856–1860	485,058	487,018
1861–1865	633,842	530,942
1866–1870	928,095	819,733
1871–1875	1,548,261	1,143,122
1876–1880	1,533,614	1,163,833
1881–1885	2,219,078	1,794,750
1886–1890	3,195,602	3,068,178
1891–1895	3,240,397	6,006,806
1896–1900	3,101,050	2,836,979

Sources: Schoonover and Schoonover, "Statistics," 108–9; Bureau of the American Republics, *Nicaragua*, 86–97; Nicaragua, Ministerio de Hacienda Pública, *Memoria* (1897).

an average yearly rate of 4.0 percent. As an indication of elite confidence, average yearly import growth for this same period rose to 9.6 percent, a rate more than twice that of exports.[32]

Incentives might have been necessary, but such a supply-oriented system was insufficient to guarantee a thriving agro-export economy. Promoting an effective transformation in Nicaragua's economy required a thoroughgoing restructuring of the country's land tenure patterns and of the meaning of land possession and use.

During the nineteenth century, land in Nicaragua was divided into three categories: communal (municipal ejidos and Indian communal lands), private (including corporate holdings, such as those of the church's various cofradías), and state-owned (baldíos). Land was abundant and the population low, providing relatively easy access to land. In most communities, local farmers usually relied on communal lands, either under the auspices of their communal rights to such land or renting. Rental of cofradía lands sometimes served the same purpose, and if these sources could not provide for local land needs, squatters would settle on baldíos. Prior to 1858, renters and communal land farmers mostly grew subsistence crops, although participation in local markets appears to have been quite high.[33] Most private holdings, on the other hand, tended to be quite large, with production concentrated in then-traditional export crops like cacao, indigo, cattle, and hides.[34]

Efforts to change the juridical structure of landholding began following the National War. Nicaragua's 1858 Constitution provided no explicit provisions for the protection of communal lands, something that E. Bradford Burns saw as "a significant and ominous legal change for the majority of the Nicaraguans, a harbinger of future problems and woe for the folk."[35] Nonetheless, ejidos were officially recognized in an 1859 law that stiffened the 1832 law that provided for ejidos in each town.[36] Although ejidos remained juridically viable throughout the nineteenth century, the state began to enact laws encouraging privatization of communal lands and the purchase and use of baldíos.[37]

In 1877, however, the state's laws regarding land took on a decidedly more aggressive character, with a greater emphasis placed on the privatization and distribution of ejidos and Indian communal lands. In that year, to more firmly link the state and perceived rights of land ownership, Nicaragua created land registries throughout the country. Subsequent laws refined this process, although their effectiveness appears to have derived from a process of attrition rather than forced expropriation. As Charlip argues, "Clearly a change was taking place; but the destruction of subsistence property through the breakup of the ejidos was not the result."[38]

Communal Land and Identity

Until the late 1870s, the majority of Nicaraguans with access to land worked communal lands. Although some privatization of communal lands had begun before this time, it was barely a trickle. As Juan Mendoza noted in his cantankerous history of his hometown of Diriamba—a center of early coffee production—during the early to mid-nineteenth century, "one could acquire land by simple occupation, without any other title."[39] Foreign visitors offered similar judgments. Ephraim Squier, U.S. minister to Nicaragua in 1849, noted the abundance and easy availability of land.[40] Pablo Lévy's account of the late 1860s boasted that "the soil is still virgin in infinite points."[41]

Between 1848 and 1877 (the latter being the year Nicaragua's land registries opened), legally notarized land transactions were uncommon. During these years the public registrar recorded 107 rural land transactions in the prefecture of Granada, representing less than 8 percent of the transactions registered between 1848 and 1897. Although private landholding would not become the dominant pattern until the 1880s, it represented the vast majority of transactions in the land registry; from 1858 to 1877, 26.7 percent of land transactions were communal, 73.3 percent private. When disaggregated to the department level, however, it is evident that communal transactions were more dominant in Masaya (57.1 percent) than in Granada (27.0 percent) and Carazo (22.9 percent). Communal transactions declined in relation to private land transactions over time, so that between 1888 and 1897 they represented 13.7 percent in Granada and 1.7 percent in Carazo. Data for Masaya are unavailable for this period; nonetheless, a marked, if not as sharp, decline was evident there as well (see table 5).

To understand the significance of changes in land tenure to the formation of the nation-state during the nineteenth century, we must first interrogate what we mean by "communal" land. Whereas, for example, Williams indicates a distinction in El Salvador between "tierras ejidales" as municipal lands and "tierras comunales" as Indian lands, Burns notes that "confusion exists whether these two corporations were in fact separate, or were always separate, or were synonymous in nineteenth-century Nicaragua."[42] Like Williams, Romero Vargas distinguishes between "ejidos" and "tierras del común" by their origin. Where ejidos were given according to royal law, tierras del común were either purchased by communities or donated by the king, and were usually accompanied by a written title.[43] The available, albeit limited, evidence suggests that Charlip's conclusion may be closest to describing the situation in the majority of the towns in the central Pacific area of Nicaragua: "It appears from the legisla-

Table 5. Percentage of ejidal and private land transactions by department, 1868–1897

	Carazo (n = 687)		Granada (n = 641)		Masaya (n = 65)	
	Ejidos	Private land	Ejidos	Private land	Ejidos	Private land
1868–1877	23	77	27	70	57	43
1878–1887	11	87	23	75	32	68
1888–1897	2	98	14	86	0	100

Source: Calculated based on RPPG-RC, 1877–1897.
Note: Due to rounding, percentages in tables may not total 100.

tion of the period [nineteenth century] and documentation in the Registro de Propiedad that all three terms [ejidos, tierras comunales, and terreno municipal] were used interchangeably to refer to town property that was available for common use; while once this may have been allocated by earlier formalities, perhaps by town elders, by the nineteenth century the land was distributed by the local government, i.e., the mayor and the municipal corporation."[44] The timing and process of this change, however, remain elusive.

The documents of an 1876 case between José Antonio Argüello and the town of Masaya offer some hints. Although they reveal neither the process nor the exact timing, they clearly show that what was explicitly recognized as Indian communal land in the original grant *became* municipal ejidos sometime after independence. Argüello, who sought to acquire 12 caballerías (768 manzanas) of baldíos in the jurisdiction of Masaya, met the resistance of Masaya's municipal council, which claimed that land as part of the city's ejidos. To prove their claim, the municipal secretary submitted to the court a copy of the original land grant. Dating from 1759 and signed by Gregorio Zelidón de Morales, "Defensor de los naturales," the document pertained to the acquisition and measurement of lands in the area known as Tisma for the indigenous community, not Masaya's ejidos. Yet at some point following independence some of this land was shifted to the municipality's jurisdiction.[45]

In her study of Diriomo, Elizabeth Dore traces this shift to a precise moment in 1852 when the leaders of the Indian community and the municipality met "to discuss where the *tierras comunes* of the Comunidad ended and the *tierras ejidales* of the municipality began. According to the minutes of that meeting, as recorded by the Junta's secretary, the ladino and indigenous leaders agreed that the latter enveloped most of the former."[46] Dore argues that the state's violent suppression of the 1845–49 rebellions—and perhaps the extrajudicial executions of its leaders[47]—led to this astonishing turn of events.

The relative wealth of indigenous communities also played an important role in their legal struggles over land. By the end of the eighteenth century most indigenous community treasuries (*cajas de comunidad*) were fairly paltry.[48] Three of the largest indigenous communities in Nicaragua (Masaya, Sutiava, and Matagalpa) accounted for more than 35 percent of the 80,693 pesos in all indigenous cajas in 1819. Masaya's 11,645 pesos, a sum that did not include their communal landholdings, would have allowed the community to pursue its interests in a way that the 670-peso treasury of the indigenous community of Jinotepe would not.[49]

In any event, when, in early March 1881, regional prefects sent a circular to the constitutional alcaldes within their jurisdictions asking them to report on Indian landholdings within their communities, the responses I found for the prefecture of Granada were unanimous: there were none.[50] One cannot conclude that no Indian communal lands existed in the prefecture of Granada by the late 1880s, only that they were very uncommon and, therefore, could not suffice as a source community identity.

Some have proposed that in many area cofradías filled this void.[51] The cofradías took in yearly contributions from members and usually invested them in cattle haciendas. From the profits of these ventures they maintained the local church and put on the events of local religious festivals. The question raised is, to what extent were the lands of the cofradías used by its membership for subsistence agricultural pursuits? Was land rented out or sold to members (or nonmembers for that matter)? This, of course, begs the question, was land suited to cattle ranching also suitable for basic grain production?

The evidence is still unclear. Romero Vargas reports that in the eighteenth century, cofradías were abundant in the prefecture of Granada. In the area that today comprises the department of Masaya there were twenty-three cofradías: nine in Masatepe, three in Masaya, nine in Niquinohomo, and two in Nindirí. In the department of Granada, Romero Vargas lists seven, five in Diriomo and two in Nandaime.[52] A century later, however, cofradías seemed much less common. During the late nineteenth century, the Roman Catholic Church sold a number of the cofradías, despite pleas from indigenous communities.[53] While evidence from the early 1880s points to the continued existence of cofradías in Niquinohomo, Catarina, Jinotepe, and Diriamba, they had clearly waned in numbers and importance.[54] Few details are available to evaluate the histories of these cofradías; however, in the case of Diriamba's Cofradía de Dolores we can trace the parcelization of its original 6.75 caballerías (432 manzanas) as it was sold to private individuals between 1881 and 1897.[55]

The governance of the cofradía in Niquinohomo, however, proves problematic for the thesis that cofradías served as a source of identity for the indigenous community. Its leadership—Nicolas Muños, Felipe Oveda, and Procopio Sandino—were, with the possible exception of Oveda, members of the local ladino elite and among the most important landowners and export crop producers in the town. Muños, the wealthiest of the three, owned 56 manzanas of land, with 30 head of cattle and 20 horses, and produced annually 29 *fanegas* (9,048 pounds) of maize, 10 *quintales* (1,000 pounds) of coffee, and 500 *arrobas* (12,500 pounds) of sugar.[56] Would these men, through their positions within the administrative structure of the cofradía, meaningfully represent the local Indian community? Muños's efforts just five years earlier to illegally confiscate cultivated ejidal lands from a half-dozen Niquinohomeños for use as his personal cattle pasture makes such a proposition moot.[57]

In any event, the lack of Indian communal lands was not necessarily an impediment to the maintenance of community identity or cohesion.[58] Rather, two additional factors threatened the cohesion of local Indian identity in the prefecture of Granada. First, the decline in communal land *in the form of ejidos* dissipated the power of one of the most important symbols with which the everyday sociopolitical fabric of communities was woven while exacerbating economic and political divisions within them. Second, the coexistence of significant populations of ladinos and Indians within municipalities and the outcomes of Indian-ladino struggles over local power resulted in a slow but inexorable decline in Indian community autonomy.

In the 1850s and 1860s, however, such a future seemed unimaginable. Land was abundant, and municipalities maintained significant autonomy from the state. Land, in particular, was conceived of as a locally controlled and allocated resource, outside the observation or intrusion of the national state. Events in Nindirí in 1857 illustrate this point, emphasizing how interwoven land and local community membership were at the time.

On 7 July 1857, Gabriel Membreño, constitutional alcalde of Nindirí, received a request from the prefect of Granada to explain why he had ordered the burning of a rural property that contained a number of small buildings on the outskirts of the town in an area called "Las Cofradías de Veracruz." The prefect's request came at the behest of Encarnación Vicente, a *vecino* (householder) of Nindirí, who claimed the property as his own and believed it had been destroyed unlawfully.

Vicente claimed that the land belonged to him and that his son-in-law, Perfecto Flores, was living on and working the land. Membreño disputed both assertions. Despite Vicente's claim to the land, Membreño maintained that since Vicente himself did not work the land, he had, essentially, abandoned it. One witness claimed: "They weren't houses, just shacks. They don't belong to Encarnación Vicente, but to his son-in-law Perfecto Flores. . . . Although [Vicente] had previously had an agricultural finca, he doesn't now and it's been many years since he lived in this town or stepped foot in this place."[59]

Other witnesses painted a similar picture, denying Vicente's claim to any rights over the land.

As to Flores, the situation was different. Although he had worked the land, his character was defective, disqualifying him from claiming ownership or usufructuary rights within the community. Under normal circumstances Flores could claim rights to the land, but he was foreclosed from this possibility because of his "evil conduct." At the time of the complaint, Flores was in jail in Masaya for having "macheted [to death] his own brother."[60] Each witness in turn testified both to Flores's undesirable qualities and to the suitability of Membreño's actions, given the circumstances.

For Membreño, the judgment was obvious. Flores's "dishonorable" character and Membreño's own duty to "assure the interests of those who live honorably" led to the conclusion that "there is no more adequate means than this for destroying men of this quality."[61] Membreño concluded indignantly, "It seems to me, Sr. Prefecto, that this report is more than sufficient to absolve me of Vicente's complaint." Because Vicente did not use the land, he had no rights to it. Although Flores may have had such use-rights, he lost them when he ceased to be an honorable member of the community.

In responding to Flores, Vicente made no effort to defend his son-in-law, never mentioning him, but he did champion his own individual and community rights. Although he claimed that the land that was burned contained "cows, pigs and fruit trees," he argued that even if it did not, "this does not authorize him [the mayor] to order the burning without the required compensation and without attending to the duties of humanity to which we are obliged, principally with the indigent."[62] He concludes by asking the prefect to find for him in his complaint and require Membreño either to rebuild the structures or pay their value, and to pay damages and court costs.

The decision of Prefect Santiago Vega seemed purposely vague. Rather than deny the veracity of Vicente's complaint or find Membreño guilty of illegal actions, Vega absented himself from considering the issues at all: "Given that this proceeding has no connection, whatsoever, with any purely governmental, economic or police matters that subject constitutional alcaldes to the departmental prefects, what is presented here refers to diverse events and consequently is outside of this authority's competence."[63] In essence, his non-finding favored Membreño, since for Vicente to continue his legal quest would require filing a case in civil court, a costly endeavor.

What is most odd about the prefect's decision is how strongly it flew in the face of clearly laid out facts. Membreño based his entire argument on his political authority as constitutional alcalde and the responsibilities that this position placed upon him. It was not as a private citizen that he ordered the houses destroyed, but as mayor of Nindirí. The law he cited to defend his decision, moreover, was nationally decreed. The reasons behind Vega's decision remain opaque—perhaps purposefully so—but the implied meaning was clear. Decisions relating to community membership and rights, of which land was a central aspect, were to be made at the local level.[64]

This struggle over municipal authority suggests how receptive rural communities could be to the language of nation. Both Membreño and Vicente laid claim to conceptions of honor, community, rights, and social responsibilities. Did someone born to a place, who owned property there, cease to be a member of a community because he or she no longer resided there? Should bad conduct deprive one of community rights? While the story that Vicente's son-in-law had murdered his own brother might evoke the biblical tale of Cain and Abel, it just as easily conforms to the narratives of patriarchal nationalism. None of this is to suggest that the idea of nation was at work beneath this conflict, but rather to point out how easily constructions of the local and the national can coincide.

Mirroring the distance between local communal land control and the state, usable ejidal land records within the public land registry are nonexistent prior to 1868. Moreover, the overall paucity of data means that analysis of changing ejidal land tenure can only be done at the prefectural level. Evident from these transactions is the relative

Table 6. Size distribution of ejidal transactions in the prefecture of Granada, 1868–1897

	1868–1877		1878–1887		1888–1897	
	Number (*n* = 13)	Total area	Number (*n* = 73)	Total area	Number (*n* = 30)	Total area
Minifundio (< 10 manzanas)	85	28	67	18	43	11
Small (10–49 manzanas)	8	10	23	28	43	43
Medium (50–199 manzanas)	8	62	10	55	13	46

Source: Calculated based on RPPG-RC, 1877–1897.
Note: Due to rounding, percentages in table may not total 100.

movement toward the concentration of ejidal land in smallholdings between 10 and 49 manzanas (see table 6).

Sufficient data exist for the decade between 1878 and 1887 to attempt to draw out differences in ejidal land tenure between Carazo, Granada, and Masaya. Carazo and Granada appear nearly identical, although minifundio-size transactions (less than 10 manzanas) accounted for slightly more ejidal transactions in Carazo (70.3 percent) than in Granada (59.3 percent). Although minifundio-size transactions dominated the ejidal entries in the land registry in all three departments, in Carazo and Granada they represented very little land, just 15.9 and 16.7 percent, respectively. In Masaya, on the other hand, minifundio ejidal holdings (32.0 percent) encompassed more than twice the area of smallholdings (14.4 percent). Masaya appears to have maintained ejidal land tenure closer to its traditional style of distribution (i.e., in 2-manzana plots) than Carazo or Granada, where the transformation in their economies encouraged larger holdings. Nonetheless, in all three cases, medium-size holdings took up nearly identical shares of land area (see table 7).[65]

In the late 1860s and 1870s, individuals began to take advantage of changing state laws to take hold of lands that municipalities believed they controlled. Rather than keeping the state at arm's length, as Gabriel Membreño had in Nindirí a decade earlier, these com-

Table 7. Size distribution of ejidal transactions in Carazo, Granada, and Masaya, 1878–1887

	Carazo		Granada		Masaya	
	Number (n = 37)	Total area	Number (n = 27)	Total area	Number (n = 9)	Total area
Minifundio (< 10 manzanas)	70	16	59	17	78	32
Small (10–49 manzanas)	22	28	30	30	11	14
Medium (50–199 manzanas)	8	56	11	53	11	54

Source: Calculated based on RPPG-RC, 1877–1897.

munities now turned to the state in order to navigate the daily more complicated tributaries of power. In their efforts to maintain local control over land, municipalities found their actions increasingly circumscribed by the state.

By the late 1860s, transformations by the state in juridical definitions of land tenure and efforts to exert local control over land began to collide. In both Jinotepe and San Marcos, for example, individuals began to encroach upon ejidos, frequently claiming them to be baldíos. Although laws in the 1850s and 1860s decreed the official measurement and demarcation of ejidos, for decades the state generally lagged in its responsibilities.

A complicated case surrounding an effort to privatize a part of San Marcos's ejidos in 1865 helps elucidate the complex relationships among the municipality, the indigenous community, and the state. On 10 April 1866, German Marques, indigenous alcalde, and Francisco García, Benancio García, Felipe Campos, Cando Sanches, Juan Felis Mercado, and Sirilo Campos, representatives of the Indian community of San Marcos, wrote to the municipal council of San Marcos to try to prevent completion of the sale of communal lands located in an area called Pochotón. Acknowledging the ladino constitutional alcalde's scope of power, Marques explained: "Being that you are charged with the interior regimen of the town and the procurement of its improvement, making every effort that can be done on behalf of the communal well-being, it is within your faculties and your duty neither to consent to nor to permit that the lands of Pochotón . . . be reduced to private dominion, because this would deprive the town of all the use rights that help it in the cultivation of those lands."[66] Despite conflicting claims to the land, the Indian community initially seemed heedless of the possibility that their claim would not prevail, since they believed they had incontrovertible documentation that the lands belonged to San Marcos. In 1848 the prefect of Granada had demarcated them, and the state had approved this measurement in 1858.

The Indian community's leaders concluded their otherwise straightforward request by noting that should the privatization of the ejidos in Pochotón proceed, they hoped to have collected sufficient funds to buy them. Again recognizing the hierarchy of power, Marques and his compatriots asked the municipal council to file the "suitable petitions." Finally, to emphasize the importance they assigned to these lands' remaining communal, they radically inverted the logic of elite nationalist discourse, revealing its limits: "Thus, we await your patriotic zeal for the good of our small society." The needs of the nation-state might trump those of the community, but to cause the community undue harm seemed incompatible with the inclusive discourse of the nation. ·

About five weeks later, on 17 May 1866, the constitutional alcalde of San Marcos petitioned the prefect of Granada to prevent the privatization of Pochotón: "Given the just protest of the entire town, the lands of Pochotón, which are communal, should not be reduced to private dominion, depriving the town of the possibility of ejidos. The reduction of the lands to private dominion would leave barely four manzanas of land for planting; and agriculture being the only source of wealth, with the sale of these lands the town will have to turn back [*retrogradar*], destroying itself, lacking the possibility of the cultivation that creates conservation and progress." Moreover, to reinvoke local control of land, the constitutional alcalde seemed to borrow the indigenous community's inversion of elite discursive logic. The town's request, he confidently asserted, was "in agreement with the aims of progress . . . which do not permit in any case that the private good be preferred over the general." Where elites argued for privatization of communal land as the means of bringing about individual progress for all, the mayor claims that privatization will bring about the enrichment of a few individuals while impoverishing the majority.

When another month elapsed without a satisfactory response from the prefect, the indigenous community's leadership, joined this time by two more community elders, again wrote to the municipal council. Perhaps sensing that their petition was on the brink of failure, they attempted in this letter to articulate in more detail the reasons behind their actions with regard to Pochotón. They explained that on 5 July 1860, Doña Manuela Aragon made a claim for eight caballerías of baldío land in Pochotón. Five year later, on 17 August 1865, a public auction was held at which the land was sold: four caballerías went to Aragon, the other four to the heirs of Guadalupe Morales. "During the five years that elapsed between the claim and the auction," explained Marques, "we remained quiet in order to enter the bidding in a better position; or perhaps to oppose it [the auction] since they are communal lands in virtue of the demarcation made in 1848 by the happily remembered Prefect Don Francisco del Montenegro, who now rests in peace." The indigenous community revealed a complicated, two-pronged approach to maintaining access to communal land in San Marcos.

On the one hand, the indigenous community argued that the municipality's right to ejidos and the precedent of their demarcation in 1848, at minimum, solidified San Marcos's hold on the lands. On the other hand, should the auction be allowed to go forward and the lands be privatized, the community was now prepared to make a higher bid than all others, and because they had worked the land they felt that they merited first rights in the bidding. In essence, although the Indians sought to work with the municipality to defend its ejidos, they were equally prepared to turn to the state and its system of distributing national lands. The latter option may, in fact, have been more desirable, since it would have provided the indigenous community with its own lands, redrawing the lines of power and autonomy between it and the municipality. To these ends, the Indians sought an injunction against the finalization of the auction until the measurement of the ejidos was completed, as well as the right to make a higher bid for any remaining land that fell outside of the ejidos. Despite these well-organized plans, neither the indigenous community nor the municipality succeeded in keeping Pochotón as communal land. The auction was finalized, with Aragon's and Morales's heirs receiving the land.[67]

The failure of the town to keep control of Pochotón, however, had nothing to do with the merits of the arguments it presented. Rather, both the town and the indigenous community were too late in making their claims. In his decision, the prefect implied that prompter action on the part of San Marcos would have produced a different outcome. Over the rest of the nineteenth century the arbitrary enforcement of deadlines would come to be a critical strategy for elites in disguising the contradictions within their ideology of nation-state. It allowed judges to recognize the justice of claims—to give hope to subaltern claimants—while legitimizing the state as a neutral arbiter. The supposedly objective quality of time cloaked the state's most unreasonable decisions in a veneer of "fairness." Consequently, the "time immemorial" rights of indigenous communities often collapsed before laws that mandated thirty-day public complaint periods.[68]

While the indigenous community of San Marcos was losing its battle to maintain part of the town's communal lands, the indigenous community of Jinotepe was succeeding in its struggle. On 1 September 1866 the indigenous alcalde of Jinotepe and a large gathering of the indigenous regidores and elders met with the municipal council to seek protection for Jinotepe's ejidos. The state's inattention to its duty to survey and mark Jinotepe's ejidos worried the Indian community. Their leaders explained that, although legislation from 1832 and 1859 called for the maintenance and measurement, respectively, of each town's ejidos, Jinotepe's communal lands remained unspecified, and thus four individuals had recently made claims to "national lands" that actually fell within the town's ejidos.[69]

As in San Marcos, the Indian community of Jinotepe took a cooperative approach to the municipality, acknowledging the municipality's authority in relation to the town's ejidos but emphasizing that these common lands represented "common interests" between the ladino municipality and the Indian community.[70] The municipality agreed. Perhaps, as Elizabeth Dore reports for Diriomo in the late 1850s and early 1860s, "Even members of the Municipal Junta, who soon claimed tracts of land, at first believed that private land was contrary to natural and common law."[71] In any event, to more effectively request amelioration of the situation, the municipal council hired Francisco Jimenes, the town's only university-educated man, to represent it before the prefect of Granada.

In arguing for the municipality, Jimenes used much of the argument developed by the Indian community. Quite succinctly, he explained that if the claims against Jinotepe's ejidos were allowed to go forward, "it will come to be that Jinotepe will be left without communal lands in which its inhabitants can dedicate themselves to the farming that is the only inheritance on which they subsist." While the consequences of privatization seemed clear, Jimenes distanced himself from the claim he was hired to defend: "The Indians have made clear to the municipality of my vicinity the damages that would befall them if the lands found in the outskirts of Jinotepe were privatized [*se venden a particulares*], and this corporation [is] convinced of the justice of the Indians' [*naturales*] complaint."[72] Despite Jimenes's lukewarm effort, the illegality of the claims made by Mariano Arana, Miguel García, Pedro Jimenes, and Salvador Espinoza was so obvious—the claimants actually admitted knowing that the lands they sought were ejidos, not baldíos—that a decision against the municipality seemed impossible. More importantly, however, the indigenous community had acted within the time period specified to contest land claims. Over the next thirty years Jinotepe continued to add ejidal lands, once in 1892 and again in 1900.[73]

Community activism around questions of communal land in the prefecture of Granada waned from the 1870s through the rest of the nineteenth century, in part a recognition of changing land tenure and the imbalance of power between the Indian communities and municipalities. The decline also reflected continuing access to communal lands effected by frequent conversions of baldíos to ejidos to replace lands that had been privatized. For example, despite the fact that La Paz had solicited and received measurement of its ejidos in 1871 and added to them in 1881, by 1891 they had again been privatized. Lack of ejidos had forced people from La Paz to rent lands within the ejidos of El Rosario. Fearing that families would have to "abandon their houses and small plots, emigrating to other parts," La Paz sought and received more land for ejidos.[74]

Throughout the second half of the nineteenth century, towns in the prefecture of Granada continued to seek and acquire baldíos for conversion into ejidos. As mentioned above, La Paz received ejidos in 1881 and 1889. Niquinohomo received 126 caballerías (8,064 manzanas) in 1884, San Marcos received 40 caballerías (2,560 manzanas) in 1886, and Santa Teresa received 8.25 caballerías (528 manzanas) in 1890. Diriomo (1883), El Rosario (1888), Jinotepe (1888, 1892, 1900), and Diriamba (1890, 1892), also got donations throughout this period, although the exact land area remains unknown.[75]

Although ejidos would continue to be a significant source of land throughout the rest of the century, their importance relative to private land in the prefecture of Granada was declining. Ejidos represented 65 percent of all land transactions between 1868 and 1877, declining to 17 percent between 1878 and 1887 and to 12 percent between 1888 and 1897. The pattern holds true even at the departmental level. For Carazo, ejidal transactions went from 60 to 13 to just 1 percent during the same period. In Granada, ejidal transactions remained more important throughout the period, revealing a less dramatic drop, from 71 to 24 to 16 percent. The limited amount of data for Masaya does not yield meaningful statistics. Nonetheless, from what is available, Masaya saw a much less dramatic decline in ejidal transactions, from 67 to 35 percent between 1868 and 1887.[76]

Neither the rise in private landholding nor the pattern of ejidal privatization, however, should be taken to indicate the disappearance of ejidos. Communities continued to plead for and receive donations of land, which they would convert into ejidos and distribute. Slowly but surely, this process brought squatters and other smallholders who lived on the agricultural frontier and outside the state's system of land titling into that system, using individual municipalities as the tool to accomplish the task. As Charlip concludes for Carazo, "the pattern emerges of continued access of smaller farms to ejidal land, at no charge, into the twentieth century."[77]

Ejidos remained common, but the laws allowing for their sale began to transform their nature. Historically, ejidal land rights were retained by one individual and could only be passed on through inheritance. If the land was abandoned or an *ejidatario* had no heirs, the land would return to the community to be redistributed to others. The ability to sell ejidal rights radically altered this system, effectively limiting the community's control over local land and divesting the community of the power to distribute and control its own ejidos.

The Rise of Private Property
and the Decline of Community

By the mid-1870s a dramatic shift in land use and holding patterns had begun. In the cases discussed above, the municipal governments in Jinotepe and San Marcos seemed to view warily the changing juridical structure of land. Ejidos served as an important source of power for the municipal government; its role as distributor of these lands should not be underestimated. Any threat to ejidos, in general, then, could be perceived as a threat to municipal power. Nonetheless, as local elites began to see their fortunes lying with the export economy, and therefore within national elite interests, their relationship to the structures of land tenure began to change, too. Francisco Jimenes, clearly powerful and well respected within Jinotepe's elite, manifested just such an attitude. Although paid to represent Jinotepe's interest in protecting its ejidos, he made it clear that he did not necessarily hold the same opinion.

This change in attitude is exemplified in an 1876 case in Niquinohomo, located in the present-day department of Masaya. Coffee and sugar production were beginning to flourish in this small town, but subsistence agriculture still predominated. As in Jinotepe a decade before, a Niquinohomo elite attempted to claim ejidal land as uncultivated baldíos. As in San Marcos, the defense of the lands attested to a cohesive local community that stood together in solidarity.

Guillermo Conto, a farmer (*agricultor*) and vecino of Niquinohomo, wrote to the prefect of Granada on behalf of himself and five others—"my brothers and neighbors"—to lodge a complaint against Nicolas Muños, also of Niquinohomo, for seeking donation of their lands for his cattle pasture: "To come forward in defense of my rights to express to you [the prefect] that for more than fifteen years I have possessed a piece of land that as a vecino I occupied in the jurisdiction of my town."[78] The complaint also questioned the municipality's role in Muños's effort, since it had certified the donation in the first place.

Conto's argument rested not merely on perceived rights to the land but also on the land's use. "Muños understands to his thinking that ranching is preferable to farming," Conto wrote, "but he is miserably wrong because the concepts of the legislative decree of 13 July 1832 and the laws of agriculture cannot be more clear and decisive."[79] This focus on the use to which the land was put evinced the penetration of national elite economic ideology among non-elites. Conto's "maize, plantains, rice, beans and grasses" certainly were not the kinds of export crops elites expected to fuel the engine of Nicaraguan progress. But for Conto and those like him, their lands and their harvests marked them as farmers and producers and merited them an acknowledged place in the nation.

When the municipality finally responded to requests from the prefect for information regarding the claim, it simply replied, "Since this junta has no private interests, just to see for the general welfare of its vecinos, it leaves to the wise disposition of the prefect to resolve that which would be just," a claim that rings hollow, since the municipality had adjudicated the lands to Muños in the first place.[80] The prefect apparently agreed. Eleven days later he decided in favor of Conto and his neighbors, maintaining their claim to the lands they worked.[81]

Four years later, according to the agricultural census taken in Niquinohomo, all five complainants still held lands. Their holdings were small but sufficient. Conto, the most well off, owned 2 head of cattle and 2 horses and worked 8 manzanas, producing 8 fanegas (2,496 pounds) of maize, 24 medios (336 pounds) of beans, and 90 arrobas (2,250 pounds) of rice per year.[82] The estimated value of Conto's land was listed as 60 pesos. The poorest of the group, Cesilio Baltodano, had just 4 manzanas but produced 4 fanegas of rice, 20 medios of beans, and 20 arrobas of rice. In contrast, Muños owned seven times more land than Conto, with a value listed at 2,000 pesos.[83] The vast differences in wealth and power, however, obviously did not impede Conto and his neighbors from demanding protection of their rights. What is more, they heralded themselves as progress-oriented Davids besieged by a backward-looking Goliath. Might should not make right in an age of reason. Lawsuits would attest to the ability of poor peasants to navigate the Nicaraguan legal system, but increasingly over the nineteenth century they tended to fight as individuals or families. Very rarely would they exhibit the kind of community or neighbor associations discussed in earlier cases.

The resolution of an 1875 conflict between Marcos Aguirre and Celendino Borge of Diriomo offers an important counterpoint to that of Guillermo Conto and his neighbors' struggle against Nicolas Muños and the municipality of Niquinohomo. Aguirre went to court against Borge, a local Diriomo elite, for encroaching on his ejidal holdings. As in Conto's case, Aguirre's claim was found to be legitimate, but he lost control of his ejidos anyhow. Borge was awarded title based on an 1858 law that allowed the municipality to expropriate land for conversion to coffee production.[84] As in the Niquinohomo case, the particular use to which the land was put proved critical and suggests both a shift in attitudes toward the state and the dangers these attitudes posed for the autonomy of rural farmers. Conto exalted the law to plead for the value of farming over ranching. Borge did the same, but to champion the elite conception of agriculture as export over Aguirre's subsistence production. These contests attested to the nation's inclusiveness, but they also augured the expansion of state authority in everyday politics.

While farmers were the common recipients of ejidal lands in Carazo, Granada, and Masaya, accounting for more than 70 percent of all recipients between 1868 and 1897, they were not the most frequent sellers.[85] In Carazo and Masaya farmers represented only about half of ejidal sellers. Although in Granada farmers made up two-thirds of sellers, this was still less than their share as recipients. It is not surprising that the merchants, artisans, housewives, and day laborers who made up the rest of ejidal recipients were not equally represented among ejidal sellers. Merchants, by and large, held onto their ejidal landholdings much more successfully than did day laborers and housewives, who were positioned on the bottom rungs of economic power. Although artisans appear to have been nearly as likely as day laborers and housewives to sell their ejidal landholdings, it is unclear whether this can be traced to the relative weakness of the artisanal economy or to growing specialization, which militated against artisans being able to work the land and their craft at the same time.

The experience of Juan Lopez, an Indian from Diriomo, illustrates the difficult, sometimes precarious situation of smallholders at the end of the nineteenth century. In 1880 Lopez filed a complaint against both the indigenous alcalde and the constitutional alcalde of his town for attempting to coerce him into accepting election as an indigenous alcalde for the following year. He refused to accept the position, claiming that acceptance would be detrimental to his personal well-being. Lopez's refusal brought down the municipality's wrath upon him, when, while working in his *huerta* (small plot), he found himself surrounded by the town's machete-wielding police. Lopez relented and accepted the position.[86]

Lopez claimed to be a farmer, but the mayor called him a laborer. While the mayor's claim may have been more an epithet than anything else, Lopez clearly teetered on the brink between these two occupations. In explaining his initial refusal to be alcalde, Lopez claimed to have contracted with Tiburcio Rivas, a local landowner with extensive holdings, to burn and clear his fields for the new planting. The work had to be completed before the first rains. Should he fail to finish the work, he would be "threatened with damages and loss" that included his own parcel of land.

Lopez's huerta had come to define the difference between his being a farmer and laborer. His private ownership of the land and his need to maintain his "personal well-being" had begun to alienate him from the very indigenous community of which he was a member. Unable to resolve this conflict within the confines of the community itself, Lopez had turned to the state. For Lopez, the balance of power and legitimacy between state and community had tilted. It was not a sudden change, but the result of the state's slow but incessant institutionalization of selfhood over community. Lopez owned land, contracted his labor power, faced lawsuits from others, and brought them himself. Slowly but surely, the functioning of the most critical facets of his life had been brought into the purview and control of the state.

Despite the apparent fissures within local identities, to say that collective action had grown beyond the pale in rural communities of the prefecture of Granada would be an overstatement. If questions of land no longer seemed to bring communities together, other communal issues did. This is not to say that disputes over land, legal complaints, or other measures relating to land ceased, but that they inevitably involved individuals, neighbors, or families. Nothing like the eighty indigenous community elders, mayor, and councilmen of Jinotepe seeking the preservation of ejidos occurred after the late 1870s.

If rural communities increasingly came to see private landholding as the norm, other features of rural life, such as water rights or access to forests, continued to be viewed in communal terms. In mid-September 1875 a large group of Indians from Diriomo gathered at the property of Nilo Ortega, a Granadino merchant and farmer. They were protesting the fences Ortega had placed on his land, closing off public access to water that flowed near his property. Ortega complained to the local *gobernador de policia* (police chief), Agripito Ortega (no relation).

Employing a common legal strategy of making as many claims as possible in the hope that one would stick, Nilo Ortega first called a number of witnesses to prove that his land was in Diriá and, therefore, not subject to the gobernador's jurisdiction.[87] The next day, however, Agrapito Ortega found against Nilo Ortega, noting that upon visual inspection he found that the fences blocked access to the water, which was public according to the law, and which it was his duty as gobernador de policia to keep open and clean. He ordered the fences taken down. Unhappy with this decision, Nilo Ortega informed the gobernador de policia that he was going over his head to the prefect. He wrote to the prefect twice, the first time claiming that his land did not really limit the Diriomeños' access to water, the second time to claim that even if his land did limit access, it was to those in Diriá, not in Diriomo.

As a last-ditch effort, Nilo Ortega solicited the privatization of Diriomo's water from the municipality. In exchange for maintaining and reselling the town's water supply, he sought the closing of "the public rights of way to rivers and lakes within the boundaries of the pueblo."[88] The ladino municipal authority demurred. Moreover, the municipality found common ground with leaders of the indigenous community to strengthen their repudiation of Ortega's plan. Not only had Ortega lied about illegally fencing off a public access route to water, but then, displeased with the local police's decision against him, he hoped to subvert local authority over resources by recourse to the prefect. The community jointly responded that the privatization effort would "deprive the pueblo of the freedom to take with complete liberty the principal element without which life itself would be reduced to a most lamentable state."[89] Whereas the relationship to land had by this time changed substantially, with many land issues now managed at the national level, water was still considered to belong under local control. As the structures of local community power and identity atrophied before the growing state, so too had community-based collective action.[90] The world in which Juan Lopez struggled—to make ends meet, to hold onto his land, to be an active member of his indigenous community—had changed significantly since he was a boy, and it would continue to change through the rest of the nineteenth century.

The rise in private property holding had inexorably altered social and productive relations. Similar trends can be observed in Carazo, Granada, and Masaya over the nineteenth century, but to say all three followed the same path would be an overstatement. While institutional developments at the national state level—be they new taxes, creation of land registries, standardization of local militias, or generalization and extension of agricultural judges—were effecting the same kinds of changes throughout the country, local social and productive relations varied tremendously. We should not expect the growth of the state to produce the same reactions in the frontier regions of Matagalpa as in the urban density of Granada, nor that the towns in the area of Masaya, most of which are unsuitable for coffee growing, would have the same experiences as those in the highlands of Carazo. Based on a close analysis of the town of Diriomo's coffee economy from the 1870s to the 1930s, Dore shows a situation of a highly stratified society in which Granadinos controlled the coffee economy while most Diriomeños shuttled between forced labor and their subsistence plots.[91] Charlip's study of the department of Carazo during this same period argues for the development of a far more egalitarian commercial agriculture system based on small-scale subsistence farming and coffee production. Whereas Dore argues that the coffee boom brought on a "peasantization" in Diriomo, Charlip finds that "Caraceños did not see themselves as peasants. In no Carazo documents does the word *campesino*, or peasant, appear." Instead, she argues, they were farmers and, whether rich or poor, "shared many of the same concerns and likely many of the same values, despite disparities in wealth."[92] By examining distinct social and economic environments across the prefecture of Granada, it becomes evident not only that Dore and Charlip have excavated key components of the rural landscape but also that these should be placed in a broader comparative context. Charlip suggests that the difference between Carazo and Diriomo may lie in Diriomo's larger indigenous population, and this is certainly a key factor.[93] Yet this, too, needs to be taken further. The relative market orientation of communities, their access to physical resources, their broader history of ethnic relations, and their historical relationship to the state led to diverging paths.

While Carazo and Granada both saw growing concentration of landholding and increasing inequality from 1848 to 1897, their paths diverged in relation to smallholdings. Landholdings of less than 50 manzanas declined in both areas, but much more severely in Granada than in Carazo. From 1878 to 1887 these holdings accounted for 46 percent of the total area in Carazo and 35 percent in Granada. Over the next decade the holdings dropped by one-half in Carazo, to 23 percent, but in Granada they fell to 11 percent, less than one-third of the previous period. In Masaya, on the other hand, smallholdings appear to have grown over time. Whereas smallholding represented 43 percent of the land area between 1878 and 1887, by the next decade they encompassed all land transactions.[94]

These size divisions are also readable in the vocabulary used to describe particular kind of landholdings. Six terms appeared in the land registry between 1868 and 1897: *huerta, terreno, finca, tierra, hacienda,* and *sitio.* Although the terms were doubtless broadly understand-

Table 8. Average area for main private landholding designations by department, 1868–1897 (area in manzanas)

	Carazo		Granada		Masaya	
	Area	Number	Area	Number	Area	Number
Huerta	9	246	15	155	9	18
Terreno	31	152	60	89	49	7
Finca	31	97	87	116	24	3
Tierra	62	9	91	9	—	—
Hacienda	63	20	257	33	—	—
Sitio	—	—	1,116	4	—	—

Source: Calculated based on RPPG-RC, 1877–1897.

able from region to region, it is clear that expectations about property size, use, and location were geographically distinct (see table 8). *Tierra* and *sitio* were used infrequently and tended to describe large holdings. The remaining terms, however, were quite common and clearly marked distinct properties. *Huerta* was the smallest designation, averaging 9 manzanas in Carazo and Masaya but slightly larger in Granada. In either case, huertas were clearly family-size plots that required no outside labor. The terms *finca* and *terreno* appeared to be almost interchangeable and marked farms that would have needed hired labor during harvest times. Although these lands averaged 31 manzanas in Masaya and Carazo, in Granada they were larger, averaging 75 manzanas. Perhaps marking the less market-oriented economy of Masaya, the term *hacienda* did not appear in its land registry records. Although the term appeared in both Carazo and Granada, Carazo's haciendas averaged just 63 manzanas, less than the average finca in Granada. In Granada, by contrast, the average hacienda covered 257 manzanas. Despite these differences, it is clear that Nicaraguans coherently distinguished landholdings by size and use, although degree of market integration certainly also informed the meanings of these terms. Most farmers, as Charlip notes, "chose the label *agricultor* whether the farm was five or five hundred *manzanas* in size."[95] Nonetheless, Nicaraguans clearly distinguished between types of farms and farming activities in ways that may well have separated a smaller farmer from a larger farmer.

In analyzing these data, we must remember that they derive from the land registry and therefore only represent land transactions, not necessarily total actual holdings. Since smallholders lived much closer to the margin of subsistence than did largeholders, their potential to fall below that line and conceivably need to sell their land was much higher. As such, we might expect the analysis of the land registry to skew toward smallholding. However, in a study of Costa Rican agricultural census and land registry records, Marc Edelman and Mitchell Seligson suggest that census records tend to underreport largeholdings because of the desire of wealthier landlords to hide from potential land redistribution policies or taxes.[96] By combining analyses from both the land registry and the agricultural census manuscripts for towns in the prefecture of Granada (carried out in 1880), I hope to provide a partial corrective to this problem.

Before looking at the distributional analysis of the agricultural census, let us broadly compare the census and the registry. Numerous comparisons could be made to assess the congruity of the sources, but two simple ones should suffice. First, we can look at the average parcel sizes recorded in each source, and second, at a ratio of the number of records in the census to the number of transactions recorded in the registry. As it turns out, Carazo demonstrates the greatest parity. The average size of all land transactions in Carazo, according to the registry, is 29.10 manzanas; according to the census, the average is 29.11 manzanas. Much more obvious differences are evident for Granada and Masaya. In Granada the registry average is 76.1 manzanas, 1.6 times higher than the census average of 46.7 manzanas. The situation is even more polarized in Masaya, where the registry average of 21.6 manzanas is 3.6 times higher than the census average of 6.0 manzanas. The ratio of census records to registry records is equally telling. In Carazo this ratio is 0.81, while in Granada it is 0.45 and in Masaya, just 0.08. Thus, whereas the land registry seems a fairly accurate representation of the actual land situation in

Figure 2. Intensity of land cultivation by size and region, 1880

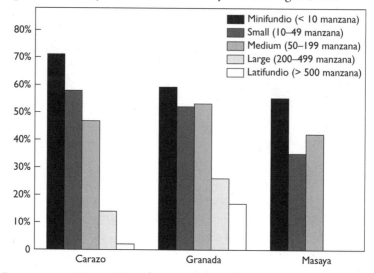

Source: AMPG, caja 158, leg. 441, "Censo agropecuaria de Catarina," 1880; "Censo agropecuaria de La Victoria [Niquinohomo]," 1880; "Censo agropecuaria de San Juan de Oriente," 1880; "Censo agropecuaria de Diriá," 1880; "Censo agropecuaria de Diriomo," 1880; "Censo agropecuaria de Granada," 1880; "Censo agropecuaria de Nandaime," 1880; "Censo agropecuaria de Diriamba," 1880; "Censo agropecuaria de Santa Teresa," 1880.

Carazo, it both underestimates landholding and skews size upward in Granada, and even more so in Masaya. Nonetheless, in all three departments the agricultural census indicates a fairly equitable distribution of land and confirms the importance of small landholdings. According to the census, the latter accounted for 84 percent of holdings in Granada, 92 percent in Carazo, and 99 percent in Masaya.

An analysis of the intensity of land cultivation—calculated as the percentage of landholding in cultivation—reveals a pattern that follows the market orientation mentioned above. The average percentage of land area cultivated, calculated from the 1883 agricultural census, was 64 percent for Carazo, 55 percent for Granada, and 52 percent for Masaya. This indicator of the intensiveness of land use is even more revealing for minifundio and smallholdings. In Carazo this ratio was 71 and 58 percent, respectively. Both Masaya and Granada showed

Table 9. Average price per manzana of private landholdings by department, 1848–1897 (in pesos)

	Carazo	Granada	Masaya
1848–1867	2.29	1.91	0.29
1868–1877	8.89	43.25	6.63
1878–1887	23.47	12.84	7.80
1888–1897	33.93	25.39	12.09

Source: Calculated based on RPPG-RC, 1877–1897

much less intensive land use of minifundio-size holdings, with ratios of 55 and 59 percent, respectively. At the level of smallholdings, however, Granada's land use much more closely approaches Carazo's, at a ratio of 52 percent, while Masaya's ratio of 35 percent indicates comparatively less pressure for such aggressive land use (see figure 2).

The transformation in landholding patterns was matched in each department by changes in land prices. Prior to the beginning of noticeable privatization in land in the prefecture of Granada, the average price per manzana was quite low. From 1848 to 1867 land sold for an average of 2.29 pesos per manzana in Carazo, 1.91 pesos in Granada, and 0.29 pesos in Masaya. From 1868 to 1877 all three departments evinced small but noticeable rises in land prices. The pressures of land claimants (such as those discussed earlier in Jinotepe and Niquinohomo) began to affect land prices, most noticeably in Carazo, where the growth of coffee production began first. From 1878 to 1887, however, prices exploded in Carazo, where the average rose to 23.47 pesos per manzana. Prices also rose in Granada and Masaya, but more modestly. As Dore has argued, a "revolution in land" had occurred in Diriomo (in the department of Granada) by the mid-1870s; however, the coffee economy, as evidenced by much lower average land prices, was still in its infancy there compared to towns in Carazo.[97] While Masaya's land prices would rise again between 1888 and 1897, they remained the lowest in the prefecture of Granada. In Granada, however, prices had nearly risen to match those in Carazo, a product of the growth of

Diriomo's coffee economy on the slopes of the Mombacho Volcano (see table 9).

Throughout the prefecture of Granada, those who claimed to be farmers dominated the ranks of private land owners, far in excess of their numbers in society. Records from towns in Carazo, Granada, and Masaya listed them as land buyers between 69 and 77 percent of the time, while farmers accounted for just 12 percent of all Nicaraguan occupations (24 percent of men's occupations).[98] Others did purchase land, even those labeled as laborers, but perhaps because of their limited experience with farming (in the case of artisans, merchants, and professionals) or their comparatively lower socioeconomic position (laborers and housewives), these groups also tended to be sellers of land more often than buyers. In the case of women, who in the land registry were almost always listed as housewives (*oficios domésticos*), the shift toward private landholding and the boom in coffee opened up new opportunities. Women showed up as buyers in land registry transactions just over 6 percent of the time, but they seemed to be slowly pushed out of landowning as the nineteenth century wore on.[99] Whether this denoted women's more limited access to capital or the efforts of men to claim the prerogatives of land ownership is unclear.[100] Nonetheless, as Charlip notes, "the new opportunities available to women were fraught with the complications of a patriarchal society."[101] Laborers present an equally interesting example within the land registry. As with women, laborers sold land more often than they bought it. What we cannot tell from the records, however, is the extent to which these are "new" laborers, stripped of their "farmer" status by dint of their land loss.

How do these statistical findings compare with the concrete experiences of individuals who lived through these changes? To attempt an answer, I have tried to trace the principal participants in the indigenous community of San Marcos's effort to retain the area of Pochotón as ejidos. Of the seven leaders of the community originally discussed, three—Cando Sanches, Juan Feliz Mercado, and Sirilo Campos—remained outside the records of the public land registry of Nicaragua. This does not mean that they did not have access to land, since as elders of their community they undoubtedly had long-standing ejidal rights. Moreover, members of the wider Sanches, Mercado, and Campos families were found frequently in the town's land transactions. Nonetheless, they clearly did not approach the growing private land market and agro-export economy, as did their fellow leaders of the indigenous community, Germán Marques and Benancio García. Although Marques's endeavors appeared limited to the 1889 purchase of a coffee and sugar finca for 400 pesos, the accumulation of such an asset is evidence of earlier involvement in the agro-export economy.[102]

Benancio García serves as a vital counterpoint to Sanches, Mercado, and Campos. Over his lifetime (and subsequent to the 1867 effort to save Pochotón) he bought and sold land in both San Marcos and Jinotepe, producing both coffee and subsistence crops.[103] As part of his integration into the coffee economy, García also mortgaged his lands, to be paid back in coffee.[104] His family members, especially Saturnino García, were also active in the San Marcos land market. Notably, both men were listed in the land transactions as agricultores. García's success undoubtedly extended from his long-established rights to communal lands, which provided him with a base of wealth within the newly privatized landed economy. Moreover, his early choice to take part in the private land economy provided him with the advantages of entry during the initial stage of what would become a booming market and helped him establish personal and political relationships that would provide further advantages down the line.[105] What is much less clear is why García made this choice when many of his fellow community members did not.

Conclusion

As communal landholding declined in the prefecture of Granada, an important new smallholding class evolved alongside the emerging pattern of private landholding. This shift attended the dissipation of municipal and community authority in the face of the growing state authority. The interrelation of the two was critical to the development of the Nicaraguan nation-state. The rise of a smallholding class out of the parcelization and distribution of Nicaragua's ejidal lands and the market in already-existing private holdings led to a generally peaceful, almost silent growth in the everyday influence of the state on local communities and their members, in effect diminishing both the power of these communities and their ability to sustain local identities. This is not to say that local identity ceased to function or be important; rather, in Clifford Geertz's words, these changes "divest[ed] them of their legitimizing force with respect to governmental authority."[106]

The majority of Nicaraguans with access to land owed their hold on that land to the state, and at times of crisis they looked less and less to community institutions to adjudicate their claims, turning instead to state institutions—be they police, courts, or prefects. Moreover, they ceased to rely on the local community for support in resisting encroachment on this land. Broad-based community uprisings occurred over the nineteenth century, but they were both infrequent and rarely related to land issues. At the same time, these changes were neither uniform nor complete. Communal lands remained, and so did community authority. Moreover, while Carazo, with its large ladino population and perfect coffee-growing conditions, experienced a rapid rise in private smallholding and market-oriented production, this was but one possible outcome. Granada and Masaya both had larger indigenous populations than Carazo, but while Granada tended toward greater concentration of land, substantial market production, and high land prices, Masaya hewed closer to its historical trend of more cheaply available land and subsistence production. Nonetheless, throughout, private smallholders became principal figures whose economic success and political participation were ever more tied to the state.

When Antonio Silva, minister of development and public works, asserted in his 1867 *Memoria* that the progress of agriculture was the goal of "*every good Nicaraguan* who desires the happiness of his fatherland," he expressed something closer to hope than actuality.[107] By the end of the nineteenth century, however, the rise of a smallholding petty bourgeoisie throughout the prefecture of Granada had created a group within Nicaraguan society that saw its interests aligned with, if not the same as, those of national elites. The elite effort to reconstruct the meaning of land and agriculture succeeded because state policies served to deepen social and economic stratification at the municipal level without appearing as a wholesale attack on communal lands, municipal authority, or indigenous custom. In so doing, these policies helped to unravel the weave of local identity, creating loose threads that were ready to be incorporated into the enveloping fabric of the nation-state.

FOUR

The Work of Their Hands
Labor, Community, and Ethnicity

"Vagrancy is more a danger to society than a suffering," wrote Liberato Dubón, the prefect of León, in a characteristic display of nineteenth-century Liberal warmth and charity.[1] Nicaragua's abundantly fertile lands and varied climes could support a diverse agriculture, but from the earliest days of the colonial period, Nicaraguan landlords felt frustrated by the unwillingness of Nicaragua's poor to labor for them on their plantations.[2] After independence, relatively easy access to land and the state's inability to control its extensive agricultural frontier made securing a sufficiently large, cheap labor force even more difficult.

From the beginning of the eighteenth century until the mid-nineteenth century, Nicaragua's population expanded relatively rapidly. Emigration from the larger towns and cities occurred largely in the first decades following independence for familiar push and pull factors. Civil war threatened the lives and livelihoods of those living near the principal cities and towns, especially León. At the same time, a short-lived boom in brazilwood in the early 1830s, growing trade relations with Great Britain, and the beginning of gold mining attracted workers to Chinandega, Granada, and Chontales.[3]

In the prefecture of Granada, in particular, by the end of the eighteenth century, people began to gather in new, small communities, occupying the spaces between the older, larger towns they had left. By the mid-nineteenth century these hamlets (which included

El Rosario, La Paz, San Marcos, and Santa Teresa)[4] had grown into full-fledged towns, juridically independent of their surrounding communities. This pattern of internal settlement, however, quickly reached its capacity to absorb people. As the state expanded following the National War the pace of migration accelerated, shifting toward the country's frontier regions: Nueva Segovia, Chontales, and Matagalpa.[5]

In late October 1860, and against this backdrop, the state polled the most important leaders and landowners in each region of the country for their opinions on improving the supply of labor for plantation agriculture. A scant six weeks earlier, William Walker, the scourge of Nicaraguan sovereignty, had been executed by a firing squad in Trujillo, Honduras. With the embodiment of foreign threats extinguished, the state began to turn more aggressively to internal issues. Facing criticism over the inadequacy of its recently enacted agricultural law of 1859, but still mindful of the disastrous experiments with controlling labor in the 1840s that ended in rebellion, the state hoped to satisfy elite concerns while avoiding renewed flare-ups.[6] Until at least the 1880s, land in Nicaragua was plentiful and cheap. Land tenure centered on communal landholding, and even as private property became more common, smallholding and minifundio (less than 50 manzanas, equivalent to 86.5 acres) predominated. Although land prices climbed in the 1880s and 1890s as coffee exports boomed, smallholding remained overwhelmingly the norm. In an analysis of the land registry for the prefecture of Granada (which included the departments of Granada, Carazo, and Masaya), smallholding accounted for 85 percent of all transactions carried out between 1878 and 1897, with holdings averaging 11.5 manzanas. An 1880 agricultural census corroborates the land registry, indicating that 90 percent of all landholders owned less than 50 manzanas, averaging 8.5 manzanas each.[7] French scientist Pablo Lévy reported in the late 1860s, "Peonage such as it is known in Mexico and other parts of Spanish America does not exist in Nicaragua."[8] Given this picture of land tenure, conflict over labor seemed inevitable.

Responses to the government's call varied by region and political temperament, but blame always fell squarely on the shoulders of the rural poor, and state policy was expected to remedy the situation. Joaquín Elizondo, a hacendado from Rivas who would become minister of war in 1879, argued in 1860 that the peasantry's lack of "that noble aspiration to improve their lot" doomed any attempt to permanently improve agriculture. Nothing short of eradicating the Nicaraguan masses' retrograde culture would make any difference. Change would come only through the slow, difficult process of "education." The minister of government, Jerónimo Pérez, voiced similar reservations in his report to Congress that same year. But rather than lobbying for education, Pérez called for a police force that could "oblige to work a multitude that does not want to because through whatever means, they have their daily sustenance assured."[9] Although a scarcity of willing laborers had aggravated Nicaraguan landlords from the earliest days of Spanish colonization, this problem took on a distinctly new cast in the process of nation-state formation.

Controlling and disciplining labor have always been central to labor exploitation, but in mid-nineteenth-century Nicaragua they need to be analyzed in relation to the ethnographic construction of labor emerging in the discourse of elites like Elizondo and Pérez. Indeed, Spanish colonial labor institutions, most notably the *repartimiento* (forced Indian labor, which lasted in Nicaragua until independence), had long suggested the equation of Indians and laborers, but until the 1850s the problems of managing labor were conceived of as largely social and economic.[10] Historically, landlords had conceived of rural laborers as lacking a political existence. Although subject to violent outbursts or rebellion, these were construed as the "pre-political" expressions of what Eric Hobsbawm once termed primitive rebels.[11] Following the National War, however, the umbrella of the nation added to the state's labor policies a political dimension that invited conflicts over the relationships among indigenous communities, laborers, and the nation-state.

Where Elizondo concerned himself with understanding the "culture" of the laborer and its relationship to the nation-state, Pérez emphasized the practical aspects of actually managing laborers. For Pérez, the cultural and political aspects were unimportant if the state could not enforce its labor laws. However, we should not make facile conclusions from the threatening cast of his discourse; although he peppered his speech with words like "police" and "force," Pérez, as much as any other member of Nicaragua's elite, had had his fill of bloodshed. The revolts of 1845–49 remained fresh in elite memory and the state shied from overtly violent action, frequently punishing officials who were excessively coercive in their daily governance. Pérez focused, rather, on the state's need to control the means of legitimate coercion and bespoke the confrontation between landlords and the state over the control of labor. To establish meaningful institutional structures to effect this control required the state, on the one hand, to insert itself into landowner-laborer relations, and on the other hand, to foster interregional cooperation among local state officials.

The prefecture of Granada is a particularly propitious location for this analysis, for it is geographically and ethnically diverse and also the place where Nicaraguan coffee production first boomed. This chapter is divided into three sections. The first examines changes in labor and agricultural law during the second half of the nineteenth century, focusing especially on how the state organized and structured its agents charged with enforcing these laws. Much of Nicaraguan historiography ascribes novel enforcement procedures and institutions to the state under José Santos Zelaya (1893–1909), but little evidence supports this claim.[12] Rather, the core of Nicaragua's labor laws and strategies of labor control developed in the decades following the National War, and it is clear that a deeper examination of Nicaragua's "labor scarcity" is needed. The second section turns to the relationship between the state's struggles to enforce its labor laws and the process of state formation. Rather than focusing on the laborer, however, this section explores the relationship of landowners to the state and the state's efforts to coordinate its locally organized institutions. Finally, the third section examines the conflicts and changes in the relationships among labor, ethnicity, and community in nineteenth-century Nicaragua by focusing on the struggles between local ladino elites and indigenous communities over the control and meaning of labor.

Labor Enforcement and State Formation

In 1859, as part of a broad new law to promote agriculture, the legislature created the position of rural magistrate (*juez de agricultura*). Each town with at least one thousand inhabitants would have its own magistrate; in smaller towns the constitutional alcalde would take on the magistrate's duties. In many ways, the position was created as a twin to the local alcalde, elected at the same time and for the same term and jurisdiction. That the law mandated the magistrate's attendance and voting at municipal council meetings further established this relationship.[13] The state's message was clear: labor recruitment and control were local concerns for local authorities.

Subsequent law slowly wrested management of labor from the municipality. By 1862 it had become clear that the municipal councils had taken advantage of the law to shift some of their work and responsibilities to the magistrate. Although the new *Ley de agricultura* maintained the magistrate's municipal-level focus, he "will now have a seat and vote in the municipality when he wants to attend." More importantly, he remained "exempt from the committees and other duties of that [municipal] body."[14] In 1869 the legislature shifted responsibility for the maintenance of books listing potential day laborers (jornaleros) in each town from the municipality to the magistrate.[15]

To improve the efficacy of rural magistrates, in 1867 the legislature created a special police force dedicated to enforcing Nicaragua's labor laws and to serve as the police arm of the rural magistrates. Each of these general agricultural agents managed four foot soldiers and a mounted corporal and covered a territory composed of several towns. Although the agents were named by the state, rather than elected locally like the rural magistrates, their orders were given by the magistrates of each town.[16]

The functions and jurisdictions of the rural magistrate and agricultural agent underscore how the state conceived of the task of controlling labor. On a day-to-day basis, the management of labor—from the evaluation of occupational status to the registration and enforcement of contracts—occurred in a fixed location: the municipality. Successful management, therefore, demanded that the rural magistrate inhabit and patrol the same orbit. The agricultural agent's jurisdiction, in contrast, had no limits, because workers frequently fled across territorial boundaries. To be tied to a place would have hampered the performance of the agent's job. However, in either case the effort to control labor was not viewed as a national task. Rural magistrates and agents formed a dense but decentralized network.

As Nicaragua's export economy began to boom in the 1880s, officials reconsidered the state's role in controlling labor, declaring in new legislation, "It is the duty of the state to pursue, capture and remit fugitive workers."[17] This new "duty" did not mean a reorganization or direct oversight of local policing efforts, since the former did not seem necessary and the latter was considered inefficient, if not impossible. In fact, agricultural law had long required police and military forces to aid the country's rural magistrates. Rather, the state took on the responsibility of centralizing and distributing information related to "fugitive" and "delinquent" workers. Beginning in 1883, hacendados and finqueros were to send monthly lists of workers who had deserted their contracts. These lists would be compiled, printed, and circulated to every police agent, alcalde, and magistrate in the country.

More importantly, the state was now to take on the costs of capturing and transporting fugitive laborers.[18] Until 1883 the agricultural laws encumbered each municipality with financing the operations of the rural magistrates. Not surprisingly, they proved loath to respond to their counterparts. The system had reinforced a form of localism—not the localism of Granada and León in the grand narra-

Figure 3. Nicaraguan coffee exports, 1865–1899 (five-year averages)

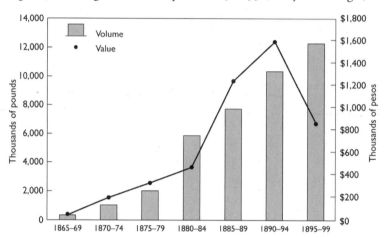

Source: Calculated from Charlip, "Cultivating Coffee," 107; R. G. Williams, *States and Social Evolution,* 265–74.

tive of Nicaraguan history, but the localism that cares not for those beyond the city limits. As the rural magistrate of Granada explained in a complaint to the treasury minister, "the ineffectiveness of the capture of fugitive workers" results "because the magistrates of other towns in the republic ignore legally issued requests."[19] Along with the assumption of these costs, the state also provided free use of the telegraph system for official communication regarding fugitive workers. While the state clearly favored the carrot with this approach, it backed it up with a stick, fining magistrates who did not act upon a legal request within three days.[20]

It is traditionally asserted that José Santos Zelaya's coup in 1893 heralded a new age in Nicaragua, the arrival of a belated "Liberal revolution" and more suitable, effective labor laws. Robert Williams is not alone when he suggests that "Growers throughout the country found relief when the Liberal government of Zelaya passed a labor code in 1894."[21] But what evidence can be mustered for this case? Can the fact that nearly 80 percent of fugitive workers evaded capture between 1897 and 1900 be considered "relief"?[22] Between 1850 and 1900 landowners cried labor shortage at every opportunity. Nonetheless, coffee production rose dramatically throughout the second half of the nineteenth century (see figure 3), as did trade in general. Significantly, where small dips in exports led to dramatic drops in imports in the first decades after the National War, by the 1880s the elite demonstrated much greater confidence in the economy's recuperative abilities.[23]

The tendency has been to focus on the post-1893 state's supposedly new responses to the problem of securing and controlling labor, especially vagrancy law, work cards, and yet another group of agricultural police. That an examination of Nicaraguan legislation over the nineteenth century shows Zelaya to have essentially followed in the footsteps of his predecessors suggests the enduring power of a Central American historiography that equates Conservative policy with colonial stagnation.[24] Moreover, Zelaya's truly novel change in labor law receives limited mention and discussion.[25] In 1901 new legislation classified all people with less than 500 pesos in capital or property as laborers. Until that time, 100 pesos had defined the limit between laborer and farmer. Over the second half of the nineteenth-century, two patterns of change converged to expand the ranks of Nicaragua's citizen-farmers. On the one hand, land tenure shifted ever increasingly toward private smallholding. On the other hand, steadily increasing land prices meant that ever smaller holdings would qualify their owners for citizenship. Thus, based on land prices gathered from transactions of private landholdings in the land registry, even most minifundio owners (less than 10 manzanas) held lands valued in excess of 100 pesos. However, enacting this law single-handedly converted the majority of Nicaragua's smallholding class into laborers and denied them citizenship rights. The law did not so much reverse the transformations in land tenure that had taken place in the 1880s and 1890s as attempt to deny smallholders their place within the nation. Zelaya would never suggest, as the government before him did in 1891, that worker fraud stemmed in great part from land-lords' "onerous and victimizing" treatment of laborers.[26] Despite (or perhaps in response to) Zelaya's expansion of state coercion and ef-forts to stifle popular sovereignty, signs pointed to both the expanded inclusiveness of the nation and Zelaya's weakness. Two years later, in 1903, the legislature voted overwhelmingly to overturn the law in the face of mounting pressure from indigenous groups, smallholders, and regional elites.[27]

Landowners, the State, and the Control of Labor

In 1867, in an inaugural speech, President Fernando Guzmán cau-tioned against state intervention in any of the fundamental sectors of Nicaraguan society, especially the economy: "When the state, going beyond certain limits, wields its influence on commerce, on agriculture, on industry, on all the branches that, in the end, form the elements of a country's culture, it becomes protectionist and centralizing. It appears to guide when it does nothing more than weigh heavily on the nation."[28] Guzmán echoed Liberal senti-ments, but the popular rebellions of the 1840s and the experiences of the war against William Walker tinged his words. If state policy had ever been directed toward simple coercion of labor, such a po-sition proved untenable after the National War. As in other aspects of nation-state formation, the state tried to balance its policy goals against the complications involved in achieving those goals. The elites' liberal project faced the countervailing forces of the nation; raw economic and political benefits of state policy needed to be weighed against the ideological costs of achieving such goals. At-tempting to ensure a ready supply of cheap labor for landlords re-quired not simply managing the hierarchy of state official involved in enforcing labor law but also dealing with the complicated rela-tionships between landlords and peasants and between municipali-ties and indigenous communities.

Most analyses of Nicaragua's agricultural laws have focused on understanding the relationships established between the state and laborers and between landlords and laborers. The frequently contentious relationship between the state and landlords, in contrast, receives little attention. Yet nation-state formation hinges, in great part, on the ability of the state to assert its authority over the individual interests of elites. It should not be surprising, therefore, that in each agricultural law from 1862 forward, regulation of landlords ("los hacendados ó patrones") tended to take up about a third of each statute's articles.[29]

The reform of the agricultural law in 1862 stipulated that landlords who expected the state's help in the recruitment of labor and enforcement of contracts had to register their properties and each contract with the rural magistrate of their district.[30] This dramatically changed the relationship of the state to landowners. The 1859 law allowed the registering of haciendas and labor contracts, but the charge of 10 centavos per contract acted as a disincentive to the system's use. The law clearly stated that "private persons may contract with one another without the intervention of the magistrate," and landlords followed economic logic.[31] With the reform, however, if landlords wished the state to act as their sword, they would have to submit to its witness. After 1862 landlords could contract laborers without going through the rural magistrate, but the decision could be costly. In a case from 1871, for example, Urbano Tifer was brought before the rural magistrate of Diriomo for failing to repay a debt he owed to Pedro Rivera. Tifer reluctantly admitted the debt but claimed it to be a personal loan, not an advance on wages. Before the magistrate could remand Tifer to Rivera's hacienda, however, Tifer complained to the prefect of Granada, explaining that there existed no registration of a contract with the magistrate and that he therefore could not hear or decide the dispute.[32]

As the state increasingly inserted itself into the regulation of labor and landlord-laborer relations, its agents occasionally generated discontent among landlords. Police and rural magistrates exercised considerable power over the distribution of labor, and landlords frequently claimed corruption. Not uncommon were complaints that state officials were in the pocket of wealthy hacendados or were forcing captured laborers to work on their own plantations.[33] One Granadino landowner went so far as to publish a handbill that charged the agricultural agent of Granada with abuse of his position, attending only to "his personal business affairs or those of any men of influence, whose feet he kisses."[34] Corruption of this sort, however, was viewed as sporadic rather than systemic, the result of bad judgment rather than malice on the part of the state.

Corrupt state agents aggravated landowners, but they could be rooted out with enough persistence. More problematic was the state's seizure of laborers for public works projects and military service, for the elite resented it even as they believed it necessary. In general, the state tried to leave to each town the organization and management of local public works, such as municipal roads, but projects more national in scope, such as wartime military recruitment or telegraph lines and roads to frontier regions like Chontales and Matagalpa, often found the state exercising seemingly unlimited, unchecked power. Foreign travelers in Nicaragua frequently reported how landowners despaired at how military recruitment could leave them without workers.[35] The practice continued throughout the nineteenth century, always in the name of national defense.[36]

Given the control the state sought to wield over landlords and the problems attendant upon accepting the state's intervention into their affairs, why did landlords do so? A significant reason was the state's promise that once labor had been contracted, it had to complete its work obligations. In discussing the labor situation for coffee growers in nineteenth-century Nicaragua, Robert Williams cut straight to the heart of the issue: "The greatest fear of capitalist growers was that the berries would rot for lack of a labor force to pick."[37] Sugar and indigo plantations nurtured the same anxiety. Significantly, for most of the nineteenth century the reality of labor scarcity seemed to far outweigh the fear that wages would rise and cut into profits.

Labor relations varied among regions in nineteenth-century Nica-

Table 10. Wages in labor contracts in the prefecture of Granada, 1881, 1885, and 1902

	N	Average monthly wages (pesos)	Contracts providing food (%)
1881	179	7.20	64
1885	193	8.88	71
1902	149	14.16	55

Source: AMPG, libro 85, "Matrículas de fincas y talleres del dpto. de Granada," 1881; libro 128, "Matrículas de operarios," 1885; libro 188, "Agriculturas contratos," 1902.

ragua. In analyzing Indian-ladino labor relations in late-nineteenth-century Matagalpa, Jeffrey Gould argues that coffee growers "had difficulty envisioning this inherently slothful 'degraded race' as a free labor force on their plantations," relying instead on debt bondage to supply their labor needs.[38] Preliminary evidence from labor contracts (including ones for coffee harvests in Managua) suggests that in the prefecture of Granada the case was different. Between 1881 and 1902, average monthly wages rose from 7.2 pesos per month to 14.2 pesos per month, an average increase of 4.4 percent per year (see table 10).[39] Moreover, agricultural law in Nicaragua from as early as 1835 specified that the act of contracting, not indebtedness, tied the laborer to employer.[40] If debt was not required for the enforcement of labor contracts, why offer it?

Food prices kept pace with wages, growing at an average of 4.7 percent per year between 1881 and 1890, while a 3,100-calorie diet consisting of one and a half pounds of corn, a quarter pound of beans, a half pound of meat, and one plantain continued to cost less than 30 percent of a day's wages (see table 11).[41] Although advances were relatively common in 1881, with laborers taking them in almost 70 percent of the contracts, the practice appeared to decline over time, so that in 1902 they were included in slightly less than 7 percent of the contracts. And where the average advance had been one month's wages in 1881, this dropped to less than a week's wages by 1902 (see table 12). Even the higher figure, however, cannot be con-

Table 11. Food prices in the prefecture of Granada, 1877, 1880/1881, 1890 (pesos per pound)

	Corn	Beans	Meat
1877	0.01	0.04	0.07
1880/1881	0.01	0.03	0.08
1890	0.02	0.07	0.10

Source: AMPG, caja 130, leg. 177, 1877; caja 150, leg. 144, 1880; Bureau of the American Republics, *Nicaragua,* 79–80.

sidered too onerous to work off. Taken in sum, wages appeared to be rising in Nicaragua, despite the fact that coffee prices did not always keep pace. Between 1901 and 1903 coffee prices averaged between 5 and 7 centavos per pound, slightly below the prices paid in the early 1880s, and less than half the 15 to 17 centavos per pound being paid between 1886 and 1895.[42]

A system of fully free labor, then, remained unacceptable not because it faced upward pressure on wages, which occurred anyway, but because of the insecurity it engendered in landowners, especially during harvest time. Not surprisingly, as much as landowners craved the stability promoted by the agricultural laws, they frequently tried to circumvent the system. A petition filed in 1875 by a Nandaime hacendado exemplifies the practice. In July of that year the agricultural agent of Nandaime fined Bartolomé Lara Rodriguez 20 pesos for illegal labor practices: 5 pesos for hiring a laborer named Cruz Mayorga without first checking his debt card, and 15 pesos for hiding Mayorga when the agent arrived to do an inspection of the workers. Rodriguez claimed that Mayorga "said he was coming from Liberia [Costa Rica] . . . and didn't carry a solvency ticket because it wasn't necessary," and asserted that the agent's charges were "completely false."[43] Rodriguez's bold assertions, however, deflated before the testimony of other workers on his own hacienda and the agricultural agent of Granada, who helped to find and arrest Mayorga. Despite being caught and fined, Rodriguez may very well have continued to try to woo workers from other haciendas. Hiring labor illegally did

Table 12. Wage advances in the prefecture of Granada, 1881, 1885, and 1902

	N	Average advance (pesos)	Contracts with advances (%)
1881	179	7.82	69
1885	193	9.16	49
1902	149	2.48	7

Source: AMPG, libro 85, "Matrículas de fincas y talleres del dpto. de Granada," 1881; libro 128, "Matrículas de operarios," 1885; libro 188, "Agriculturas contratos," 1902.

not diminish hacendado acceptance of state intervention in labor control; instead, it represented the paradoxes inherent in the process of nation-state formation. Initially, at least, the growing smallholder population only exacerbated a situation of increasing demand for laborers and labor mobility.

Like the efforts of the state to eradicate contraband aguardiente production, its labor policies suffered at the hands of the local officials charged with their enforcement. In contrast to the often hostile attitudes of municipal officials to the state's aguardiente policies, local officials generally supported the state's efforts to control labor. To the extent that local officials failed to enforce the agricultural laws, this arose out of the frequent struggles of these officials both against the hierarchy established by the laws and with officials from outside their jurisdiction.

In the first years after the National War, the state had to contend with municipalities that had for decades experienced tremendous autonomy. Officials at the municipal and regional level continually tested the strength of the state and its ability to organize and control them. In 1857, for example, Pio Echaverri, the constitutional alcalde of Masatepe, wrote to the prefect of Granada, seeking to name the local police agent rather than accept the one chosen by the prefect. Echaverri expressed an understanding of the hierarchical relationship between himself and the prefect, but felt he was in a better position to determine the needs of the municipality.[44] Even as the relationship between the prefect and his subaltern authorities became established, however, squabbles persisted.[45]

On 10 February 1873, Ygnosente Fletes, the agricultural agent of Granada, wrote to the minister of development to complain that the rural magistrate of Granada had tried repeatedly to order him to travel far outside his jurisdiction in an effort to capture a number of different laborers who had deserted their contracts. In recent months Fletes had received orders to go to remote areas, including Rivas, Tipitapa, Chontales, and Masatepe. Fletes explained, "The rural magistrate of Granada believes that I, as agent, am obligated to carry out orders from him outside his jurisdiction."[46] But the magistrate, Fletes argued, misunderstood the law and its applicability.

Rather than respond to Fletes, however, the minister simply turned the complaint over to the prefect of Granada for investigation. The prefect, in turn, requested that Rosario Vivas and Marcos Urbina, the rural magistrate and his deputy, explain why and under what authority they had ordered Fletes to assist them in capturing laborers outside Granada. The answer to the first question was simple: it's his job. Determination of authority, on the other hand, required interpretation of law, law that was occasionally unclear and contradictory. Their interpretation, Vivas explained, brought together two aspects of the law governing rural magistrates and agents. First, the rural magistrate can order the agricultural agent to capture fugitive workers. Second, the agent's territorial jurisdiction is understood to have no limits. As such, Vivas and Urbina argued that they could order the agent to capture workers who were outside their own jurisdiction, since the workers were always necessarily within the agent's jurisdiction.

An exasperated Fletes also sought support from Minister of Agriculture Anselmo Rivas. Rivas responded, but not to the complaint. Instead, he railed against Fletes's disruption of hierarchal authority and order. Fletes "is a subaltern employee of the prefecture," Rivas lectured, "subject to it in all ways by law, and for these reasons, has no rights to approach the government directly about this or any other issue of his responsibility." Separately, Rivas sent a letter to the prefect containing the government's interpretation of the law and issues involved in this case. In it he wrote that the president "has ordered me to express to you the opinion of the government about this particular issue" to help guide the prefect's actions in this case. The state concurred with the rural magistrate in this case, but with certain limitations. Vivas had argued that the rural magistrate could order the agricultural agent to pursue laborers anywhere in the country, since, although the agent was assigned to a particular jurisdiction, the territory of his authority was without limits. The state, however, asserted an important distinction: for the agent to cross out of the territory to which he was assigned, he must be requested by an authority in the jurisdiction into which he will enter. Thus, if Vivas wanted, for example, to order Fletes to capture a laborer in Chontales, Vivas would have to consult with his counterpart in Chontales and have him request Fletes's assistance in that jurisdiction. Although this was slower and less direct than the method Vivas wished to employ, Rivas cautioned that "Any other way would introduce disorder and confusion into the actions of public functionaries."

The struggle between the rural magistrate and the agricultural agent of Granada reveals the critical problems involved in the state-building process at this level. Policy—labor or otherwise—was meaningless if it could not be implemented. Consequently, Anselmo Rivas concentrated his lecture to these agricultural officials on the dangers implicit in circumventing the hierarchical organization of the state as laid out in both the constitution and the law. Although Fletes had a legitimate complaint against the rural magistrate, his decision to bypass his immediate superior led to reprimand rather than resolution. To flatten these hierarchies across local communities would dilute the state's power and promote local autonomy, the very antithesis of the state-building project. Only once the state had reestablished the hierarchy was it worth focusing on the actual management of cross-jurisdictional requests.

For the most part, conflicts between state officials within individual jurisdictional units had declined by the 1880s as the hierarchy of municipality-prefecture-state congealed.[47] Struggles between authorities across territorial borders—from city to city and prefecture to prefecture—however, proved significantly more vexing and intransigent. Since people were highly mobile, especially after the National War, coordinating officials in geographically distinct places became a primary aspect of the state's labor policies. Figures reported in 1900 by the agricultural agent of Managua speak volumes for this need and the state's failures in this area. Of nearly six thousand warrants issued by the agent, 73 percent were for workers who had fled to other departments; less than 9 percent of these were ever captured.[48]

In 1882, Narciso Arévalo, a Granadino hacendado, became embroiled in the kind of cross-jurisdictional dispute that frustrated labor coercion. Arévalo saw himself as an ideal Nicaraguan: he grew coffee and sugar on his hacienda and actively participated in the state's system of labor contracting and control. He duly went before the rural magistrate of his jurisdiction to register his hacienda and the contracts he signed with workers (*operarios*). Moreover, given the frequently limited resources of the state, Arévalo aggressively pursued his own fugitive workers.[49]

Despite his efforts, however, Arévalo found himself stymied by the state's own agents. He had hired two laborers from Niquinohomo, Máximo and Francisco Pavon Negro, but they subsequently fled back home. Arévalo requested that the rural magistrate of Niquinohomo, Rumualdo Espinoza, capture the Pavon brothers, but Espinoza and his secretary, Agustín Vega, proved recalcitrant in their duties. Prodded by Arévalo's lawyer, they eventually arrested the Pavon brothers, but just as quickly let them go. The magistrate claimed that Arévalo had no evidence of contract or debt, despite the proof that Arévalo's lawyer had sent to the magistrate. Only after Arévalo himself journeyed to Niquinohomo to show the contracts did Espinoza and Vega comply.

Naturally enough, Arévalo found this treatment unacceptable and complained to the prefect of Granada, seeking to punish Espinoza and Vega as harshly as the law would allow. In his original petition, Arévalo noted that this was not his first incident involving Niquinohomo's rural magistrate; however, this was the first time he had approached the state to force its officials to comply with the law. Faced with pressure from their superior, Espinoza and Vega admitted their errors and genuflected before Arévalo: "[He] is of noted good conduct, incapable of charging what he is not owed."[50] Given their apology and the "harmony and goodwill" expressed by the magistrate and his secretary, Arévalo decided to drop the charges.[51]

Although the prefect appeared ready to fine Espinoza and Vega, and perhaps remove them from their positions, that result does not appear to be what Narciso Arévalo desired. Significantly, the resolution of this conflict occurred not before the prefect in Granada but in Niquinohomo amid the members of the municipal council. Given the increased mobility of Nicaragua's labor force and the growing reliance of landowners on state officials in disparate locales, "harmony and goodwill" may well have been a more useful result.

The documents shed little light on the reasons behind the magistrate's original actions or for the flight of the Pavon brothers. Through the mid- to late nineteenth century, fleeing to home, as the brothers did, had been the preferred site for escape. David McCreery noted the same pattern in late-nineteenth-century Guatemala, suggesting that "the purpose of flight usually was less to evade obligations than to initiate or to stimulate negotiations."[52] Perhaps the Pavons simply sought respite from their work or felt that local officials in Niquinohomo would serve as a negotiator between them and Arévalo. In any case, the increasingly harsh labor regime of the Zelaya government and the declining power of local communities in the face of the national state led ever greater numbers of workers to avoid capture by escaping across departmental borders.[53]

Labor, Ethnicity, and Community

In 1862 the *Ley de agricultura* defined a laborer as someone who "is without occupation and without the means to subsist."[54] Far from novel, this definition had been in place, legislatively at least, since as early as 1835.[55] In the context of the transformations occurring in Nicaragua following the National War, however, the definition took on a new character. In the new nation-state the laborer occupied a place on the political spectrum at the opposite end from the landholder. Where the landowner was the ideal citizen, the laborer became the marker for the "non-citizen," truly a "mozo," a boy, socially immature and unable to exercise the rights of the national citizen.

This politicization of the discourse on labor proved immediately problematic. Although the elite had historically equated Indians with laborers, the definition of the laborer as landless (or at least land poor) butted up against the (landed) reality of the indigenous community, the prevalence of subsistence agriculture, and the indigenous self-identification as farmers (*agricultores*). In the process of nation-state formation, members of indigenous communities struggled to differentiate themselves from the poor, individual laborer. Unlike in Guatemala, where the state explicitly tied Indians to the status of laborers (especially in the form of the forced labor system of the *mandamiento*), in Nicaragua the state never discursively placed laborers and Indians together in the same discussion.[56] At the local level, however, ladinos continued to view Indians as their largest and most important source of labor. Indeed, in her study of labor in nineteenth-century Diriomo, Elizabeth Dore argues that rural magistrates nearly always assumed laborers to be Indians, only actually applying that label when a laborer's "physical and cultural characteristics jarred with elite Diriomeños' notions of Indianness."[57] In post–National War Nicaragua, the struggles of ladinos and indigenous communities to define the meanings of labor and ethnicity through everyday practice became deeply tied to the process of nation-state formation.

Rural Magistrates, Community Rights, and Authority

In May 1868, Pedro Calero, the indigenous alcalde of Masatepe, wrote to Santiago Guerrero, the town's rural magistrate, to complain of the unfair and illegal treatment his community faced: "You oblige the unhappy Indians [*indígenas*] who have no commitments, to work in the haciendas of the ladinos, without taking into consideration that these people have to cultivate their own lands."[58] Calero asserted that the 1862 agriculture law only allowed the rural magistrate to force contracted laborers to work. Since those within the indigenous community had their own lands, they should not be subject to the magistrate's authority. Guerrero denied that this distinction provided any special status to the indigenous community or its members. As he understood it, the law empowered him to determine who is and is not a laborer. In his reply he insisted that he made no distinction between "Indian and ladino" laborers. Whatever the truth of Guerrero's statement,[59] it is evident that he and Calero faced each other from diametrically opposed understandings of Nicaragua's labor law.

Given Guerrero's intransigence, Calero sought to at least insert the indigenous community into the magistrate's decision making. The agricultural law instructs the rural magistrate that if he is unsure of someone's occupational status, he should bring the person before the constitutional alcalde for a determination. Hoping to incorporate his position as indigenous alcalde into the magistrate's interpretation of this article, Calero requested: "In the case that you insist in [your policy of actively pursuing Indians] . . . I ask that you certify with me everything that you do . . . to deduce the rights of the Indians [*indígenas*] whom I represent."[60] If Calero could not achieve the indigenous community's autonomy from the rural magistrate, he hoped that Guerrero would view his authority as parallel and equivalent to that of the municipal alcalde. Julie Charlip notes a similar case from 1871 over the authority of the indigenous alcalde of Jinotepe. According to a letter from the indigenous community, the indigenous and constitutional alcaldes had in the past worked in "a truly fraternal harmony," but recently the ladino alcalde had sought to undermine his Indian counterpart's authority by relying on the ladino sheriff for future dealings with the indigenous community. The experiment apparently failed as members of the indigenous community ignored the sheriff's orders, claiming that "being Indians they had no greater authority than [the indigenous alcalde]."[61] Indigenous community authority might not last through the coffee boom, but at this point indigenous leaders like Pedro Calero were not alone.

Two months after Calero's initial complaint, and still unsatisfied with Guerrero's response, Masatepe's indigenous community hired Granadino lawyer Francisco Noguera to represent them before the prefect of Granada. Although he wrote more formally than the indigenous community's original petition, Noguera essentially recapitulated Calero's contention that Guerrero was forcing Indians to work on the haciendas of ladinos even though they had not previously contracted themselves for such labor. Noguera argued that Guerrero's "erroneous interpretation" of the law had led him to act unfairly and arbitrarily, exercising power far beyond that granted him by the law. Moreover, when Guerrero forced Masatepe's Indian farmers (*agricultores*) to go to the haciendas of ladinos, "the agricultural works that provide to these poor people the grains that they consume throughout the year become abandoned." He concluded, "If [the law] is understood in this way, it would be an attack on the individual guarantees that our constitution so protects."[62]

The tenor of Calero's argument, promoted by Noguera, is one of rights, as defined in the constitution and the law. By forcing Masatepe's Indians, even the landholders, to labor on ladino haciendas, Guerrero constructed Indians as a laboring class. In replying to Calero's initial complaint, Guerrero had not denied that he arbitrarily forced Indians to work; rather, he asserted that he viewed all laborers, be they Indian or ladino, as equally subject to the labor law and his authority. His treatment of Indians, however, implied that he viewed all Indians as laborers naturally subject to the law by dint of their race. In contrast, in seeking to have the state fulfill its obligations as codified in the law, the indigenous community asserted its membership in the national community, and in so doing it problematized ladino racial discourse and the discourse of national identity. Significantly, even when Calero offered the compromise position that not all members of the community were necessarily landholders, he did so in an effort to assert his equivalence to his municipality's ladino officials.

It is unknown if the indigenous community prevailed in this case, but in any event it petitioned the state again just three years later. In October 1871, Cornelio Lopez, indigenous alcalde of Masatepe, representing himself and the community, wrote to the president of Nicaragua to complain of the treatment they suffered at the hands of the new rural magistrate. Like Calero before him, Lopez focused on the arbitrary nature of the magistrate's actions: "Repeatedly and without any recognition of the qualities or circumstances of the individuals . . . the rural magistrate puts our names on a piece of paper, and with this list delivers us to work for some of the property owners that had solicited us from him."[63]

Whereas the community and Calero had approached the rural magistrate timidly in 1868, Lopez seemed emboldened by the community's willingness to resist. With almost casual indignation he explained to the president, "Of course, Sir, more than a few resist, whether because they are not day laborers or because they have previous obligations, sickness or whatever other cause. And in refusing, they are taken to the stocks where they remain for the whole day." The community's response, Lopez implied, reflected "the violence exercised upon us without any law authorizing the magistrate to act in this way, that is to say, against our will." The community's struggle remained to redefine the indigenous community as "we who have fincas on which we work," not as an endless pool of degraded laborers.

In turning the complaint over to the prefect of Granada, the proper authority for such issues, Rafael Zurita, representing the president, summarized in clear and concise terms the rural magistrate's power in relation to laborers as laid out in the agricultural law: "Rural magistrates can only deliver for service on haciendas the day laborers or artisans that the contractors ask for, but in no way the farmers [*agricultores ó labradores*] that for themselves, their family or servants, are occupied in the cultivation of the earth." The members of Masatepe's indigenous community clearly grasped that their access to land placed them and the rest of Nicaragua's Indians at the edge of a new relationship with the emerging national community. Their landholding meant membership in that community, despite the efforts of local ladino authorities to deny it to them. In reprimanding Masatepe's rural magistrate, the state precisely articulated the indigenous community's position: "These people cannot be placed in the lineage of those that live by the work of their hands."[64]

The state's decision went beyond defining and contrasting those who produced ("cultivation of the earth") and those who labored ("work of their hands") to the explicit equation of smallholding with citizenship. Zurita ended his order by pointing to an 1853 executive decree that exempted from regular militia service all farmers who grew as little as three medios of beans or a half fanega of corn. That such a right would be granted over a service so vital to the security of the state, Zurita argued, made the state's decision in this case all the more important.[65] Since such harvests could be reaped from even the most modest holdings, Zurita's remarks suggested the equation of subsistence production with an intrinsic political independence.[66] How actively this policy was pursued is unclear, but in legally deferring this level of military service in favor of subsistence production, the state at least provided rhetorical support for the promotion of smallholding over and above the value of labor coercion. By the end of nineteenth century, the Zelaya government had not only abandoned any such rhetoric but sought to compel even the most successful small farmers to work the harvests of the country's largest coffee haciendas.[67]

Labor and Ladino Racial Discourse

Municipalities and indigenous communities frequently worked together in the first two decades after the National War, especially when confronted with threats to local autonomy. Their cooperation, however, showed itself to be mostly strategic, and at times it disintegrated into open conflict.[68] Indeed, the indigenous communities and municipalities struggled on a daily basis, constantly remapping the boundary lines of power and autonomy between the two. By the early 1880s most indigenous communities in the prefecture of Granada were struggling to maintain their salience and cohesion. The shift toward private landholding patterns and the disruption of the relationship between the community and communal landholding strained the fabric of indigenous identity in ways that proved difficult to repair. This situation was compounded by increased state and landlord pressure on labor as coffee came to dominate Nicaragua's exports.

Nieves Ramírez of Diriomo exemplified the transitions occurring at this time. In December 1882, only days after the death of his mother, Juana Muñoz, Ramírez found himself compelled by the rural magistrate to complete the contract that his mother had signed to harvest coffee on a hacienda in Managua. Ramírez protested to the prefect, implying that the magistrate pursued such an aggressive and illegal course because Ramírez was born an Indian, that "race that has always been looked down upon in the towns." Ramírez, however, sought not to defend his indigenous heritage but to distance himself from it. He recognized the position he had been born into, but with a past-tense proviso that echoed ladino racial discourse: "I *had* the misfortune of belonging to the indigenous race." Now Ramírez signaled his status as a buyer of labor, not a seller; as a ladino, not an Indian: "I offered to the magistrate to send my servant [*moza*], at my cost, to carry out my mother's commitment."[69] The magistrate, however, refused, demanding that Ramírez himself labor at the hacienda.

Ramírez's case was not unique. Although two-thirds of Diriomo's Indian men were listed as laborers in the 1883 census, nearly a quarter of them were farmers like Ramírez. Ladino men were less likely to be laborers, but with almost 45 percent of them so classified, it was still their primary occupation. Despite this, 80 percent of the laborers who passed before the rural magistrate's gaze were Indians.[70] Where the magistrate looked at Indians and saw laborers, Ramírez simply looked at what he had left behind.[71] Ramírez, the ladino agricultor, had struggled to escape the toil of the Indian jornalero, yet he remained caught between these two identities, caught between cultural and biological conceptions of ethnicity.[72] Both he and the magistrate accepted the ladino equation of class and ethnicity, but where Ramírez lived his life predicated on the fluidity of his identity, the magistrate made no such concessions.

Conclusion

In analyzing official efforts to foster a large, cheap labor force—one of the key emblems of the elites' liberal project—it is evident that the state's means did not match its ambitions. Abundant opportunities to avoid wage labor necessitated the creation of an institutional framework for managing and coercing labor. Although local state authorities questioned both the wisdom and prerogatives of applying national policy at the local level, they grasped the congruence of local and national interests. Nonetheless, the fortifying of the hierarchy from municipality to prefecture to national government failed to produce official cooperation across regional borders. The state, for example, overcame the resistance of rural magistrates to their immediate superiors at the prefectural level, but it failed to abate their disdain for their compatriots in other communities.

Subaltern resistance, especially among Indians, posed a different kind of challenge to the nation-state than did the instability of state hierarchy. Doubtless the petty subterfuge that James Scott has characterized as the "weapons of the weak" sapped the strength of both state and landlords. Alongside these daily acts of subversion, however, landlords and government officials faced the efforts of indigenous communities to construct an alternative modernity. Rather than reject the nation as either insignificant or inimical to their interests, indigenous communities recognized the inherent malleability of national identity. They sought to equate community membership with landholding and in so doing to redefine Indians as farmers who "worked their own lands." Landlords may have equated Indians with barbarism and labor, but the nation admitted a new calculus from within its own discourse. The radical potential of indigenous claims to the nation should not be underestimated. As Jeffrey Gould has argued, "to accept the validity of indigenous claims to citizenship and communal rights would be to delegitimize and destabilize local ladino identities and power."[73] In the three decades that followed the National War, they did just that.

By the 1890s, however, Indian communities in the prefecture of Granada no longer challenged elite conceptions of modernity. Especially after the 1881 indigenous rebellion in Matagalpa and parallel riots in León and Masaya, state authorities at all levels increasingly closed off political and discursive spaces for indigenous communities within the nation. Those in urban centers, such as Sutiava in León and Monimbó in Masaya, continued to be politically and socially active, as did those in the agricultural frontier regions of Jinotega, Matagalpa and Chontales.[74] In both cases, access to community wealth and land resources proved vital to their long-term struggles. Moreover, for those on the frontier, distance from the centers of state authorities worked for decades to keep these at arm's length. For the majority in the prefecture of Granada, however, social and economic transformations attenuated the salience of their indigenous communities just as the political climate became more stifling.

The dominance of communal land tenure had given way to private landholding. Access to land increased for some but disappeared for others. The mounting landless population induced a parallel transformation in the labor system. In the past, indigenous communities worked to protect their members from the predations of landlords and the state, but now, unable to maintain the vision of Indians as farmers and without another base of power, the communities began to disengage from the state.[75] A newspaper editorial from 1888 titled "The Artisan" is suggestive of this shift:

> The Indian looks towards the desert, the artisan fixes his gaze on the city; the Indian can return to the animal skins of the

ancient aborigines, the artisan can get dressed in a fashionable suit; the Indian isolates himself, the artisan associates with others; the Indian is a passive agent of production, an instrument in agriculture, an arm [*brazo*] in the collective; the artisan is an intelligent factor in industry, a voter in public opinion, a citizen of the state, a patriot in the campaign; the salary is imposed on the Indian, while the artisans prices his contract; you track down and drag back the Indian, you look for and make an offer to the artisan; in a word, the Indians sinks, the artisan rises.[76]

Without the kind of indigenous leadership and resistance that characterized the 1860s and 1870s, the idea of Indians as laborers became reentrenched in an increasingly hegemonic ladino racial discourse that excluded Indians from the nation, except as markers of a mythic origin.

FIVE
Customs of the Nicaraguan Family
Ethnic Conflict and National Identity

While traveling through Central America around 1870, a French scientist and explorer named Pablo Lévy believed he had stumbled upon a unique anthropological circumstance. Whatever merits he found in the other countries, it was Nicaragua, with its diverse ethnic mixture derived from "the white race, the black race and the red American race," that fascinated him.[1] He estimated Nicaragua (excluding the Atlantic coast) to be 55 percent Indian, 20 percent mestizo, 20 percent mulatto, 4.5 percent white, and 0.5 percent black.[2] Such diversity had long been recognized by colonial officials in Nicaragua, who worried that it might destabilize the Spanish empire.[3] These concerns briefly waned after independence, but Nicaraguan elites of all stripes increasingly viewed this reality as a fragile foundation for a stable nation-state.

Beginning in the late 1840s, Nicaraguan leaders faced a series of obstacles to state building and political consolidation, including indigenous uprisings and British reassertion of their protectorate over the Mosquitia. These were not entirely new, of course, both having antecedents in the Spanish colonial era, but in the context of Nicaragua's assertion of full independence in 1838 they took on a decidedly (anti)nationalist tone that altered how officials understood them. As one observer noted in 1847, the state's response to fighting between Indians and ladinos had bred in the former "an implacable hatred of all authority and social order."[4] In the colonial era, Indian communities could rail against local authorities while claiming fealty to the Spanish empire with chants of "Long live the King! Death to the Government!" Now, however, such protests challenged the nascent nation-state. In the wake of these popular uprisings and their threat to the state power, Nicaraguan Conservative Fruto Chamorro signaled the need for a new constitution that would vest more power in the hands of the executive and promote political stability. In this context, Chamorro worried about Nicaragua's racial diversity and the place of Indians in Nicaraguan society. According to Chamorro, "The racial heterogeneity of which the state's population is comprised is a topic that . . . deserves your most esteemed consideration, for the desire to establish absolute equality between the races causes great detriment to social well-being." Despite this, Chamorro argued that rapid changes in ethnic relations would simply return Nicaragua to the insurrections of the 1840s: "The indigenous race, more backwards in everything than the other race [ladinos], possesses exclusive habits, preoccupations and uses that are so old that only time and civilization will modify them. To instantly banish them would bring on altercations, violence and fights; as such, prudence dictates that the indigenous system have exceptional institutions adapted to their customs and character."[5] Chamorro's paternalistic and racist attitudes were nothing new for Nicaraguan elites, but placing these at the center of debates over a new constitution and the social order reflected a growing inclination that ethnic divisions "that are so old" were more dangerous than political ones.

Concerns over the Atlantic coast region, which had eluded both Spanish and Nicaraguan control since the colonial period, mirrored anxiety about Indian resistance to the nation-state. After independence, Nicaraguan officials generally refused to recognize Miskitu political authorities, much less Miskitu sovereignty, limiting the possibilities for negotiation.[6] Nicaraguan minister of foreign relations Sebastián Salinas made this argument to Frederick Chatfield, British general consul in Central America, in 1847 when he urged that any acknowledgment of the Miskitu "would confer a right upon the savage hordes [to] form kingdoms . . . and establish universal anarchy and disorder."[7] Salinas did briefly flirt with recognizing the Miskitu through a convention signed with Princess Agnes Anne Frederick, the youngest daughter of the deceased Miskitu king Robert Charles Frederick, but this appears more as his effort to circumvent British intervention in the region. In wooing Princess Agnes Anne, he told her that "the sovereign government of Nicaragua . . . has always lived with the most ardent desires to protect them [the Miskitu] and form *one single family as sons of the same state*" and that Nicaraguans saw the Miskitu as "our brothers," but these words concealed a deeper antipathy toward the peoples of the Atlantic coast.[8] Indeed, when British forces took the Caribbean port city of San Juan del Norte and reaffirmed their protectorate over the Mosquito Coast, the people of the region returned to being "hordes" with a false "king" whose sovereignty "is neither a principle of international law, nor do cultured nations recognize such phantoms."[9]

The British compounded the intervention by snubbing Nicaraguan attempts to be treated as international equals. Writing in 1889, historian José Dolores Gámez described the humiliation that Nicaragua's chargé, Francisco Castellón, faced during his 1849 assignment in England; Castellón "was officially received by the English government, but every effort he made to arrange the current difficulties was in vain, for the English government avoided dealing with Nicaragua, as it seemed very depressing to call such a small fraction of Central America a 'nation.'"[10] Not surprisingly, as Frances Kinloch Tijerino has noted, "The usurpation of the port [of San Juan del Norte] . . . provoked the ire of the Nicaragua authorities." But as she concludes, "Lamentably, this was directed not just against the British usurpers, but also against their Miskito allies."[11] Increasingly, the peoples of the Caribbean coastal region came to symbolize ethnic threats to Nicaraguan sovereignty. While these conflicts had no direct effect on Indian-ladino relations in the prefecture of Granada, they increasingly came to serve as claims of proof of the potential of Indian "savagery."

Within the emerging discourse of the nation-state, ethnic heterogeneity came to reflect potentially distinct political legitimacies, since varied claims to autochthony, natural law, and rationality appeared discursively compatible even if their political ends were not. Prior to the war against William Walker, there was little to suggest that Nicaraguan elites viewed these ethnic distinctions as carrying much of a political charge. The international dimension of Nicaraguan dealings with the Mosquito Coast certainly complicated the threat of ethnic autonomy, but the physical distance between the Atlantic and Pacific coasts attenuated the perceived consequences. Indian revolts in Matagalpa and Masaya threatened to bring the state to its knees and devolve society into "anarchy," but the Miskitu, by contrast, were seen as "savages who roam the desert and the forests of the coast of Honduras and Nicaragua . . . without a known language, illiterate, without arts, without commerce, without laws, and without religion."[12] As it was, the extent of Nicaraguan authority on the coast was generally limited to collecting customs taxes at the port of San Juan del Norte, and even intensified British interests in the region failed to stymie the Nicaraguans from levying this key source of revenue.[13] Walker's invasion, however, placed the conflicts of the 1840s into high relief by exposing how local conflicts (the kind that Fruto Chamorro fretted over at the constituent assembly) were linked to internal divisions. Such divisions also included the kind of inter-elite violence that plagued the early independence years, but these were frequently couched as inherently petty differences (e.g., personalism or "party colors"), while ethnic ones came to be constructed as fundamental distinctions.

While national leaders fretted that Indian ethnicity imperiled the nation, at the local level Indian-ladino relations were far more ambivalent. Histories of resistance, land tenure, and ethnic composition all played important roles in the everyday politics of ethnic conflict in different communities. The notion that Nicaraguans shared a homogeneous mestizo national identity—what Jeffrey Gould has called the "myth of mestizaje"—would come to dominate Nicaraguan constructions of the nation, but they remained decidedly more complicated throughout the nineteenth century.[14] This chapter takes up the struggles over Indian and ladino identities in the prefecture of Granada and their relationships to the nation-state. In exploring these issues, I first examine how ethno-racial language was used in Nicaragua and, particularly, how the state attempted to construct a deracialized homogeneity through its census taking. Despite these efforts, ethnic terms structured Indian-ladino conflicts throughout the nineteenth century. Using the prisms of Indian-ladino ethnic relations and of state, municipal, and Indian community interrelationships, I then examine competing conceptions of political authority that inform Indian and ladino constructions of the nation and of each group's place within it. The outcomes of these conflicts provide the foundation upon which we can then understand the uneven decline of Indian communities and identities in the prefecture of Granada. Against the tendency to see these relations in continually oppositional terms, this chapter proposes a more negotiated and interdependent approach.[15]

Race, Ethnicity, and the Census

Reflecting on the relationship of the census to the nation, Benedict Anderson comments: "The fiction of the census is that everyone is in it, and that everyone has one—and only one—extremely clear place. No fractions."[16] It is not just that censuses and other such measures try to reduce the complexities of social and economic relationships into easy-to-read cross tabulations. By trying to capture any particular relationship, the state simultaneously creates two parallel narratives, one qualitative, the other quantitative. With racial categorizations, the census functions not only to tell us *how many* of this or that group there are among "us" but also to tell us what these groups are, in other words, *who* "we" are. Yet it is also both an act of self-discovery—especially during the nineteenth century, when national censuses were inevitably tallied by local officials—and of self-definition through the choices of categorization. By analyzing the changing taxonomies of successive censuses, we encounter the history of racialization in its most public and national form.[17]

Throughout the nineteenth century, local and national officials collected immense amounts of census-like data, especially at the municipal level. While age, occupation, and sex were regularly recorded, race was almost never enumerated. The exceptions to this rule were the national censuses carried out in 1846, 1867, and 1883.[18] Some evidence also suggests that birth and death registries may have distinguished between Indians and ladinos, since one observer at the end of the nineteenth century offered departmental statistics to that effect.[19] Nonetheless, to whatever extent such data were collected, it was not a nationally regulated or regularized policy.

The most systematic census of the nineteenth century was undertaken in 1883. Although carried out more than sixty years after independence and the abolition of caste terms, it relied, as the censuses before it had, on racial categories used during the colonial period. As a point of comparison, the 1776 censual listing of those who could purchase indulgences[20] divided Nicaraguans into Spaniards, mestizos, mulattoes, and Indians.[21] The 1867 and 1883 censuses kept these categories (although "Spaniard" now became "white") and added black and zambo (splitting them off from the category "mulatto"). All of these categorizations also appeared in Nicaragua's colonial-era parochial baptismal registries.[22] The next full census was carried out in 1920, at which point the state abandoned the caste categories in favor of a spectrum of colors.

Much of the scholarship on nineteenth-century Nicaragua argues not simply that "Indian" and "ladino" provide the most meaningful way of understanding race but that other systems of categorization or racial imagination had been in such decline by the end of the colonial period as to have become meaningless. A nineteenth-century North American observer made the case plain: "The fusion among all portions of the population of Nicaragua has been so complete, that, notwithstanding the diversity of races, distinctions of caste are hardly recognized."[23] Such a contention would make it difficult to understand the continued use of caste terms in the censuses. It certainly was not for lack of alternatives (such as Indian and ladino or the abandonment of race as an aspect of the census).

In 1883, just as the majority of indigenous communities in Nicaragua seemed to be losing their integrity—or to have submerged within cofradías or into more secretive forms—the Nicaraguan government decided to carry out its most complete census to date. Surprisingly (and seemingly uniquely for Central America at this time), among the numerous categories of information the state decided to collect was a column for race (*raza*). The Office of Statistics worked assiduously to ensure a common form and a common set of responses for this census. In particular, however, the director worried about how race would be marked, and outlined in detail how this should be done and the responsibility of local census officials to see that it was done properly. As he noted in a circular sent to the departmental head of statistics of Granada, "The races that populate Nicaragua have six classes of types more or less well manifested and that can be easily known. These types are: the pure white, the pure Indian [*indio*], the pure black, the mestizo, the mulatto, and the zambo."[24] True to his request, none of the manuscript censuses deviate from these terms.[25] The emphasis on "pure" races reflects scientific racist theory of the era, but it also may have been in response to Pablo Lévy's calumnies against mestizos, mulattoes, and zambos.[26]

Although most of the returns from the 1883 census have been lost to the numerous earthquakes and fires that have plagued Nicaragua's archives, the departmental figures were published in the 1885 *Memoria* of the Ministry of Government, and manuscript pages have survived for at least nine towns in the prefecture of Granada. The regional and municipal returns attest to a racially diverse Nicaragua. Perhaps as important, however, is the wide range in this diversity, from highly indigenous towns like Catarina and San Juan de Oriente to highly mixed ones like Diriamba and Diriá (see tables 13 and 14). Overall for the prefecture of Granada, Indians accounted for 50 percent of

Table 13. Racial and ethnic distribution of Nicaragua and the prefecture of Granada, 1776–1883 (in percent)

	Indian	Mestizo	Mulatto	Black	Zambo	White
1776 (national)[1]	46	13	37	—	—	5
1867 (national)[1]	50	26	14	3	7	0
1883 (national)[1]	32	18	30	7	6	7
1883 (prefectural)[2]	50	17	17	3	9	5
1883 (selected towns)[3]	60	14	13	1	5	7

Source: 1776: Romero Vargas, *Estructuras sociales,* 174, 177, 181, 298–300, 302; 1867: Lévy, "Notes ethnologiques," 47; 1883, prefectural and national: Nicaragua, Ministerio de Gobernación, *Memoria* (1885); 1883, towns: AMPG, caja 184, leg. x5, "Estadísticas," 1883, caja 188, unnumbered leg., "Estadísticas," 1883, caja 191, leg. x7, "Estadísticas," 1883; caja 192, unnumbered leg., "Estadísticas," 1883.

[1] These figures do not include Mosquitia, which was not censused. The census of 1776 used "Español" rather than "White."

[2] Calculated as the sum of the departments of Granada and Masaya.

[3] This figure is calculated from the 1883 manuscript censuses collected in Catarina, Diriá, Diriamba, Diriomo, La Paz, El Rosario, San Juan de Oriente, San Marcos, and Santa Teresa. These towns form part of the prefecture of Granada and represented approximately 20 percent of its inhabitants and 7 percent of Nicaragua's total population (259,894).

the population, the other half divided between mestizos (17 percent), mulattoes (17 percent), blacks (3 percent), zambos (9 percent), and whites (5 percent). With the exception of "white" replacing "Spaniard," these racial categories are identical to those commonly used in colonial censuses, including that carried out in 1776. Where figures are available, it is evident that those identified as mixed race were a growing population in many towns, most notably due to migration from the larger cities after independence.[27]

How were these categories assigned in the 1883 census? Did people choose from the designations when asked by the census takers, or did the census takers assign the values themselves? And what factors determined the assignment: descent, physiognomy, community consensus? The Office of Statistics expressed great concern about these issues. On the one hand, it suggested that the white, Indian, and black were "well defined and offer no difficulty whatsoever in being determined." As to mestizos, mulattoes, and zambos, these were explained as "the mixture of the Indian and the white . . . the white and

Table 14. Racial and ethnic distributions for selected towns in the prefecture of Granada, 1883 (in percent)

	Indian	Mestizo	Mulatto	Black	Zambo	White
Masaya						
Catarina (1,107)	95	3	1	1	0	0
San Juan de Oriente (432)	93	2	0	4	1	0
Granada						
Diriá (1,375)	46	42	5	7	0	0
Diriomo (2,310)	74	0	19	7	0	0
Carazo						
Diriamba (3,411)	49	25	10	6	1	9
La Paz (378)	89	5	1	0	0	5
El Rosario (293)	83	3	3	9	1	0
San Marcos (1,079)	65	0	0	2	1	32
Santa Teresa (813)	3	5	67	5	5	16
Total (11,198)	60	14	13	5	1	7
Department of Granada (32,829)	39	18	23	6	6	8
Department of Masaya (23,433)	65	15	8	0	12	0
Prefecture of Granada (56,262)	50	17	17	3	9	5

Source: See table 13. The prefecture is the sum of the two departments. Total population figures are in parentheses.

the black . . . [and] the black and the Indian," respectively. Clearly, however, these words or notions of mixture were considered too inexact. Departmental prefects were instructed by the director of the Office of Statistics: "I must insist on this issue of race. I believe it is indispensable that you expand upon these explanations to the local agents [of the census], given the lesser capacity for comprehension they have for want of education." To properly fill out the census, then, the local agents would need to understand how "facial features, hair and skin color" identified race. The circular continued, "Give them [the local agents] various examples, such as this: an individual with a skin color of *negro claro*, very curly hair, short and stout body is obviously a zambo; the hair reveals the pure black and the color and size the Indian."[28]

At least by the assessment of the Office of Statistics, most Nicaraguans (even those of inferior or limited education) would know the meaning of "black," "white," and "Indian" and be able to attest to these on sight of such individuals, but mixed-race peoples were another matter altogether. The circular questioned whether established and accepted definitions of mestizo, mulatto, and zambo existed or were employed in nineteenth-century Nicaragua. While these might not be so self-evident, the circular does appear to posit a fairly well established set of physical descriptors (and differences) that could easily be linked to the appropriate terms. In other words, race as the descent of bloods may have had little significance, but descent as appearance did. As one foreign observer noted at the end of the nineteenth century, "Among them [Nicaraguans] still exists a kind of caste based on color."[29]

The 1920 census took a new approach to race, eschewing the colonial caste terminology in favor of five color designations: white, black, *trigueño* (variously translated as wheat-colored or swarthy), *cobrizo* (copper-colored), and yellow. In the western and central departments, where 81 percent of the population lived, however, the first three colors accounted for almost 99 percent of the population. Yellow was used for the Asian population and comprised less than 420 individuals.[30] Cobrizo was used more widely than yellow, but it was limited to the central and eastern regions of Chontales, Jinotega, Matagalpa, Bluefields, and Cabo Gracias.[31] Trigueño seemed to play a multifaceted role, mapping to Indian, mestizo, and mulatto populations with equal ease.[32] Given this apparent diversity and the existence of an intermediary color term, "cobrizo," why was it not used? Based on usage it appears that the term "cobrizo" allowed the census to racialize the Atlantic coast and the Atlantic frontier regions (notably, Matagalpa and Chontales) as distinct space. In other words, against the claims of simply being a color descriptor, it was used as an ethno-racial label.[33] The 1920 census seemed to codify this shift with its use of skin color in place of "race," but this proved quite the contrary. Appearance mattered, and would continue to do so, but so too did community and ethnicity.[34] Anthropologist Richard Adams's research in the 1950s suggests how true this remained. One of his informants, a mestizo from the town of San Ramón, located to the east of Matagalpa, claimed that speech, custom, and appearance made it possible to distinguish Indians (what his informant termed "*indios*") from mestizos.[35] Indeed, for Adams, what most distinguished Indians from ladinos was "customs, which include the place of residence."[36]

From the welter of collected census statistics emerges an official narrative of Nicaraguan national identity. Until 1883 the censuses portrayed a multiethnic Nicaragua made up of Indians, Africans, Europeans, and their mixed descendants. Still, this discursive pluralism sat in tension with the Enlightenment ideals of human equality that underpinned the abandonment of the caste system after independence. By the turn of the century these were abridged to just two broad divisions—Indian and ladino—that implied cultural distinctions more than biological ones. As the "history" of ethnic and racial diversity seemed to melt away the imagined destiny of national unity, Indians and indigenous communities held fast to claims of a unique place in the nation. For ladinos, however, diversity linked them to the colonial caste system's narratives of degeneracy and inequality. Racialized language continued to exist, of course, but increasingly it displaced race onto the Atlantic coast and identified it with foreignness.

Although the Atlantic coast region figures only marginally in the historiography of Nicaragua, it has come to have a fundamental role in the construction of Nicaraguan identity. Throughout the colonial period the region remained outside Spanish control (and, in fact, often seemed to be invading the Pacific), an unconquered territory of "savage" Indians and blacks.[37] Even successful steps toward claiming possession of the Mosquitia proved ambivalent. The 1860 Treaty of Managua, for example, ended the British protectorate in the region and granted Nicaragua sovereignty over the entirety of the territory Nicaraguans claimed as their own, yet the treaty also specified the creation of the "Mosquito Reserve," a territory within which the Miskitu were to "enjoy the right of governing, according to their own customs."[38] As with the brief effort to claim the Miskitu as "our brothers" in 1849, Nicaraguan officials did take moderate steps toward culturally incorporating the Atlantic coast in 1872 when an accord was established to promote Catholicism, the Spanish language, and the rudiments of Nicaraguan institutional authority over the region. By the end of the decade, however, whatever efforts had been carried out were abandoned in the face of budgetary restraints and the undoubtedly arduous task of "nationalizing" the Mosquitia's dispersed populations.[39] Miskitu resistance to the Nicaraguan campaign added to already tense Miskitu-Nicaraguan relations and forced a revisiting of the Treaty of Managua. The emperor of Austria agreed to arbitrate the dispute, although the Miskitu were left out of these discussions because they were not signatories to the treaty. The emperor's decision in 1881 reiterated Nicaraguan sovereignty over the Mosquito Reserve, but in a highly restricted form. Political, economic, and social regulation were now to be shielded from Nicaraguan interference and fully assigned to the Miskitu authority.[40] As I have argued, these kinds of everyday engagements are fundamental to the process of nation-state formation. As local authority in the Mosquito Reserve grew after the arbitration, a Mosquitian nationalism appeared to emerge, one that imagined the region as a sovereign and independent territory.[41]

Increasingly, the Mosquitia was constructed as an "Other" against which to measure the "true" Nicaragua. The Austrian emperor's arbitration simply exacerbated this situation. For nineteenth-century historian José Dolores Gámez, the indigenous people of the coast were "a tribe of savages," and even that conclusion was tempered by an attitude that questioned their true indigeneity.[42] From Gámez's perspective, "the inhabitants of the Mosquitia were no longer the ancient *Caribisis* that Columbus met . . . . [but] had mixed themselves with them [blacks], and their descendants, true zambos, composed the majority of the new population." Moreover, this history had disengaged them from Nicaragua, leading them to hate the Spanish and "happily receive the English."[43] Still, even if the Miskitu were generally perceived as "inauthentic Indians," Nicaraguan nationalists never wanted to fully write them out of the nation.[44]

With the military incorporation of the Mosquitia in 1894, debates over nation and ethnicity shifted away from the complex local struggles between indigenous communities and ladinos and toward starker comparisons with the Atlantic coast. Political antagonisms may have flared in the wake of José Santos Zelaya's rise to power, but as one newspaper editorial declared, "this issue of the Mosquitia is of such a nature that it is in unadvisable to apply to it either a conservative criterion or a liberal one, but rather a Nicaraguan criterion."[45] Part of that Nicaraguan criterion meant distinguishing between Mosquitian Indians and blacks. While Rigoberto Cabezas, who commanded the annexation campaign, welcomed the integration of the Miskitu as "a great mission to fulfill," Mosquitian blacks, who referred to themselves as Creoles, were almost always referred as "foreign" or "Jamaican" and were increasingly seen as a race apart from Nicaraguan nationality.[46] Black resistance to Cabezas, for example, led one Nicaraguan newspaper to imagine a race war on the coast, publishing an account that "all the Spaniards [Nicaraguans]" had to flee "for fear of being murdered."[47]

By the 1920s the more overtly racialized terms "mestizo" and "indo-hispanic" began to slowly supersede the use of the more culturally suggestive "ladino." In this context the Atlantic coast became an enclave within the nation, the otherness against which Nicaraguan intellectuals like Gustavo Alemán Bolaños could hold up "the indo-hispanic race that is called the Nicaraguan."[48] If Nicaragua had no "racial question . . . because we share a common race," then there was little room for the people of the coast.[49] Rather, as an official report on the Atlantic coast argued, avoiding the "triumph of barbarism" would require "populating the coast with Hispano-Nicaraguan blood, language, customs and culture."[50] By the early 1930s, Carlos Cuadra Pasos, one of Nicaragua's most important twentieth-century nationalist intellectuals, solidified this discourse in the emerging sociological language of "race relations." To him, the people of the Atlantic coast were "ethnic minorities," ill at ease with the purportedly mestizo "racial majority."[51] In this language, the coast was a part of Nicaragua, yet apart from it. The Atlantic coast served as the foil to the discourse of mestizaje, enhancing Nicaragua's image of homogeneity.

By the mid-twentieth century, the history of people of African descent in western Nicaragua had largely been expunged from popular and academic renderings. For example, in discussing Rivas, which by colonial estimation had one of the largest African-descended populations in Nicaragua, Adams noted that "The beginning of a negroid component in the otherwise mestizo population is significant. . . . This suggests that the movement of the Negro population has been, at one time or another, up the San Juan River, into Rivas and south into northwestern Costa Rica."[52] Such a conclusion accords well with the common popular and scholarly belief that blackness in the Pacific region of Nicaragua came from "some Negroes who had come over from the Atlantic Coast."[53] Anthropologist Mary Helms's assessment of Nicaragua's racial history from the early 1980s comes to much the same conclusion: "Most of Nicaragua's black population also reside on the Atlantic Coast. These English-speaking creoles, largely of Antillean (particularly Jamaican and Cayman Islands) ancestry, are the predominant population of the few port towns."[54]

Nationalist intellectual Pablo Antonio Cuadra distilled this transformation into an origin tale of *el nicaragüense*, who emerged from the intersection of "two bloods, two cultures."[55] After independence, the Nicaraguan may have struggled with a divided soul, but at least it resided in a unified body. The 1920 census, with its listing of 71 percent trigueños, made this point abundantly clear, providing the statistical grist for nationalist mills. Nicaraguans now differed from one another merely in shades of a single color—from light to dark—having become culturally and ethnically homogeneous.

The Politics of Identity and the Nation-State

While the language of the caste system endured beyond independence, "Indian" and "ladino" had begun to dominate the lexicon of race and ethnicity in Central America as early as the late eighteenth century. Both terms were Spanish inventions whose meanings began evolving from the earliest days of the Spanish empire in the Americas.[56] Throughout much of the colonial period, indigenous peoples maintained a certain distance from non-Indian communities, a distance favored by the Spanish Crown and most evident in the survival of communities of monolingual indigenous language speakers. These were not static communities, and change and interaction did come. In his travels through Nicaragua at the beginning of the seventeenth century, Antonio de Herrera described the common use of Spanish in many of the region's indigenous communities.[57] Although indigenous language, dress, religious practice, and community membership all evolved over the colonial period, Spanish notions of Indians living in telluric communal societies functioned to define them in fairly stable terms. In its earliest use, "ladino" was used for African slaves who had learned to speak Spanish and had become Christians.[58] By the end of the colonial period the term invoked both biological and cultural meanings, referring both to people of mixed-race descent and to indigenous people who lived a culturally Europeanized life outside an indigenous community.[59]

In the main cities and new mixed-race towns, the hubbub of urban plebeian life made racial distinctions difficult to maintain. Until the mid-seventeenth century, skin color, dress, and hairstyle still allowed city-dwelling Indians and non-Indians to be categorized and divided along supposedly racial lines. But as Paul Gilroy has noted, race is not a natural category that sustains itself; rather, it survives through constant ideological intervention.[60] Colonial officials worked to contain the profusion of racial mixtures within the *sistema de castas* (caste system), an increasingly complex system of racial designations meant to sustain a world ordered along Spanish hierarchies.[61]

Over the next century, as differences in plebeian lifestyles blurred, the lines of official racial distinctions began to collapse. Nonetheless, as mixing increased and made it ever more difficult to distinguish mulattoes, mestizos, zambos, Indians, and Spaniards from one another, Spanish officials struggled ever harder to differentiate them.[62] While in theory racial distinctions became finer and clearer, in practice they began to devolve to the most commonly used categories of Indian, black, Spaniard, mestizo, and mulatto. The depths of Spanish anxiety over racial mixture are clearly evident in such fantastical mixtures as *negro torna atrás* (black turn back), in which a black child may be produced from the union of a Spaniard and a nearly white *albina* (one-eighth black from a single black great-grandparent). While such fanciful categories never appear in the mundane documents of everyday life, they figure prominently in theoretical and descriptive works on the New World.[63] The figure of the *negro torna atrás* implied that the taint of African blood could lurk as an unpleasant and socially devastating surprise to supposedly pure Spanish families. The failure of Spanish ideologies of race and purity to be functional in everyday life doubtless encouraged such neuroses. As the nineteenth century approached, Enlightenment ideals of equality, freedom, and citizenship further undermined the philosophical underpinnings of these racial distinctions. Still, although the discursive structure of race was changing, race would remain pivotal to the formation of postcolonial Latin American societies.[64]

The public discourse recorded in government documents and newspapers of the nineteenth century appeared to accept Nicaragua as divided into two groups, Indians and ladinos. The Nicaraguan state, in particular, seems for the most part to have dropped the use of colonial racial terms as part of the effort to institute a liberalism free of inequality and labels. Just as honorific terms like "highness" and "majesty" were to be abolished and replaced with "citizen," so too should the terms of caste.[65] This did not mean that Nicaraguans ceased to think or act in racialized terms. The power of European racism, on the one hand, and the effort to maintain European values after independence, on the other, built structures of difference that did not easily settle into either biological or cultural terms. Instead, they tended to oscillate uncomfortably between the two.

Discourses of Political Authority

Archival records from after the National War indicate that more than a dozen indigenous communities still functioned in the prefecture of Granada. By the end of the nineteenth century most of these seemed to disappear, or at least left no further imprint on the archive. Most explanations of this process focus on the state's efforts to destroy communal landholdings. Yet, unlike the less densely populated regions of Matagalpa, Chinandega, Jinotega, Nueva Segovia, and Chontales, where Indian communal lands continued to exist, the evidence for the prefecture of Granada suggests that most of the indigenous communities located there had not had their own communal lands since the late eighteenth century.[66] Ejidal lands belonging to the municipality continued to exist, but usually outside the control of the Indian communities themselves. As more Indians began to shed native languages, their communities stood as important levees against the rising waters of ladino society. Examining the indigenous communities in the prefecture of Granada highlights how the reductive focus on communal lands glosses over the complex relationships of Indian communities with local, regional, and national officials as well as their struggles with these authorities and among themselves.

Despite opinions to the contrary, the disappearance of tribute requirements, common indigenous language, distinct dress, and communal lands in many of these communities did not necessarily signal the demise of Indian ethnic identity.[67] The critical issue is whether an identity continued to function in communal terms that distinguished it from other identities.[68] In the case of nineteenth-century Nicaragua, no specific "custom and use," religious activity, or particular pattern of landholding or labor provided the meaning of Indian identity; rather, it arose out of how these and other aspects functioned relationally to delineate the boundary between Indians and ladinos. Population size and concomitant access to capital also clearly played a role in community survival. Sutiava, Matagalpa, and Monimbó, the three largest indigenous communities through the colonial period, have remained the most vital to this day.[69] Still, understanding this history at the community level demands attention to environmental, social, and economic considerations.

Although the elite ideology of "civilization and progress" would eventually permeate ladino society, immediately following the National War ladinos remained divided as to how such "civilizing" should be accomplished and what "civilization" meant. Government officials initially focused attention on the reorganization of the military and police forces, the assertion of solid political control over the municipalities and local caudillos, the improvement of (mostly indirect) tax collection to achieve fiscal health, and the maintenance of social order. Only the first of these tasks required more than a nominally active relationship between the state and Indian communities. Efforts at more thoroughgoing social and cultural change—and attendant conflicts—would only arise in subsequent decades when state policy turned to economic goals. In the meantime, ladino municipalities and local leaders endeavored to maintain as much autonomy from the state as possible while solidifying and expanding their control over local labor and land resources. To the extent that these overlapped with Indian communities, conflict inevitably ensued.

Although the juridical relationships among the state, municipalities, and indigenous communities appeared straightforward, their meaningful interpretation proved rather more complicated.[70] Following independence, all towns (*pueblos*) were renamed municipalities and given a juridical status; indigenous communities, however, lost all such status. In the prefecture of Granada, relatively high population density led to indigenous communities being coterminous with pueblos, whereas in Matagalpa, for example, a single community came to encompass multiple municipalities.[71] In the few cases where purely Indian towns survived—Catarina, La Paz, and San Juan de Oriente, for example—it appears that the Indian community's structures were assimilated into the municipality's form. The tremendous emigration of ladinos from the major cities (Granada, León, and Rivas) into rural pueblos, however, led frequently to the maintenance of

Indian communal authorities alongside the municipal government.[72] The result was an indigenous alcalde and regidores, whose existence and community authority remained legal but unspecified under the constitution of 1858, and municipal authorities, who formed part of the state and whose powers were legislatively defined.[73] In these cases, struggles revolved around municipal intervention in the lives of Indians and their communities and Indian efforts to break free of the municipality's antagonistic embrace.

Soon after the 1861 elections for indigenous alcalde were held in Masatepe, Juan Gutiérrez, the ladino constitutional alcalde, attempted to prevent the newly elected regidores, Juan Hernández, Pedro Gaitán, and José María Moraga, from taking office. Believing they lacked the necessary qualifications, he named three Indian replacements for them. Infuriated by this "capricious" abuse, Celedón Ampie, the newly elected indigenous alcalde, complained to the prefect of Granada, Salvador Sacasa, reminding him of the state's responsibilities to Indians: "[We come] before you, . . . the one specially charged with vigilance for the preservation of the guarantees, privileges, preeminences and legal customs of the Nicaraguan family."[74] In response to Ampie's claims, Gutiérrez justified his actions by citing a 9 May 1853 law that ceded regulation of local elections to municipalities. "How could it be possible," he asked, "that if these are properly its [the municipality's] powers, that the Indians want to take on for themselves such duties, its [the municipality's] untransferable rights? Or in other words, if said [indigenous] alcaldes are ancillaries of the constitutional ones, how can they certify and elect themselves?"[75] Gutiérrez certainly believed that municipal authority trumped indigenous authority, but the relationship between the two remained ambiguous. His implication that Indian alcaldes "are ancillaries to constitutional ones" seemed to legitimate Indian officials, but as subordinates. This reflected post-independence patterns of municipalities needing indigenous alcaldes to enact community-wide demands such as labor drafts.[76]

For Gutiérrez, legitimacy arose because "modern" law "day by day is improving and enlightening our ancient customs." Despite his use of "our" rather than "their" to modify "customs," he nevertheless constructed the difference between custom and law as a dualism. Ampie, on the other hand, looked to the past, to "time immemorial," for legitimacy. The legitimacy of Indian customs emanated not from their codified recognition in the *Leyes de Indias* but rather as a natural consequence of the "legal" status they inherited from the historical experiences of Indian communities throughout Nicaragua. Ampie denied the dualism employed by Gutiérrez by collapsing the division into Indian "legal customs."

Although the state sided with the Indian community, affirming that Indians "are permitted to preserve their customs and uses insofar as they are compatible with the general principles of the common legislation," the state's response left ambiguous the relative legitimacy of local Indian and ladino political authorities.[77] The Masatepe Indian community's size and history of rebellion may have led to the state's limited and conservative decision, but the possibility of limiting municipal autonomy was undoubtedly appealing. Although the decision was favorable to the Indian community, it left open the possibility for significant decisions against Indian communities in the future.

Two years later, what appeared to be a very similar situation in Diriomo produced a decidedly different outcome. In the indigenous community's annual election held on "Santo Viernes," Ubaldo Peinado was named alcalde. A week later, Peinado and the community were informed that he had also been chosen by the municipality to serve as a *jefe de cantón* (local constitutional official). In response, Indalecio Quesada, a former indigenous alcalde, wrote to the new prefect, Narciso Espinoza, to complain of interference with Indian elections.

As Celedón Ampie had done in representing Masatepe's Indians, Quesada demanded the state's protection for the community's customs, further defending them as "of the most useful and advantageous nature, as much for the good of the *pueblo* . . . as for the better service of the church."[78] How, Quesada asked, could Peinado carry out his important duties as indigenous alcalde if he also had to do the work of a jefe de cantón? His responsibilities as a member of the indigenous community clearly outweighed his responsibilities to the municipality, Quesada argued. Abrahám Alfaro, constitutional alcalde of Diriomo, responded much as his counterpart in Masatepe had, asserting municipal responsibility for local elections. Moreover, Peinado's status as a citizen obligated him to accept government service when called upon.[79]

Despite the similarities between these two cases, Espinoza's response bore little resemblance to Sacasa's. Although he acknowledged the preservation of indigenous customs, Espinoza tried to do so as restrictively as possible. Against Quesada's argument, he resolved that "the election of the jefes de cantón is preferable to that of the Indian alcaldes of the pueblos, and to whatever other namings of pure custom." Espinoza pointedly circumscribed the weight of custom to whatever the state tolerated: "The creation of the jefes de cantón emanates directly from the law, with a subsequent character to the customs of naming indigenous alcaldes . . . which is only respected as a consequence of the tolerance and dissimulation of the sovereign in attention to various considerations that do not operate here." For Espinoza the phrase "legal customs" would have been meaningless. For him, law and custom defined poles that clearly delineated the differences between Indian and ladino culture.[80] Mediation or accommodation was unimaginable; the dialectic would be solved only through the dissolution of Indian culture and identity.

Espinoza's decision expanded beyond these issues and the localized context, however, to clarify the relationship between Indian communities and the state: "The election of the jefes de cantón is of greater rank, not only because a greater number of citizens compete for them than for Indian alcaldes, but also because these absolutely lack the jurisdiction with which the jefes de cantón are endowed." The communities would be tolerated so long as they in no way threatened the functioning of the state. Although this conflict centered on the relationship between Indian communities and municipal authorities, Espinoza actually left this area unresolved.

As had been the case in Masatepe, Diriomo's ladino authorities had sought to control Indian elections to expand their local power base, and similarly, a municipal claim of authority over the indigenous community was ignored by the state. This may have been because Indian communities provided a check on the municipalities, serving as a barometer of social and political conflicts at the local level.[81] If indigenous communities funneled their discontent at what they perceived as local injustice through national state institutions, the communities could be tolerated within the elites' nation-state project.[82] By evading the overriding issue of power, the state obscured the broader relationship of local discourses of political authority to the nation-state project.

Given these complex relationships, therefore, it is not surprising to find, twenty years later, the municipal secretary of Masatepe still complaining of Indian autonomy and trying to justify to the prefect the constitutional alcalde's interference in Indian elections: "If such [Indian] alcaldes, which are no more than purely customary, do not have to remain subject to the immediate supervision of the municipalities, they will turn into a constant menace to local tranquillity. The autonomy and efficacy of municipal power would do well to destroy them."[83] Like prefects before him, this one was nonresponsive to the central issue of municipal power. Municipal autonomy, perceived as a greater threat to state authority than the continued existence of supportive Indian communities, received no support. It is these complex interrelationships and struggles that inform the following discussion of Indian and ladino constructions of the nation-state and their respective roles within it.

Ladino and Indian Constructions of Nation and Other

Indians and ladinos struggled over the parameters of the nation for most of the nineteenth century, offering varying constructions and contesting each other's constructions.[84] Local politics, of course, was frequently more complicated than discourse would seem to indicate. We have already seen how the relationships among the state, municipal authorities, and Indian communities cannot be characterized as top-down and linear but rather as interconnected at multiple levels based on congruency of goals sought by each party. Although the evidence is scant and a fuller understanding of these relationships awaits, available data evince internal cleavages within the indigenous communities, within municipalities, and within the state itself that made for a less-than-seamless ladino construction of the nation-state.

Ladino conceptions of the nation oscillated around a core tension in the civilization-barbarism dichotomy.[85] Were Indians irredeemable savages, defining one side of an unresolvable dialectic, or were they salvageable through an assimilative "process" of civilization? At the individual level, the abandonment of signs of ethnic difference collapsed the dualism separating an Indian from ladinos, thereby resolving an Indian's barbaric status.[86] At a collective level, however, the process proved more complicated. Could aspects of Indian identity deemed "barbaric" be eliminated through "civilization" and yet allow for the continued functioning of an Indian ethnic identity? Or, was Indian identity a "barbaric" unity that demanded complete elimination?

In 1866, Rosalío Cortés, then minister of foreign relations for President Tomás Martínez, delivered a commemorative address in celebration of the forty-fifth anniversary of Nicaraguan independence. Constructing independence as the liminal moment in which the national character was born, Cortés used the opportunity to present an official ladino vision of national identity. Using "Indian" and "ladino" both literally and metaphorically, he structured a narrative of sometimes explicit but more frequently implicit dualisms: tribe versus nation, atavism versus progress, myth versus history, barbarism versus civilization, respectively. "The America of Moctezuma and the America of the Incas," Cortés intoned, "were the Americas of the savage, the idolater, the cannibal." Counterposed to a ladino America requiring no reference—how could it possibly have any of those qualities?—an Indian America was unthinkable.[87] "Humanity," Cortés continued, could not accept then, nor can it accept now, "such backwardness, adorned with bloody, repugnant, and revolting fetishes."[88] Like many dominant ethnic ideologies, Cortés's address expressed a core denial of Indian humanity.[89]

Despite the settled appearance of his dogmatic intolerance, Cortés manifested the ambivalence inherent in ladino civilization-barbarism discourses. Indian savagery would seem to preclude their national membership, yet when Cortés spoke, just a year later, at the opening of his *colegio* in Masaya, he seemed to offer up the contingent possibility for such membership, noting that "Ignorance, lack of knowledge, is weakness and innocence. . . . The savage is the first and most visible type of ignorance."[90] The "savage" was at once a racial type and a cultural condition.

Ladino discourses of national identity thickened and localized as specific struggles with Indians became empirical touchstones in mytho-historical narratives. As ladinos increasingly challenged Indian identity, they eschewed metanational symbols like Cortés's "America." To understand the process by which the ladino discourse of national identity solidified is to focus on the struggles that helped define and specify it.

An 1861 conflict in Nindirí reveals the weakness of the state following the National War and the lack of fixity in ladino ethnic ideology. Around midnight on 19 October, the majority of the leadership of the indigenous community gathered together to replace the indigenous alcalde, Máximo Dinarte, and his regidores.[91] Dinarte, they claimed, had colluded with Emiliano Cuadra, a Granadino elite, to remove the local parish priest without first seeking the approval of the community. Not only did Dinarte no longer represent their interests, they argued, but he had taken actions detrimental to them.

Two days later, both the constitutional alcalde and the judge of first instance wrote to Prefect Narciso Espinoza to recount the events and recommend appropriate responses. Nicolás Ríos, the alcalde, reported that Dinarte was dispossessed of his office peacefully and according to custom. The judge, José Mariano Bolaños, however, described a scene of terror and disorder, the pacification of which demanded the coercive powers of the state. According to Bolaños, the machete-wielding Indians had rioted, "threatening the old one [indigenous alcalde] and championing the new one."

The competing interpretations of these events function as a prism separating different strands of ladino ideology. For Ríos the events pivoted on concepts of autonomy and authority, while Bolaños constructed them in terms of ethnic conflict. The testimony of Indians who participated in the election bear out Bolaños's description of the events, but without his pejorative connotations. What for Bolaños threatened "order," for the Indians followed "custom," and therefore had been the appropriate response to an internal conflict in the Indian community. Ríos concurred, trying to defuse Bolaños's explosive rhetoric by reporting to the prefect: "There is no intranquillity whatsoever here; rather, good order and the conservation of good harmony has been observed as has been the case in the past. For this reason, there has been no reason to importune the police chief of San Fernando [Masaya]."

For Ríos to accede to Bolaños's interpretation meant acquiescing to state intervention to resolve what Ríos perceived as local affairs. During this same era, Elizabeth Dore has also found Indian-ladino unity in Diriomo in the face of outside threats to local autonomy.[92] Significantly for the Indian community, Ríos's refusal is tantamount to a denial of the civilization-barbarism dualism.

Given evidence of state, municipal, and Indian community relationships already discussed, the prefect's decision is not surprising. Dinarte had to be restored as indigenous alcalde, Espinoza declared, because Nindirí's Indians had overstepped the acceptable limits of use and custom by resorting to arms. No doubt the prefect felt justified, given Dinarte's "civilized" insistence that "the legal principles and recognized customs of the pueblos must not be subject to the will of the dregs of society." By siding with Dinarte's faction, Espinoza enunciated a limit on both the notion of custom as a standard of governance in Indian communities as well as the limits of municipal autonomy within the ladino elite's emerging conception of the nation-state.

Espinoza's ideological convictions bumped up against political reality when Ríos responded that he had neither the authority nor the means to reimpose Dinarte's leadership. Moreover, even if Ríos could do so, Dinarte had lost all legitimacy in the eyes of the Indian community and they would simply ignore his dictates. Bolaños, exasperated with what he considered the constitutional alcalde's ineptness and lack of resolve, reiterated his position with even greater hyperbole. Alluding to Indian uprisings of 1845-49, he claimed that nightly riots by the town's Indians placed the community on the verge of a bloodbath.[93] The judge's assertions clearly alarmed the prefect, who dispatched the regional police to Nindirí and headed up his own investigation. Although none of the prefect's subsequent reports corroborated Bolaños's claims, Espinoza intervened directly, rerunning the election and forbidding the leaders of either faction from running.

In the following decades, as the state consolidated authority over the municipalities, the elites' ethnic ideology came to dominate other ideological currents. This is not to say that the tension surrounding the civilization-barbarism dualism declined. Nicaragua's most famous nineteenth-century historians—José Dolores Gámez, a Liberal, and Tomás Ayón, a Conservative—exemplified the continuing debate.[94] In their general histories of Nicaragua neither wrote about events in the second half of the nineteenth century, yet both appear to have allegorized earlier events to draw connections with contemporary ones, such as the 1881 Indian war in Matagalpa and León.[95]

Just seven years after the 1881 war, Gámez described the participation of what he called Matagalpa's "semi-savage Indians" in a mid-1840s uprising led by Bernabé Somoza. Gámez offers few details, but he informs us that "The Indians waged *their customary caste war*, and entire towns fell at the edges of their machetes, terror and desolation sown wherever they went."[96] Morphologically, it is just a short jump from "customary" to "custom" and to the construction of Indian culture as a culture of violence, subject to the capricious direction of charismatic caudillos.[97] For Gámez such "anarchic" opposition required the iron fist of the state to ensure the survival of ladino "civilization." Jeffrey Gould's research in late-nineteenth-century Matagalpa found this attitude widespread.[98]

Ayón, whose history of Nicaragua appeared in 1882, never denied the need to "civilize" Nicaragua's Indian population, but he argued for their peaceful incorporation. "Who would argue that Europe's peoples did not descend from savage races?" he reminded his readers.[99] Ayón's allegory comes from a more distant source than Gámez's: the 1740–41 imbroglio between Antonio Padilla, the mulatto captain of the mulatto militia of León, and José Antonio Lacayo y Briones, the newly named governor of colonial Nicaragua.[100] For more than a decade Padilla's militia had navigated Spanish power in their efforts to achieve greater autonomy and authority for themselves.[101] Worried about the militia's loyalty, especially in an era of increased British aggression, and jealous to affirm white authority, Lacayo y Briones challenged Padilla's command and accused him of treason. Padilla and his men protested, with repeated chants of "Long live the King" and "Death to bad government."[102] For Ayón this attested to their good intentions and indicated that their actions were "more from ignorance than from wickedness."[103] Nonetheless, Padilla was hastily condemned for treason and executed, his body drawn and quartered and his body parts displayed throughout the city.[104] In his conclusion to this episode, Ayón inveighed against the hypocrisy of elite liberalism. "The internal anxiety of [León] and the threats of foreign enemies," he argued, were simply excuses for the

> zeal for the preservation of order [which] cannot fail to recognize that the trial was incomplete for lack of a defense and that the punishment was excessive and applied with a cruelty

repugnant to the good government of a Christian people. . . . It is a terrifying spectacle, a man—perhaps honorable—and the good father of a family, dead at the executioner's blow, hung afterward in the gallows to instill terror in the weak, indignation in the brave and intense pain in the his grieving children, and finally quartered so that parts of his body would remain unburied, like an advertisement. . . . And this was executed in this small country of America when in Europe J. J. Rousseau, Montesquieu, Montaigne, D'Alembert, Voltaire, Condillac and other very wise men were establishing the philosophy of the penal system in the solid trials of law, teaching "that the end of punishment is not to torment and mistreat a sensitive being, nor to undo a crime already committed, but rather to prevent the criminal from causing further damage and keep the rest from committing others." Neither the principles of Spanish laws of that time, the claim of Nicaragua's political situation, nor the nature of the crime committed authorized the stratocratic proceeding.[105]

Ayón never doubted the treasonous nature of Padilla's acts, but Padilla's punishment represented vengeful caprice that instilled within the mulatto population feelings of hate and fear rather than security and allegiance. The suppression of state threats could not justify recourse to terror and torture. The state had to come to terms with its "uncivilized" populations, and do so without becoming uncivilized itself. Failure to do so, Ayón warned, would lead to future conflicts, such as the mulatto uprising in León that occurred four years after Padilla's execution.[106]

Such tensions within the civilization-barbarism dichotomy remained, but they no longer served to split the state and ladino municipalities. By 1880 municipal intervention in Indian communal affairs turned on a discourse of ethnic and national identity that linked local ladino interests with those of the nation-state. When, for example, Masatepe's Indians complained to Rafael Baldino, the subprefect of Masaya, about ladinos and the treatment the Indians received from them, Municipal Secretary Ramón Navarro responded: "It would be better . . . to make them understand that *we* now lead the life of a republic and that the nation recognizes no special character for *them* and, as such, they must abandon their customs, which are as prejudicial to themselves as they are to society."[107] Echoing ladino ethnic ideology, Navarro placed Indians outside both the nation and the state.

But Navarro's discourse went beyond the usual construction that Indians must abandon their culture—abandon themselves—to become part of the nation.[108] Navarro denied their very existence as a community: "Would it be justice if for fear of offending *this or that person*, the *public good* was left undone?"[109] His discursive logic erased the Indian community, transforming the complaint into the work of individuals, who, in Hobbesian logic, had no recourse against the broader community, be it the municipality of Masatepe or the state of Nicaragua.[110] If indigenous alcaldes continued to exist, it was not because they represented a true community but "for purely political reasons and the generosity and tolerance [of the state]."[111] While Navarro's statements may have reflected increased Indian acculturation, they also signaled the hegemony of elite ethnic ideology across ladino class divisions.

Indian constructions of the nation-state tended to develop in one of two directions, what sociologist Paul Gilroy calls the "politics of transfiguration" and the "politics of fulfillment."[112] Through the politics of transfiguration, Indian communities sought a utopian reconstruction of the discourse of nation-state that would countenance Indian culture. Through the politics of fulfillment, on the other hand, Indian communities sought to force ladino society to live up to the principles and promises of their nation-state discourse, most importantly justice and equality before the law. The politics of transfiguration manifested counterideological struggles which, in the case of the Indian communities of the prefecture of Granada, frequently gave way to the politics of fulfillment, signaling the first steps in the construction of ladino hegemony.

Until the 1880s, Granada's Indian communities evinced strength and unity in the face of the fractured ideology of the nation-state. Returning to 1861, when the indigenous alcalde, Celedón Ampie, complained against the ladino authorities of Masatepe, the Nicaraguan state was still weak and both it and the nation stood naked as the ladino elite's ideological constructions. Although we have already discussed how the Masatepe conflict underscored discourses of political authority, it also drew together a complex set of discursive strands to create an Indian conception of the nation.

Ampie asserted his claim for the "preservation of the guarantees, privileges, preeminences and legal customs of the Nicaraguan family" not just for Masatepans but for an ethnically Indian *national* identity.[113] Without overstating the meaningfulness of his words, they certainly show a radical political astuteness and self-awareness not normally given to Indians in the mid-nineteenth century, especially in Nicaragua. Nicaragua's mostly illiterate Indians needed no daily newspapers, tombs of unknown soldiers, or state-sponsored commemorative parades in order to imagine a broader, deeper cultural-political community of kind.[114] Their uses and customs, annual elections, and religious processions, the sum of their experiences over "more than three centuries of the despotic [Spanish colonial] government and more than forty years of the current one," had forged a meaningful identity. Moreover, custom, writ broadly, the basis for such identity and its value and legitimacy, was recognized "by customary law [*ley consuetudinario*] throughout the world."[115] Ampie's construction of the nation-state dismissed the vision offered by ladino elites, promoting a transfiguration of the nation-state. For Masatepe's indigenous community, the fair adjudication of ladino and Indian authority claims could not rely on semantic clarification; ladinos must contend with and integrate an Indian ethnicity that perceived itself as legitimate and as historically rooted as their own.

The discourses on Indian elections and political authority point to one aspect of Indian identity; the relationship of ladinos and Indians to the church and religious activity in general provides a different perspective. Parish priests frequently took paternalistic views of the Indians to whom they ministered,[116] but they could also act to emphasize the salience of Indian ethnicity and its "naturally" national character. Difficulty in accessing church archives and their general disarray has, to date, provided little opportunity to examine these issues fully. Nonetheless, some preliminary analysis based on available data is possible.

The economic, political, and cultural aspects of the church's relationship to its parishioners were intertwined, and separating the strands is sometimes difficult. Events surrounding the decision of Diriomo's parish priest, Tomás Pereira, to demolish part of the chapel in 1866 demonstrates these complexities. The documents fail to reveal why Pereira ordered the demolition, but Indian parishioners were already at work when ladino authorities got wind of the project. The constitutional alcalde and a number of ladino vecinos rushed to the church to demand a stop to the work, but according to witnesses, Pereira treated the gathered ladinos "like madmen," claiming that "'the town belongs to the Indians,' that they were its only representatives because the ladinos were not born here."[117] The church may have been the locus of the claim, but Pereira went beyond it to indicate that the entire town belonged to the Indians, both politically and culturally, because they were natives to it. The ladinos, whom Pereira labeled as foreigners, had no legitimate recourse to decisions made by the Indians.

Pereira's outburst seemed to reflect Indian resentment at recent ladino actions. Two years prior to this confrontation, for example, Diriomo's indigenous community had accused Urbano Morales, a local ladino elite, of illegally collecting and then keeping alms for the church.[118] The church represented resources to the Indian community, both because of the structures it specifically organized around Indians (most obviously the saint images and religious processions of Indian community and cofradías) and because of Indian belief in their singular contribution to the maintenance of the church.[119] Diriomo's elites engaged this discourse, not by negotiating shared legitimacy, but by claiming complete sovereignty over the church and its property within the municipality.

Within two decades the church as locus of transfigurative redefinitions of the nation-state gave way to the politics of fulfillment. While Indians continued to claim themselves as the only true contributors to the church, their discursive construction of this changed. An important conflict in this politics of fulfillment erupted in Masatepe when the ladino municipality sought to take over the parsonage from the local parish priest and convert it into a school.[120] At stake were important elite symbols of the nation-state: the church, private property, governmental authority, and education.

The Indians claimed that the confiscation was unacceptable because the parsonage did not belong to the municipality. How could it be municipal property, they argued, if, over the years, only the Indians had provided the necessary money and labor for its repair and improvement? Framed in these terms, the issue hinged on Indian property rights, not on obstinacy in the face of progress. They were not against the building of a school, but insisted on fair exchange. If a school was to be built, it should be in the isolated valleys, where Indian children could make use of it. To come into the town was too dangerous, they argued, because the children would have to cross a steep gully and ford a river that had no bridge.

By using the parsonage, the municipality would take away the Indian community's property and convert it into something that the community could no longer benefit from. Significantly, Indian ownership of the property is not defined by "time immemorial" possession but by contemporary work and money placed into it. Discursively, then, there is no opposition to property and education, but rather an acceptance of these within a framework of fairness and equality.[121] Rather than disregarding Indian contributions and their right to participate in municipal affairs, the municipality responded by claiming that ladinos paid a *fair* and commensurate share of taxes to the church and other municipal works programs, thereby entitling them to as much of a voice in decisions as the Indians.[122] By the end of the nineteenth century, the Roman Catholic Church despaired to preserve itself under the anticlerical pressures of the Zelaya dictatorship. Some churchmen may have advocated rebellion, but more common would be electoral pressure such as that encouraged by Masatepe's parish priest in 1895.[123] At the national level, the church girded against Zelaya's new financial and ideological constraints by levying a regressive "first fruits" tax on parishioners and closely controlling church properties, including cofradías. These measures angered indigenous communities and marked an emerging rift with the church.[124]

While the relationship of Indian communities to citizenship remained a point of conflict, the tenor of Indian arguments shifted, suggesting the growing hegemony of the liberal state. In 1880 Masatepe's Indian community complained that, although a significant number of their members met the 100-peso capital requirement, they were systematically left off the voting rolls.[125] The municipal authorities did not deny the charge but did deny responsibility, simply saying they had no control over who received citizenship, the determination lying with the state's Directorate of Supreme Authorities. However, they added for good measure that if Indians did not appear on the lists it was because they chose not to enroll on them unless a pressing political issue came up.[126] In other words, in contrast to true Nicaraguans, Indians were selectively and self-interestedly "national."

As the ladino nation-state became increasingly fundamental to the politics of everyday life, the transfigurative politics of the past no longer seemed possible. This is not to say that Indians did not avail themselves of more covert means of resistance, but rather that the foundations of more radical communal resistance were daily being undermined. To continue negotiating social and economic change, Indian communities increasingly found themselves accepting the state as the legitimate arena in which to do so. Yet their access to that arena was increasingly limited by their inability to qualify for citizenship.

To understand the relationship of Indian access to citizenship requires disentangling a number of complicated issues. The 1883 census manuscripts help by bringing together information on both race and citizenship. Citizenship, which meant the right to vote and hold elected office, was not freely given. Only men over eighteen could be "qualified" for citizenship, and it required them to possess at least 100 pesos in capital. Moreover, potential citizens had to present themselves to the Directorate of Supreme Authorities, who would evaluate their request and also ensure that neither moral nor physical impediments precluded such qualification. Although citizenship could potentially stand as a proxy for a broad class division—that is, those with at least 100 pesos in capital and those without—it proves a weak indicator. Indeed, no correlation existed between occupation and citizenship unless the census's race classification was factored in.

An analysis of the census manuscripts reveals that the average rate of citizenship qualification was just over 51 percent, but this masks tremendous diversity in citizenship opportunities. The eight towns for which data are available divide into two groups: Catarina, Diriá, La Paz, and San Juan de Oriente, which offered citizenship to 79 percent of men over eighteen; and Diriamba, Diriomo, San Marcos, and Santa Teresa, where the average rate citizenship was just 23 percent. Still, the patterns that link these towns are neither straightforward nor obvious.

Race clearly mattered in access to citizenship, but not simply as a consequence of generalized discrimination against Indians or based on their weight in each town's population. Indians formed the majority in Catarina, La Paz, and San Juan de Oriente, all of which had above-average rates of Indian citizenship, but they also did so in Diriomo and San Marcos, where an average of just 11 percent of adult male Indians had citizenship. Similarly, while Diriamba and Santa Teresa had minority Indian populations and a very low Indian citizenship rate, Diriá's 46 percent Indian population saw an Indian citizenship rate of nearly 95 percent.

A pattern emerges, however, when the agricultural focus of each town is examined through the agricultural censuses carried out in

Figure 4. Indian citizenship and export orientation in the prefecture of Granada, 1880s

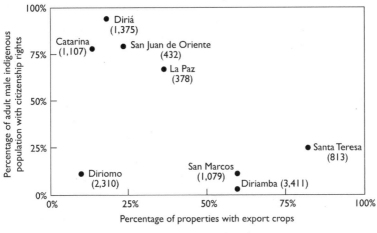

Note: Figures in parenthesis are total populations for each town.

Sources: Citizenship statistics (percent of adult male population listed as citizens) calculated from the sources used in table 13. Property analysis calculated from AMPG, caja 158, leg. 441, "Censos agropecuarias," 1880; caja 182, leg. 490, "Censo agropecuaria de Diriamba," 1882.

the 1880s (see figure 4).[127] Catarina, Diriá, La Paz, and San Juan de Oriente—towns with high rates of Indian citizenship—were all dominated by subsistence agriculture. These towns also produced export products, such as sugar and coffee, or raised cattle for regional commercial markets, but to a far lesser degree than did San Marcos, Santa Teresa, and Diriamba, all of which had rural economies driven by commercial agriculture and all of which throttled Indian citizenship.[128] Diriomo appears as an outlier to this pattern, having what the 1880 agricultural census showed to be a subsistence-centered economy, but this obscures the fact that Diriomo provided much of the foodstuffs for the neighboring city of Granada and that it once had been an area of significant cacao production.[129]

Catarina, Diriá, La Paz, and San Juan de Oriente all had significant Indian populations, focused on subsistence agriculture, and provided

183

both relatively high and equitable access to citizenship. While the economy of Diriomo still relied on basic grains, its proximity to and tight relationship with Granada and emerging coffee production had led to ladino domination and the political disenfranchisement of its Indian majority.[130] Diriamba and San Marcos had politically—if not numerically—dominant ladino populations and emphasized export agriculture; both restricted and highly skewed access to citizenship. Few Indians lived in Santa Teresa, which, unlike the other towns in this analysis, had no indigenous community. Given this and an economy driven by sugar and cattle, limited Indian citizenship is unsurprising. Diriamba, San Marcos, and Santa Teresa also shared significant "white" populations, something hardly found in the other towns. Whether this contributed to discrimination against Indians or was rather a sign of these people's efforts to distance themselves from Indians and Indian heritage remains to be debated.[131]

It would seem that Indian access to citizenship was dependent on their ability to control the municipality. In towns where ladinos formed a numerically powerful bloc and controlled municipal government, conflict inevitably erupted over the radically different Indian and ladino visions of the proper use of local resources—most obviously land and labor. Since, in towns such as Diriamba and San Marcos, the uninterrupted promotion of ladino priorities required their control of the municipal government, control of citizenship could effectively limit such an avenue of attack on ladino. In towns where such conflicts appeared absent, both because of Indian numerical dominance and the subsistence nature of their agriculture, access to citizenship could prove a less volatile issue. Furthermore, while Indian communities frequently complained about municipal authorities who limited Indian citizenship, few if any similar complaints were found in those with open political access.

Returning to the indigenous community of Masatepe's complaint about access to citizenship, it would appear that Masatepe fit the pattern outlined for Diriamba and San Marcos above. For ladinos in Masatepe, a flourishing coffee-growing area, their long history of conflict with the town's Indian community demanded limiting Indian power wherever possible. Inasmuch as Indians saw citizenship as a meaningful stage for contention, ladinos would, in turn, see limiting access to citizenship as necessary.

Indian Identity in Transition

By the late 1880s, indigenous communities rarely appeared in the archives of the prefecture of Granada. Although some of this may have to do with Masaya becoming a separate department, that cannot account for everything. The new department only contained the towns of Masaya, Masatepe, Nandasmo, and Nindirí. Diriomo, Diriá, Diriamba, Jinotepe, and San Marcos—all of which had active indigenous communities—remained within Granada's jurisdiction.[132] In contrast to the active indigenous community engagements of the 1860s and 1870s, Julie Charlip notes, "By 1887 the indigenous people seemed to be petitioning ladino authorities with complaints, but without the protection of an alcalde indígena."[133] Still, no documents detail the disbanding or extinguishing of these communities. Despite limited evidence, three conflicts that arose in the 1880s provide clues to their disintegration.

In 1881, Juan Lopez, an Indian farmer from Diriomo, complained to the prefect of his maltreatment at the hands of both the constitutional and indigenous alcaldes of his town.[134] He had recently been elected an indigenous alcalde but did not want to accept the position, declaring: "Despite my being one of the most active townsmen, in terms of social responsibilities, they want to constrain me to exercise an office to which I am not obliged, an exercise which would cause notable damage to the well-being to which all honorable men aspire, even one so poor as I." As it was, Lopez added, he already provided free weekly labor for the construction of the new church and was currently contracted with Tiburcio Rivas, a local hacendado, to clear and burn his fields before the winter rains came. Rivas had threatened to sue Lopez for damages if he did not complete the task in time. Despite these grounds for exception, Lopez concluded, they wanted to force him to accept the position "against my will." Indeed, by the time Lopez finally complained to the prefect, he had been surprised on his small plot of land by a machete-armed patrol that on orders of the constitutional alcalde "convinced" Lopez to accept the position for one week. Since that time he had tried to quit, but was continually threatened against such action.

Lopez's argument highlights the confusing and changing situation of Indian identity. Lopez charged that the constitutional alcalde lacked jurisdiction over Indian elections and therefore had no right to force Lopez—through violence or any other means—to accept the results. Although this implied Lopez's belief in the autonomy of the indigenous community, his attitude and explanations in response to his election suggested a slippage in his own relationship to the community. As he noted, he did his "social duties" and was merely trying to protect his personal "well-being." Lopez's discourse fit perfectly into the elite vision of the liberal nation-state. Indeed, he already mouthed words that would appear six years later as lessons in a state-sponsored political catechism.[135] Such an acceptance, however, threatened the very autonomy of the Indian community. Lopez stood with one foot in the community and one foot out.

Just as citizenship required that all men elected to hold office accept such positions, so membership in the indigenous community implied the same of its male members. While people often sought to avoid their civic duties, such refusal was never couched in an attack on the legitimacy of the state. Men pleaded sickness, poverty, or a death in the family, but never that the state held no authority over them when it called them against their will.[136] Lopez's refusal signaled a serious breakdown in the indigenous community. The prefect's finding for Lopez made the situation that much more difficult to repair.

Lopez's argument is not so surprising given the discourse coming from indigenous leaders in a conflict over their annual election in Masatepe in 1883 and the complex responses of different civil authorities to the conflict. Following the election, an Indian named

Felipe Hernández protested to the constitutional alcalde and then to the prefect that the election was fraudulent because the former indigenous alcalde, Cornelio Lopez, and his successor, Mateo Mercado, had not followed the prescribed custom.[137] The subprefect of Masaya, Marcelo Vijil, had originally decided to allow the election.[138] However, after interviewing witnesses and receiving statements from the complainants to the election, it became obvious to Prefect Ascención P. Rivas that the election had not been carried out in accordance with custom and as such needed to be held again.[139] What might otherwise have been an uninteresting and unimportant decision, however, reveals the fraying of Indian identity.

In the original complaint, Hernández and fourteen other members of the Indian community described the role of indigenous alcaldes in Masatepe: "There is a laudable and religious custom of electing an alcalde of the community. . . . [H]is functions are purely religious and of piety, and for this reason we are interested that this custom remains in its total purity."[140] Although Hernández and the first four signers of this petition were *mayordomos de santos* (their duties specifically related to the care of images of saints for processions and festivals), their emphasis was exceptional; they equated custom directly with religious practice. Their description squared perfectly with nineteenth-century liberal ideology: Indian communities and religion were tied together through backward customs, and all three needed to be eliminated. Thus, although Hernández may have constructed this equation in positive terms, it actually fit the discursive logic by which the Indian communities and their religious festivals were vilified as "the greatest obstacles to progress and civilization."[141]

Twenty years after Celedón Ampie's radical claim for Indian "legal customs," Hernández and his compatriots slid to the other extreme, denying the ability of their community to adjudicate its internal claims and complaints: "Our foundation for this petition is custom, because we have no national laws that regulate the elections of the alcaldes of the community [*común*]. But there are the *Leyes de Indias* that recommend to your authority what to do: keep and respect the customs of the Indians inasmuch as they are not against the religion and laws of the kingdom."[142] The relationship of Indian communities to the *Leyes de Indias* is completely inverted. Custom no longer provided the means to resolve internal conflicts; for that the community had to turn to the established laws of the republic.

Mateo Mercado, the newly but fraudulently elected indigenous alcalde, responded in entirely different terms. Having had his claim to election overturned, he argued that the customs of the community were beyond the provenance of the state. They were "purely private," he noted, citing article 13, section 3 of the 1858 Constitution to explain why they were not subject to dictates of the prefect or, for that matter, to any other civil authority.[143] Mercado's stand was radical, delegitimizing all state authority in relation to the Indian community, yet his reliance on the constitution also marked that same state's hegemony. Mercado had cited the constitutional protection accorded to political parties. In principle, for an effective opposition to operate, its internal functioning, membership, and publications had to be outside the purview of the state. In contrast to Hernández and his compatriots, Mercado asserted complete autonomy for indigenous communities. Yet Mercado's use of the constitution signaled the disintegration of Indian ethnic identity, for it denied the historical legitimacy of Indian identity in favor of legislative recognition. Autochthony is forever, while law can be abridged or abrogated.[144]

The last of these episodes concerns Diriamba and leads to some final questions. In 1883, after first complaining to the prefect of Granada, but without apparent success, Seferino Hernández, Francisco Davila, Marcos Pérez, and Doroteo García had written to the Ministry of Government seeking help.[145] They represented themselves as "alcaldes and regidores" and charged that properties belonging to their community were being mishandled. First they railed against a man who had apparently sold a community-owned house in order to buy a piece of land. Second, they named Nicolás Díaz as treasurer of the Natividad cattle finca, only to find that he had left it in total disrepair and absconded with its profits. Perhaps given this recent chaos, they turned to the constitutional alcalde, Enrique Baltodano, but he "will neither hand over the accounts to the pueblo, represented by its alcaldes, nor care for the finca."

Not once does the word "Indian" (in any of its variations), or even "natural" (native), appear within the petition. Hernández and his associates indicated simply that they represented "a body organized by means of annual election that traditionally has been transmitted from one generation to the next in order to administer and preserve the interests that it has provided for itself through periodic voluntary offerings from the sons of this town."[146] They went on to explain:

> The members of the body thus organized are called alcaldes and regidores, who at the same time that they preserve peace and harmony with the good customs of the pueblo, attend to the good administration of the property of the community. . . . So have things marched along with nothing more than ecclesiastical intervention in the area of management, without civil authorities having to interfere in these matters, except when we have called for protection in cases of illegal intervention from outsiders or of embezzlement and wrongdoings by those charged with their administration.

What was this "body" of alcaldes and regidores? The grumbling over the Natividad finca points toward these men representing the cofradía of the Imagen de Natividad. Yet the larger claim to communal property and the administrative structure point toward an indigenous community. Cofradías were headed by mayordomos and *priostes* (festival hosts), not alcaldes. Yet priostes and mayordomos also appeared in Dore's description of "officeholders in the indigenous community in Diriomo" in an 1885 grievance of labor coercion by the rural magistrate.[147] Indian cofradías and Indian communities have been intertwined since the colonial period, but perhaps the declining autonomy of indigenous communities—at least in the prefecture of Granada—had begun leading Indians to relocate the political core of the community in the cofradía. Writing about late-nineteenth-century Guatemala, Virginia Garrard-Burnett noted just such a practice: "the Indians reconstructed the brotherhoods as religious loci of community identity, political coherence, and economic parity."[148] Although indigenous communities in Nicaragua may have seen the cofradías as potential bulwarks against ladino intervention, they were hardly immune to conflicts with both the church and the state.[149] In 1889, for example, when a new law called for cofradía property to be titled in the land registry, it was the ladino constitutional alcalde of Diriamba and the parish priest, not the leaders of the indigenous community or Seferino Hernandez and the cofradía's other mayordomos, who met with a local judge to hammer out the Imagen de Natividad cofradía's holdings.[150] Similarly, in a dispute with the Matagalpa cofradía in 1893, the local priest complained that the Indians "still think they run the cofradías."[151]

Conclusion

All three of the conflicts discussed above illuminate the intense political creativity of Nicaraguan indigenous communities. These efforts are neither James Scott's "weapons of the weak" nor the isolating strategies of closed corporate communities.[152] Instead, they express the almost schizophrenic pursuit of both the politics of fulfillment and the politics of transfiguration, of efforts to embrace (or at least acknowledge) the power of the state and yet to reject its legitimacy and authority.

In 1850 Indian identity appeared solidly grounded in a history of community and custom; ladino identity, if it existed at all, exhibited deep fissures. Perhaps ladinos shared in certain Enlightenment ideals, but in Nicaragua's first post-independence decades these were hardly enough to establish common cause between elite ladinos and their subaltern brethren. The popular rebellions of the 1840s, in fact, suggested greater links between poor ladinos and Indians, as they struggled against the encroaching state and challenges to community authority and autonomy. Moreover, the majority of Indians and ladinos—like those who lived in the towns and villages at the heart at this study—drew from the same well of cultural referents of rural, communal life. Ladinos, of course, were *not* Indians, but "not" was hardly the makings of an affirmative, let alone national, identity.

By the 1880s these worlds seemed inverted in the prefecture of Granada. Indians saw an erosion of community authority and the transformation of the social and economic bases of their world. Juan Mendoza noted this shift in his 1920 history of Diriamba, writing of the Indian alcalde: "Some thirty years ago, his administrative role disappeared."[153] Some rode the waves of change to an affluence and individualist independence their forebears had never known; others sank into poverty and alienation. These may be the extremes, but they represented the key challenges to indigenous communal identity. Ladinos, by contrast, increasingly found their social, political, and economic roles reinforced by expanded municipal authority and by their growing sense of the municipality as a ladino institution and the legitimate building block of the nation.

The examination of Indian-ladino struggles over political authority and national identity reveals two key factors that underpinned this change. First, the complex and at times seemingly contradictory relationships among the state, municipalities, and Indian communities frequently obscured the state's role in promoting a nation-state project that fundamentally altered Nicaragua's social and economic structure. Second, as the state consolidated its power and extended the scope of its activities to participate more forcefully in municipal life, it nurtured increasing congruence between national elite and local ladino ideologies.

Taken together, these factors help explain why Indians in Matagalpa and León rose up in 1881, while no similar rebellion occurred in the prefecture of Granada then or at any other time between 1850 and 1900. The state's imposition of a work requirement to build the telegraph line from Managua to Matagalpa highlighted the state's authorship of change perceived as unacceptably detrimental to Indian life, an authorship never made explicit in the state's relations in the prefecture of Granada.

In daily conflicts over the nature and legitimacy of competing political authorities, Indians and ladinos struggled over the meaning of national identity, the determinants of inclusion and exclusion, and the direction of socioeconomic transformations. But while ladinos manifested growing unity, Indian communities began to fragment. As those communities weakened, continued attempts to negotiate change with the state required increasing concessions to the state's legitimacy in everyday life. Moreover, the advance of the nation-state project engendered new forms of internal stratification within Indian communities that damaged the ability of these communities to carry on meaningful communal action for their members. Stratification itself was not new, but when it was coupled with the loss of both material resources such as land and symbolic ones like language and political authority it disrupted the ability of communities to smooth over such cracks in the boundary lines of Indian identity.

Until about 1880, Indian identity had the potential to radically negotiate the meaning of the nation-state. This process of negotiation and struggle, however, led to the inexorable, though not inevitable, decline of Indian identity and the emergence of what Jeffrey Gould has called the "myth of Nicaragua *mestiza*."[154] This decline signaled both the crushing of ethnically centered oppositional ideologies and the identification of the state as the legitimate locus of political activity. Although the elites' state project would continue to face challenges, these would increasingly spring from broadly class-based resistance or from within the confines of nationalist discourse itself. In some ways, the extent of this change can be gauged not just in the destruction or submergence of Indian cultural identity but by the narrative reconstruction of this process in biological terms. What was essentially a process of ladinoization was so complete—at least in the prefecture of Granada—that few questioned nationalist rewriting of this process as one of historical miscegenation originating in the early colonial period. Until recently, who could (or would) argue with Pablo Antonio Cuadra, one of Nicaragua's foremost national-ist intellectuals, when he wove together Nicaraguan culture, society, and history with the thread of Indian-Spanish mestizaje, a thread he followed in a linear progression from the seventeenth-century folk play, *El Güegüense*, to Rubén Darío to the nationalist avant-garde movement Cuadra himself cofounded.[155] Evidence to the contrary was dismissed as exceptions that proved the rule, the last gasp of "el problema del indio."[156] The nationalist discourse that represented Nicaragua as a historically homogeneous society—culturally ladino, biologically mestizo—had become hegemonic.

Conclusion

The discourse of the nation-state is necessarily popular in nature. Simple state forms can exist when resource extraction and warmaking needs are relatively limited. However, as Nicaraguan elites learned, the competitive world of states in the nineteenth century doomed such countries to colonization or control by stronger, imperialist powers. Survival required an exchange between the state and its subject peoples, a negotiation over resources and rights, responsibilities and opportunities. This negotiation necessarily complicates society, because it often contradicts better-established ideologies of race, class, gender, and community. These problems arise from the fact that the elites do not simply invite the masses into history, as some scholars would have it, but invite them into a complex, shared future. As the Nicaraguan nation-state formed, the interests of landlords, merchants, political leaders, ladino municipalities, and indigenous communities coincided and clashed. Transfigured through the discourse of nation-state, the changing relationships among these groups created a new and dense network of alliance and resistance that simultaneously made governance more difficult while embedding it more deeply in people's daily lives.

The Nicaraguan state grew at a remarkable pace following the National War. The stability of postwar elite relations enabled the government to be more successful at collecting taxes and expanding its coercive forces. This success, in turn, provided the means to assert dominion over aspects of social control and organization long entrusted to the Roman Catholic Church. Whether Liberals or Conservatives, Nicaraguan elites always understood the need for effective taxation and coercion, but only with the crisis of the war against William Walker did they see how critical the creation of Nicaraguan "citizens" was to maintaining sovereignty. In the end, the patriarchal social forms and identity embedded in church doctrine did not differ radically from that inculcated by state institutions. The church, however, did not serve the primary duty of legitimizing the state, and for many it appeared as a threat to the state's consolidation.

At first, attempts to wrest social control and organization from the church only highlighted how inadequately prepared the state was for these tasks. The church hierarchy, from bishop to parish priests to cofradía leaders, provided the means to coordinate and structure parishioner action and ideology. Beginning with census and statistical information gathering, the state encountered resistance from local communities. Activities like these could only be carried out effectively by municipal officials, but these officials, who had for so long remained relatively autonomous from earlier experiments in state formation, questioned the advantages of such intrusions. In this and similar tasks, national governments were confronted with the need for new approaches to creating institutions and establishing policy. Success came when activities and ideas bound national and municipal authorities together around seemingly shared goals.

As its core institutions began to expand, the Nicaraguan state slowly implemented the broad goals of elite progress. Having temporarily put aside the dreams of an interoceanic canal after the National War, the elites turned more intensively to export agriculture. As was common throughout Latin America, the mid-nineteenth-century elites sought the privatization of communal lands. Initially, ladino and indigenous communities frequently worked together to resist what they perceived as a threat to community integrity, autonomy, and well-being. After all, communal lands provided their means of subsistence and reproduction. Ladino and Indian officials asserted a set of "common interests" in maintaining communal lands, but expansion of private landholding illuminated critical differences between the two groups. As the ladino communities became more involved in export-oriented agriculture, they altered their views toward ejidos. For indigenous communities, communal lands formed a critical locus of political, economic, and social organization. For ladino municipalities, however, these lands came to serve simply as a means of grounding a potential labor force to a specific place by tying it to the land.

Broadly speaking, between 1858 and 1900 the state succeeded in shifting the vast majority of Nicaragua's communal lands into private hands; however, ejidos remained an important aspect of land tenure well into the twentieth century. Although the evidence does not support the belief that communal lands disappeared entirely in the nineteenth century, ejidal lands in 1900 clearly did not function in the same way that they did in 1850. Until the late 1870s, ejidal lands conferred use rights that could be inherited or passed back to the community, allowing the community to determine the form and distribution of its lands. In this way, communal lands provided one of the most important mechanisms for reproducing local identity and reinforcing its salience. Community members generally ignored the state's laws promoting the privatization of ejidal lands, but they frequently took the opportunity to buy and sell these rights, which these laws also conferred. The transformation was dramatic, for while the community maintained ownership of the land, its control had disappeared. In some ways, the post-1870s ejidos acted like a virus. Communities continued to recognize the ejido form, which had existed for centuries, but instead of promoting community solidarity, it now tended to inculcate private landholding relations and subvert the power of local community. In the new world of private landholding, the state took over the community's role in the control, distribution, and use of land.

In parallel with these efforts to transform land tenure, the state acted to create a sufficiently large and stable labor force to meet the demands of the expanding export agriculture economy. Not surprisingly, government officials met with resistance both from individuals who simply wanted to control their own labor power and from indigenous communities seeking to create a place for themselves within the new nation-state. Historically, ladino landlords had viewed Indians as laborers. The codification of new laws aimed at organizing, controlling, and disciplining labor, however, opened new spaces for indigenous communal landholders to transform themselves within the ladino ethnic and racial discourse.

In the first decades after the National War, the most common reply of indigenous communities to the state's new labor policies was to acknowledge them with the following response: We have our own lands, we are not laborers. At the same time, governments struggled with the local officials charged with enforcing these laws. Whereas the fixity of land meant that a direct vertical relationship between national and local officials could be used to manage the land privatization effort, the mobility of labor demanded a more complex, horizontally coordinated set of relations. By the early 1880s, the land privatization process was well under way and the power of indigenous communities had diminished considerably. Against this backdrop, the elites' equation of Indians with laborers reemerged newly strengthened.

In the aftermath of the war against Walker, indigenous communities struggled more to maintain autonomy from the mostly ladino municipalities with which they coexisted than against the state. To some extent this expressed the state's success in hiding itself behind the actions of local officials, yet it also revealed the state's willingness to serve as a brake on municipal power and act as a seemingly neutral arbiter of Indian-ladino conflicts. However, the social and economic transformations discussed previously began to weaken and undermine the indigenous communities. Some indigenous communities continued to assert their autonomy, but only at the expense of increased oversight by the state. The decline and disappearance of other indigenous communities, however, began to be reflected in the shifting locus of racialized discourse toward a mestizo nationalism that both dismissed indigeneity and increasingly confronted the looming prospect of incorporating the incompatible "otherness" of Atlantic coast peoples. The military annexation of the coast in 1894 complicated the already tense and frequently racist engagement of Nicaraguan officials and intellectuals with the coast. Where mestizo nationalism could imagine an Indian past to the Nicaraguan nation, a Costeño heritage seemed inconceivable. This dynamic has frequently proved volatile, if not corrosive, and militated against the more negotiated nation-state formation that occurred on the Pacific.[1]

Until recently, most narratives of nineteenth- and early-twentieth-century Nicaraguan history argue that inter-elite divisions and subaltern struggles were tied together through a simplistic notion of caudillo politics: local elites controlled the masses through patronage and coercion and deployed them like pawns in political demonstrations, strikes, and regional uprising.[2] In these interpretations, regionalism and personalism explain elite and subaltern, and ideology is either dismissed entirely or expressed in overly rigid terms. Enrique Guzmán made this same argument in 1888 in his classic essay "El Torre de Babel," and while his work is frequently cited, this account of political frustration has never been systematically examined.[3] This is not to deny the influence of caudillismo in Nicaraguan politics, but we clearly need a more nuanced and historicized approach to the topic.

The war against William Walker (1855–57) marked a turning point in Nicaraguan politics and state formation. As the decades passed, Nicaragua appeared more stable, more economically prosperous, and more politically mature. In the wake of Walker's ouster in 1857, Conservative Tomás Martínez and Liberal Máximo Jerez formed the "binary presidency." In contrast to the first decades after independence, people from all political stripes and regions were now included as cabinet ministers, prefects, and judges. Still, leadership at the highest level—the presidency—became increasingly exclusive. Between 1821 and 1871 at least three of Nicaragua's presidents (or supreme directors) were mulatto.[4] The last of these, Vicente Quadra, was the grandson of the mulatta ex-slave Juana Augustina Montenegro. Still others from this period, including the "Solentiname Carib" José Núñez and mestizo Fruto Chamorro, attest to this social and political opening.[5] But by the end of Quadra's presidency in 1875, these mixed-race parvenus were shunted aside for the white scions of the colonial aristocracy's most powerful families: Chamorro, Zavala, Sacasa.[6]

Arturo Cruz's recent study of the same era—what he calls the "Conservative Republic"—is equally suggestive of these paradoxes. Cruz notes both the geographical shift in presidential power from Granada to Rivas and eventually to León with the succession of Roberto Sacasa after Evaristo Carazo's death cut short his term, and the increasingly liberal economic and ideological stances of the office's holders.[7] This coincided with the growth of urban artisans, who accounted for nearly 20 percent of the male population in Granada, Masaya, Managua, and León in the 1880s.[8] The founding of the Sociedad de Artesanos de Managua in 1884 responded to this surge and artisan desires for political participation.[9] Rather than pursue these calls for political opening, the "grandees of the Conservative circle" (as Cruz calls them) increasingly closed ranks. Cruz, however, minimizes this conflict and concludes that the period's end came when "Conservative" probity and thrift fell to "Liberal" perfidy and intemperance.[10]

The regime of José Santos Zelaya marked the reemergence of an intense political factionalism reminiscent of the 1820s and 1830s. Political divisions had existed in the post–National War period, whether as "Arriba" (Above) and "Abajo" (Below), the common distinctions found in many municipalities, or in the form of regionalist parties like the Liberal Rojos and the numerous Conservative splinters, such as the Iglesierios, the Genuinos, and the Progresivos.[11] But a new violence, both rhetorical and physical, permeated the Zelaya period. Although he was a Liberal, journalist Carlos Selva detected a dangerous and quixotic new politics in the offing, claiming that Zelayistas like Manuel Coronel Matus were "seeing ghosts" when they claimed "There are in Nicaragua three allied elements that intend to overthrow the government, that is to say: the clergy, fanaticism and the conservative party."[12] This echoed the kind of anti-Liberal rhetoric that Conservatives employed before the National War, calling Liberals "the most odious delinquents" and accusing them of the kind of political "vandalism" that threatened to plunge Nicaragua into barbarism.[13] Cruz rightly notes that "With Zelaya in power, new surnames appeared in the pages of Nicaraguan history." But Zelaya also sought to tear some of the old pages from the same book.[14] The dramatic clashes raised the antipathy between Liberals and Conservatives to new heights. Newspapers in the 1870s and 1880s may have bristled with prickly political barbs, but by the early 1900s, politics exploded with shocking fury.[15]

The rise of Zelaya's dictatorship is often attributed to an emerging Liberal coffee elite whose economic, ideological, and regional interests distinguished them from the merchant/cattle-raising Conservative oligarchy. Zelaya certainly broke with previous administrations, but not necessarily in the "Liberal" or "revolutionary" terms so often ascribed to him.[16] Nonetheless, his rule did reflect important but frequently overlooked changes throughout society. Jeffrey Paige, for example, has argued that Zelaya's nationalist project "was based on an extremely circumscribed view of the nation essentially limited to the leading Liberal and Conservative families."[17] As much as these elites may have hoped for this to be the case, however, reality proved quite the contrary. The inclusiveness of the nation and the local thrust of its politics placed tremendous pressure on ruling politicians to live up to their discourse of nation. It was one thing to claim that Nicaragua would be moved forward by farmers, but it was another to find these farmers making political demands. It was one thing to urge education and trades as sources of progress, but it was another to find artisans and tradesmen forming social organizations and seeking representation.

Understanding the development of the everyday nation-state in the nineteenth century illuminates the political possibilities of the twentieth century. As Michel Gobat has argued, even if Conservatives in 1910 sought a return to a pre-Zelaya political order, such efforts met stiff resistance from a growing civil society seeking its place at the national table.[18] As leading Conservative Carlos Cuadra Pasos, whose uncle Vicente Quadra served as president from 1871 to 1875, succinctly explained, "this was not possible because the political structure and social consistency of the nation had been altered."[19] Peasants, indigenous communities, and urban artisans all struggled for a place in the nation and to define its parameters. Their growing strength and autonomy, the increasingly divided elite, and their common language of nation established the framework for much of the struggle over the next three decades.

U.S. intervention in Nicaragua from 1910 to 1933 highlighted the depth of Nicaraguan popular nationalism and often served as a catalyst for subaltern political action. Augusto Sandino's anti-imperialist guerrilla war is perhaps the most famous manifestation of this period's nationalist struggles. Michael Schroeder's study of Sandino argues that his "rebels seized on a language and a set of practices that had long been employed by the dominant classes and grafted them onto a radically different vocabulary and project of nationalism and social justice."[20] But they were far from alone, even if other subaltern groups were not as radically anti-capitalist. Smallholding peasants and medium-size producers that had emerged from the 1870s with the decline of communal landholding and the rise of private property proved a potent political force through the end of U.S. intervention.[21] As Gobat persuasively argues, whereas the agro-export boom of the 1920s saw "an unprecedented concentration of wealth and power in much of Central America, in western Nicaragua the boom instead weakened elite control over the rural economy."[22] Small and medium-size producers, who often saw themselves as Nicaragua's ideal citizens, forced their political and economic interests into the national dialogue. By contrast, during the first half of the twentieth-century, peasants in the Chinandega region faced mass evictions and expropriations. What had been impossible in the prefecture of Granada during the coffee boom was accomplished rapidly in Chinandega as the coercive strength of both capitalists and the Nicaraguan state plunged almost entire communities into the ranks of semi-proletarians and landless field laborers. In his seminal study of the region, Jeffrey Gould notes the common belief in the 1920s and 1930s among field workers at the region's largest sugar mill that the mill's owners had made a pact with the devil. As Gould argues, "Such myths attempted to make sense of the exploitative nature of wage labor and the loss of land, to a Nicaraguan audience that was undergoing the transition from a peasant-based to a wage labor economy."[23] This shift would produce new identities, too, but ones whose engagements with the state and political demands would be quite different from the prefecture of Granada, where the more inclusive economic transition to private property seemed far less diabolical.

Artisans had begun to articulate a political identity by the 1880s. As a newspaper article from 1888 claimed, the artisan was emerging as a prototype of the Nicaraguan citizen: "the artisan is an intelligent factor in industry, a voter in public opinion, a citizen of the state, a patriot in the campaign."[24] By the time of U.S. intervention in 1910, artisans had become key figures, articulating a nationalist discourse that rallied for urban modernization, state-sponsored secular education, and local economic development.[25] Their social clubs and political activities helped "forge among the heterogeneous artisan population a more common identity."[26] Artisans took seriously the promises of national citizenship proffered after the National War and found particular resonance in the radical liberalism espoused by Zelaya and the Liberals of his generation.[27] Depending on the opportunities and the stakes, artisans could be counted on for an array of political mobilizations: voting, organizing, striking, rioting. By the 1930s, these artisans and a growing urban workforce became the seeds of a labor movement that would prove crucial to the Somoza dynasty's rise to power and to its demise.[28]

Following the National War, indigenous communities approached the nation-state from a variety of perspectives, but it was hardly alien or unknown to them. Some sought to escape the pressures of the growing nation-state and maintain the indigenous community as culturally and politically autonomous. But others engaged the nation head-on, either reimagining the nation within an indigenous framework or seeking a place for the community as an integral part of it. Indian-ladino relations took a particularly violent turn in the 1880s, but indigenous communities remained politically active. Indian responses intensified with the Zelaya dictatorship's effort to abolish indigenous communities and the political ascent of a new Conservative leadership under Emiliano Chamorro, which claimed Indians as a key political constituency.[29] By the early 1920s, indigenous communities, particularly urban-based ones, stood at the forefront of a number of nationalist anti-imperialist protests, although their indigenous identities often appeared sublimated in nationalist language. On the eve of Anastasio Somoza's rise to power, every political party appeared to recognize the need to accommodate indigenous communities within the discourse of the nation.[30] Still, as Jeffrey Gould argues, indigenous leadership in "the nationalistic and popular fights . . . enabled them to incorporate themselves ideologically into the Nicaraguan mestizo nation. But ironically, at the same time that it facilitated their integration into the nation at the ideological level, it marginalized them as ethnic communities, since they were considered like every other citizen and lost their right to cultural autonomy."[31]

Sergio Ramírez once noted, almost offhandedly, that three of the early twentieth century's key figures in Nicaraguan political history emerged from the small towns of the prefecture of Granada: "An irony of destiny would be that within a small radius of territory of not quite ten kilometers [Augusto] Sandino would be born in Niquinohomo and, in other small villages a bit to the south, José María Moncada in Masatepe and Anastasio Somoza in San Marcos."[32] While Ramírez implies chance, others have argued that this region's pioneering coffee-growing economy produced an emergent Liberal elite.[33] Lost in both of these discussions, however, are the quite humble origins of these towns and so many of their leading figures and the popular quality of their liberal tradition.[34] Liberalism came to other regions, too, but often as a Hobson's choice or at the barrel of a gun.

The revolution that overthrew the Somoza dictatorship and the local conflicts that engulfed the Frente Sandinista de Liberación Nacional (FSLN) place the importance of these local histories in sharp relief. In his classic study of the "social subject" of the Sandinista revolution, sociologist Carlos Vilas argued that Carazo and Chinandega should be placed together based on the agricultural focus of their economies (coffee in Carazo, sugar and cotton in Chinandega) and the similar occupational profiles of Sandinista combatants in the two departments. Whereas the petty bourgeoisie of artisans and tradespeople dominated the ranks of combatants in most departments, in Carazo and Chinandega it was agricultural workers.[35] Not surprisingly, this was also "where the FSLN's political work with agricultural laborers started earliest."[36]

Yet as both this study of the prefecture of Granada and Gould's study of Chinandega make evident, Vilas's snapshot obscures as much as it reveals. While Carazo's turn-of-the-century history was notable for its smallholding and emergent middle class, Chinandega's was marked by radical social dislocation and impoverishment in the face of rapid capitalist expansion. That the two regions appeared similar by the 1970s owed to the declining fortunes of Carazo's smallholders.[37] The Chinandegan campesinos of Gould's research initially embraced Somoza's Liberal populism, but generations of shared poverty and collective struggles forged an autonomous movement and regional identity that challenged the popular limits of Somocismo.[38] Many of Carazo's land-poor farmers and landless workers, by contrast, shared memories of smallholding and bourgeois achievement.[39] Carazo may have provided the highest proportion of "obreros y jornaleros" to the Sandinista's fight against Somoza, but it also fielded the highest proportion of students.[40] Perhaps not surprisingly, then, while Chinandega has remained an FSLN stronghold in post-1990 elections, until the 2004 municipal elections, Carazo had voted Liberal. The struggle for inclusion in the nation and to mold its form has animated local communities throughout Nicaragua and continues to do so, a process that is at once conflictive and shifting. To understand this process in Nicaragua and elsewhere, we must eschew the hegemonic grip of "destiny" in favor of the everyday struggles and contingencies of history.

Notes

Abbreviations

AGCA   Archivo General de Centro América,
Guatemala City

AMPG   Archivo de la Municipalidad y de la
Prefectura de Granada

RPPG-LH   Registro Público de la Propiedad de Granada,
Libro de Hipotecas

RPPG-RC   Registro Público de la Propiedad de Granada,
Registro Conservatorio

Introduction

1. On such projects in Central America see, e.g., Woodward, *Central America*; Gudmundson and Lindo-Fuentes, *Central America, 1821–1871*; Palmer, "A Liberal Discipline," ch. 3.

2. Newson, "Depopulation of Nicaragua," 255, 284. When the Caribbean lowlands, which remained outside Spanish control, are excluded from Newson's calculations, her depopulation calculation rises to 97.5 percent (see table 4, p. 269).

3. See Romero Vargas, *Sociedades del Atlántico*.

4. The following two paragraphs are based on MacLeod, *Spanish Central America*; Wortman, *Government and Society*; Newson, *Indian Survival*; and Romero Vargas, *Estructuras sociales*.

5. Newson, *Indian Survival*, 84–88, offers an excellent discussion the debates over the native population of Nicaragua on the eve of contact. Although her own estimate of over 826,000 may be high, Newson argues persuasively for a figure over 500,000. For her discussion of the post-contact population decline, see 101–6, 117–24, 335–37.

6. Newson, *Indian Survival*, 318–19.

7. On these occupational patterns see Romero Vargas, *Estructuras sociales*, 129–66, 223–55, 307–23.

8. The text of the 1893 Constitution as well as preliminary documents related to its drafting are reprinted in Esgueva Gómez, *Constituciones políticas*, 1:358–94. Although civil marriage and divorce were provided for by Nicaragua's 1871 Civil Code, these were augmented under Zelaya. See Charlip, *Cultivating Coffee*, 182; Cobo del Arco, *Políticas de género*, 79–108.

9. For the 1896 reforms see Esgueva Gómez, *Constituciones políticas*, 1:397–404. Full manhood suffrage was granted by the 1905 Constitution (often called the "Autocratic" Constitution), but Zelaya's rule had already lasted thirteen years by this time, suggesting the fiction that voting had become in Nicaragua. See Esgueva Gómez, *Constituciones políticas*, 1:408–27.

10. This paragraph is based on a summary taken from the 1858 Constitution. See Esgueva Gómez, *Constituciones políticas*, 1:331–50.

11. Cruz, *Nicaragua's Conservative Republic*, 46–52, provides an excellent discussion of these provisions and their functioning.

12. J. L. Gould, *To Die in This Way*, 42–43.

13. See, e.g., Breuilly, *Nationalism and the State*.

14. Barth, introduction.

15. Comaroff, "Of Totemism and Ethnicity," 52; B. F. Williams, "A Class Act," 418–20.

16. Comaroff, "Of Totemism and Ethnicity," 59.

17. Comaroff, "Of Totemism and Ethnicity," 62. See also Alonso, "Politics of Space"; A. D. Smith, *Ethnic Origins of Nations*; cf. Brass, *Ethnicity and Nationalism*.

18. Anderson, *Imagined Communities*.

19. Hobsbawm, "Inventing Traditions"; Hobsbawm, *Nations and Nationalism*; Gellner, *Nations and Nationalism*. For a more general overview of theories of nationalism see A. D. Smith, *Theories of Nationalism*; Calhoun, *Nationalism*; B. F. Williams, "A Class Act."

20. Tilly, *Coercion, Capital, and European States* 115–17, 83; A. D. Smith, "Origins of Nations," 349–50.

21. Thomas Holt makes a call for such an approach in the study of race and race making: "The task of sorting out how these different levels of analysis are linked—that is, understanding how the large and 'important' are articulated with and expressed through the small and 'unimportant,' and vice versa—requires that we explicate more precisely the relation between individual agency and structural frameworks, on the one hand, and that we conceptualize more clearly just how one's consciousness of self and other are formed, on the other" ("Marking," 8).

22. Although we depart on the relationship of nation to state, Duara, "Historicizing National Identity," argues for much of this same reconceptualization of nation.

23. Although "primordialist" analyses of nations exist (see Brass, *Ethnicity and Nationalism*, 69–108, for a discussion of these), most theorists now focus as these identities as constructed. See, e.g, Anderson, *Imagined Communities*; Hobsbawm and Ranger, *Invention of Tradition*; Deutsch, *Nationalism and Social Communication*. The nation-state, like all collective identities, is defined relationally and requires other states or rival powers for such an identity to exist. Although this is

tacitly acknowledged in many studies of nation-states, the specifics of these relationships tend to be left unexamined, the emphasis instead on internally driven national "imagining."

24. Chatterjee, *The Nation and Its Fragments*, 220–39; Geertz, "Integrative Revolution," 306–7; Geertz, "After the Revolution," 239; Brass, *Ethnicity and Nationalism*.

25. Weber, *Peasants into Frenchmen*. While pioneering, Weber's work has been critiqued for, among other things, its failure to take seriously local politics and the possibilities of cultural negotiation. See, e.g., Sahlins, *Boundaries*.

26. Holt, "Marking," makes a similar call to action in studying the history of race. The literature on the history of everyday life is vast and methodologically varied. While de Certeau, *The Practice of Everyday Life*, is particularly influential, my own work is more in concert with Ludtke, *The History of Everyday Life*, and Lefebvre, *Critique of Everyday Life*.

27. Comaroff and Comaroff, "The Colonization of Consciousness," 236; Hobsbawm, "Mass-Producing Traditions"; Geertz, "Integrative Revolution," 308.

28. Geertz, "Integrative Revolution," 276–77.

29. Nairn, *The Break-up of Britain*, 41, quoted in Anderson, *Imagined Communities*, 47–48.

30. Anderson, *Imagined Communities*, 48, would have none of this apply to Latin America, arguing that "At least in South and Central America, European-style 'middle classes' were still insignificant at the end of the eighteenth century. Nor was there much in the way of an intelligentsia."

31. Mallon, "Promise and Dilemma"; Thurner, *From Two Republics to One Divided*; Guardino, *Mexico's National State*; Urban and Sherzer, *Nation-States and Indians in Latin America*; Grandin, *Blood of Guatemala*.

32. Mallon, *Peasant and Nation*, 4. See also Gilroy, *The Black Atlantic*; and Comaroff and Comaroff, "Homemade Hegemony."

33. See Duara, "Historicizing National Identity," for an engaging discussion of these issues. Although Duara's analytical focus is different than my own, we concur on both the negotiated, fluid nature of the nation and on the need to break with the traditional/modern dichotomy at the heart of Anderson's theory of nation.

34. On these "activities" of the state see Tilly, *Coercion, Capital, and European States*, 96–97. See also Tilly, "War Making and State Making."

I. Brothers and Others

1. Burns, *Patriarch and Folk*, 1–13.

2. Pinto Soria, *Centroamérica*; M. Rodríguez, *Cádiz Experiment*; Wortman, *Government and Society*. For Nicaragua see Zelaya G., *Nicaragua en la independencia*; Coronel Urtecho, "Introducción."

3. On these various political identities see, e.g., "Acta de la Orfandad," León, 17 April 1823; "Tratado declarado suspendidas las hostilidades," Masaya, 26 April 1823; "Decreto de Independencia Absoluta," 1 June 1823; all reprinted in Esgueva Gómez, *Documentos*, 99–102, 118–19, 119–21, 125–28.

4. "Decreto del Congreso Federal anexando Nicoya a Costa Rica," 9 December 1825, reprinted in Esgueva Gómez, *Documentos*, 142–43. See also Wortman, *Government and Society*, 271, on the viability of Nicaragua in these years.

5. An excellent exception is Kinloch Tijerino, *Nicaragua*.

6. See, e.g., Belli, "Luchas políticas"; Burns, *Patriarch and Folk*; Zelaya G., *Nicaragua en la independencia*; Coronel Urtecho, "Introducción"; Lanuza, "Formación del estado nacional"; Velázquez, *La formación del estado*.

7. Lanuza, "Formación del estado nacional," 106. All translations are mine unless otherwise indicated.

8. For a wonderfully detailed and nuanced history of colonial Central American city government and politics, see Dym, "A Sovereign State of Every Village."

9. Coronel Urtecho, "Introducción," 41.

10. Belli, "Luchas políticas," 51, 53.

11. Tilly, "War Making and State Making"; Tilly, *Coercion, Capital, and European States*.

12. For the first assertion see Coronel Urtecho, "Introducción," 41. The second is from Radell, "Historical Geography of Western Nicaragua," 179, cited in Burns, *Patriarch and Folk*, 42.

13. See Stevens, *Origins of Instability*.

14. Burns, *Patriarch and Folk*, 35–50, 145–59.

15. The son-in-law and major political ally and booster of Tomás Martínez (president, 1857–66), Jerónimo Pérez held numerous ministerial posts. Most of his writings were originally printed in *La Tertulia* (Masaya), which he published. His works are collected in Pérez, *Obras*.

16. Pérez, "Biografía de Don Manuel Antonio de la Cerda," 478.

17. Tomás Ayón, José Dolores Gámez, and Enrique Guzmán all helped to create the "historical" narrative for this belief. See, e.g., Ayón, "Apuntes"; Gámez, *Historia de Nicaragua*, 248–52; Guzmán, *Editoriales de La Prensa, 1878*, 141. Subsequently, this conception has found expression in the works of José Coronel Urtecho, Alberto Lanuza, and Humberto Belli, among others. Cf. Burns, *Patriarch and Folk*, 14.

18. Pérez, "Biografía de Don Manuel Antonio de la Cerda," 477.

19. Wortman, *Government and Society*, 271.

20. Kinloch Tijerino, *Nicaragua*, 112–21.

21. Burns, *Patriarch and Folk*, 120–30.

22. Kinloch Tijerino, *Nicaragua*, 101–41.

23. See, e.g., Chamorro Zelaya, *Fruto Chamorro*; Valle, *Los Somoza y la estirpe sangrienta*. A more thorough evaluation of this period's historiography is Casanova Fuertes, "¿Héroes o bandidos?"

24. This approach is suggested implicitly in Burns, *Patriarch and Folk*, 145–59, and explicitly in Casanova Fuertes, "Hacia una nueva valorización."

25. De la Rocha, *Revista política*, 7; Coronel Urtecho, "Introducción," 47; Casanova Fuertes, "Orden o anarquía," 285–87.

26. Casanova Fuertes, "Orden o anarquía," 287–88.

27. Téllez Argüello, *Muera la gobierna*; J. L. Gould, "*¡Vana Ilusión!*"

28. See Burns, *Patriarch and Folk*, 147–59.

29. Esgueva Gómez, *Constituciones políticas*. Two other constitutional projects were organized (in 1848 and 1854) but were never implemented.

30. José Guerrero, "Mensaje del director supremo en la inauguración de la Asamblea Constituyente," 3 September 1847, reprinted in Vega Bolaños, *Gobernantes de Nicaragua*, 132–34.

31. See Burns, *Patriarch and Folk*, 10, 16; M. Rodríguez, *Cádiz Experiment*, 118–19, 142; Wortman, *Government and Society*, 261.

32. José Núñez, "Mensage que el Presidente del Consejo, encargado del Poder Ejecutivo presenta a la A. L. al abrir sus sesiones," León, 28 November 1834, reprinted in Vega Bolaños, *Gobernantes de Nicaragua*, 60–66.

33. José Núñez, "Contestación de Núñez," León, 5 March 1837, reprinted in Vega Bolaños, *Gobernantes de Nicaragua*, 74, my emphasis.

34. See, e.g., Burns, *Patriarch and Folk*, 78–79, in which he cites an article published across four issues of the *Mentor Nicaragüense* that takes the form of a letter written from a father to his son who is about to take office as head of state. In it the father explains how the statesman is like a father, whose role is the same to the state as it is to his family. See also "El honor," *Gaceta de Nicaragua* (Managua), 4 November 1866; Fernando Guzmán, "Manifiesto de S. E. el Presidente D. Fernando Guzmán a los pueblos de la república," *Gaceta de Nicaragua* (Managua), 9 March 1867.

35. Gillis, *A World of Their Own Making*, 28–31.

36. Lanning, *Eighteenth-Century Enlightenment*, 209–14.

37. José León Sandoval, "Discurso," 30 April 1846, reprinted in Vega Bolaños, *Gobernantes de Nicaragua*, 104–6; see also Fruto Chamorro, "El director del estado de Nicaragua a sus habitantes," *Gaceta Oficial de Nicaragua* (Granada), 23 April 1853, reprinted in Pérez, *Obras*, 327.

38. José León Sandoval, "A los pueblos del estado," Managua, 10 December 1846, reprinted in Vega Bolaños, *Gobernantes de Nicaragua*, 113–14. See also José León Sandoval, "El director supremo del estado, á sus habitantes," Managua, 3 Novem-

ber 1846, reprinted in Vega Bolaños, *Gobernantes de Nicaragua*, 112–13. For similar expressions made when addressing the population as a whole, see Fruto Chamorro, "El director del estado de Nicaragua a sus habitantes," *Gaceta Oficial de Nicaragua* (Granada), 23 April 1853, reprinted in Pérez, *Obras*, 327; Fernando Guzmán, "Manifiesto de S. E. el Presidente D. Fernando Guzmán a los pueblos de la república," *Gaceta de Nicaragua* (Managua), 9 March 1867, reprinted in Pérez, *Obras*, 791.

39. Esgueva Gómez, *Constituciones políticas*, 1:348.

40. See José León Sandoval, "Mensaje leído al Asemblea Lejislativa," 1846, reprinted in Vega Bolaños, *Gobernantes de Nicaragua*, 107–9.

41. See, e.g., Tomás Balladares, "El senador que ejerce el S. P. E. del estado de Nicaragua, á los habitantes del mismo," León, 24 March 1840, reprinted in Vega Bolaños, *Gobernantes de Nicaragua*, 82.

42. AGCA, B5.4, leg. 62, exp. 1660, transcribed as "Fragmentos de la proclama del P. José Antonio Chamorro justificando el por qué está a favor del Plan de Iguala (Nov. de 1821)," in Esgueva Gómez, *Documentos*, 102–3.

43. See Burns, *Patriarch and Folk*, 10, 16; M. Rodríguez, *Cádiz Experiment*, 118–19, 142.

44. Woodward, *Central America*, 112.

45. On Jerez's life and politics see Chamorro, *Máximo Jerez y sus contemporáneos*; Gámez, *Apuntamientos para la biografía de Máximo Jerez*; Salvatierra, *Máximo Jerez inmortal*.

46. See Karnes, *Failure of Union*, 204–28. On Mendieta see Mory, "Salvador Mendieta."

47. Blas Antonio Sáenz, "Discurso pronunciado por el Senador Director Sr. Blas Antonio Sáenz al instalarse el cuerpo legislativo del estado," San Fernando [Masaya], 10 March 1845, reprinted in Vega Bolaños, *Gobernantes de Nicaragua*, 88–90.

48. Folkman, *The Nicaragua Route*; Kinloch Tijerino, "Canal interoceánico."

49. José León Sandoval, "Discurso pronunciado por el Sr. Director José León Sandoval al presentarse á la A. L. del estado en la sesión del 22 del presente mes de Marzo de 847," reprinted in Vega Bolaños, *Gobernantes de Nicaragua*, 119–20; José Núñez, "Contestación de Núñez," León, 5 March 1837, reprinted in Vega Bolaños, *Gobernantes de Nicaragua*, 71–72.

50. Gootenberg, *Imagining Development*.

51. José León Sandoval, "Mensaje leído al Asemblea Lejislativa," 1846, reprinted in Vega Bolaños, *Gobernantes de Nicaragua*, 107–9.

52. José Guerrero, "Contenstación del presidente al Congreso," 3 September 1847, reprinted in Vega Bolaños, *Gobernantes de Nicaragua*, 134–35, my emphasis.

53. Naylor, *Penny Ante Imperialism*, 152.

54. Naylor, *Penny Ante Imperialism*, 158–67. On the deep scars this event left see José Guerrero, "El director supremo del estado de Nicaragua á los habitantes del mismo," 1 January 1848, reprinted in Vega Bolaños, *Gobernantes de Nicaragua*, 135–36.

55. This concept, now generally accepted in international law for the demarcation of international borders, was first embraced in Latin America following the region's independence from Spain.

56. M. Rodríguez, *Palmerstonian Diplomat*, 288; Van Alstyne, "Central American Policy," 345.

57. Kinloch Tijerino, *Nicaragua*, 155–63; Naylor, *Penny Ante Imperialism*, 148–76.

58. M. Rodríguez, *Palmerstonian Diplomat*, 289.

59. Lanuza, "Estructuras socioeconómicas," 97.

60. Naylor, *Penny Ante Imperialism*, 189.

61. On the struggles between British Foreign Office and Colonial Office officials over Britain's role in the region, see Naylor, *Penny Ante Imperialism*, 140–67.

62. See, e.g., José Guerrero, "El director supremo del estado de Nicaragua á los habitantes del mismo," 1 January 1848, reprinted in Vega Bolaños, *Gobernantes de Nicaragua*, 135–36; "La doctrina de Monroe," *Gaceta de Nicaragua* (Managua), 10 February 1866.

63. Herrera C., *Bongos, bogas, vapores y marinos*, 59–68.

64. Olien, "Micro/Macro-Level Linkages," 275–77.

65. Woodward, *Central America*, 145–46; Karnes, *Failure of Union*, 140–42.

66. May, "Young American Males," 859.

67. M. Rodríguez, *Palmerstonian Diplomat*, 301. Squier's speech was reprinted in the 16 July 1849 issue of *Correo del Istmo* (León).

68. *Correo del Istmo* (León), 7 March 1850, quoted in Kinloch Tijerino, *Nicaragua*, 203.

69. Kinloch Tijerino, *Nicaragua*, 201–13.

70. Gobat, *Confronting the American Dream*, ch. 1.

71. The literature concerning Walker and the National War is voluminous. An important starting point is Walker's own book on his campaign, *The War in Nicaragua*. See also Scroggs, *Filibusters and Financiers*; Burns, *Patriarch and Folk*, 194–237; Bolaños Geyer, *William Walker*.

72. Kinloch Tijerino, *Nicaragua*, 298–99.

73. Patricio Rivas and Máximo Jerez (Chinangdega) to José María Estrada (Choluteca), 14 June 1856, reprinted in Esgueva Gómez, *Documentos*, 185, my emphasis. Although Liberals sought reconciliation, they did not wish to accept sole blame for Nicaragua's dire situation. In a public call to unite against Walker, Rivas refers to

Liberals and Conservatives as "those two parties guilty of fostering so much unhappiness." Rivas's plea is reprinted in Barquero, *Gobernantes de Nicaragua*, 106–7.

74. Estrada to Rivas and Jerez, 18 June 1856, reprinted in Pérez, *Obras*, 383–84.

75. "El Pacto Providencial del 12 de septiembre de 1856," reprinted in Esgueva Gómez, *Documentos*, 190–92.

76. See Pérez, "Revolución de Nicaragua en 1854" and "Campaña nacional."

77. Pérez, "Campaña nacional," 242.

78. *Gaceta de Nicaragua* (Managua), 6 June 1866.

79. See also "Cambio de instituciones," *Gaceta de Nicaragua* (Managua), 11 March 1865; "A los pueblos de Nicaragua," *Gaceta de Nicaragua* (Managua), 25 August 1866; "Las pasiones," *Gaceta de Nicaragua* (Managua), 1 September 1866; "Los últimos 10 años desde 57 al presente," *Gaceta de Nicaragua* (Managua), 1 December 1866. "La doctrina de Monroe," *Gaceta de Nicaragua* (Managua), 10 February 1866, makes the explicit connection between the weakness created by internal divisions and the threats of stronger foreign powers, such as the United States.

80. Fernando Guzmán, "Manifiesto de S. E. el Presidente D. Fernando Guzmán a los pueblos de la república," *Gaceta de Nicaragua* (Managua), 9 March 1867.

81. See, e.g., "Redención," *Gaceta de Nicaragua* (Managua), 24 December 1864; "Observaciones," *Gaceta de Nicaragua* (Managua), 9 June 1866; "El honor," *Gaceta de Nicaragua* (Managua), 4 November 1866.

82. See, e.g., Wheelock Román, *Imperialismo y dictadura*, 14–17; Biderman, "Class Structure," 42; cf. Charlip, *Cultivating Coffee*; Cruz, *Nicaragua's Conservative Republic*.

83. Pérez, "Biografía de Don Manuel Antonio de la Cerda," 479, emphasis in the original.

84. Gobat, *Confronting the American Dream*.

85. While government reports and *memorias*, correspondence, and newspaper articles and editorials contain pieces of this ideological vision, it is most succinctly stated in a series of articles that appeared in 1865 and 1866: "La autoridad," *Gaceta de Nicaragua* (Managua), 7 January 1865; "El pueblo," *Gaceta de Nicaragua* (Managua), 22 July 1866; "Policia," *Gaceta de Nicaragua* (Managua), 25 August 1866; "La propiedad," *Gaceta de Nicaragua* (Managua), 27 October 1866; "La justicia," *Gaceta de Nicaragua* (Managua), 10 November 1866; "La educación," *Gaceta de Nicaragua* (Managua), 17 November 1866.

86. Woodward, *Positivism in Latin America*, x.

87. Woodward, *Positivism in Latin America*, xii.

88. Arellano, *Brevísima historia*, 38–44. On Mexican positivism see Leopoldo Zea, *El positivismo en México* and *Apogeo y decadencia del positivismo en México*. See also Raat, "Leopoldo Zea and Mexican Positivism."

89. Arellano, *Panorama de la literatura nicaragüense*, 23. On Krause and his influence in Latin America, see Stoetzer, *Karl Christian Friedrich Krause*.

90. For Guatemala see McCreery, *Rural Guatemala*.

91. Twinam, "The Negotiation of Honor," 94.

92. In the Nicaraguan case, see, e.g., Dore, "Property, Households, and Public Regulation," 598–601.

93. The profound impact of nation-states on nineteenth-century European thought is evident in the fascinating reversal of the flow of discourse made by the renowned German physician Rudolf Virchow, who in his 1858 study, *Cellular Pathology*, suggested that the body be understood as a "cell state in which every cell is a citizen," where disease was but a form of civil war.

94. Only in the twelfth edition (1884) of the dictionary of Royal Academy of Spanish was the term "brazos" noted to imply laboring. The first edition (1726) and those thereafter suggested a rather different meaning: "Metaphorically signifies effort, power, valor and vitality."

2. Death and Taxes

1. "Mensaje del Excmo. Señor General Presidente Don Tomás Martínez en el acto de su inauguración el 15 de Noviembre de 1857," *Gaceta de Nicaragua* (Managua), 22 November 1857.

2. Wortman, *Government and Society*, 271.

3. Unless otherwise noted, all references to currency are to Nicaraguan pesos fuerte, with 1 peso equal to 100 centavos. Nicaraguans often also used the colonial peso system, according to which 1 peso is equal to .8 pesos fuerte. For purposes of calculations and consistency, I have converted all figures in pesos into pesos fuerte.

4. Lévy, *Notas geográficas*, 351.

5. Lévy, *Notas geográficas*, 477.

6. Lévy, *Notas geográficas*, 351.

7. Wheelock Román, *Imperialismo y dictadura*, 14–17; Coronel Urtecho, "Introducción."

8. See Edelman, *Logic of the Latifundio*; Fernández Molina, "Colouring the World in Blue."

9. Nicaragua, *Código*, 24–28; Nicaragua, Ministerio de Hacienda Pública, *Memoria* (1865–66).

10. Burns, *Patriarch and Folk*, 52.

11. Nicaragua, *Código*, 38–39.

12. Nicaragua, Ministerio de Hacienda Pública, *Memoria* (1865–66).

13. See Nicaragua, *Código*, 23–25, for the more than a dozen laws decreed to control tobacco growing and selling.

14. Burns, *Patriarch and Folk*, 147–50.

15. Burns, *Patriarch and Folk*, 147.

16. On these projects see Cruz, *Nicaragua's Conservative Republic*, 81–84.

17. AMPG, caja 51, leg. 171, Buenaventura Selva, Government Minister (Managua), to Departmental Prefect (Granada), 2 May 1866.

18. AMPG, caja 146, leg. 418, García (Managua) to Departmental Prefect (Granada), 19 November 1880. The plan called for two days of work, or 70 centavos per day to avoid such work, an unheard-of sum at the time. See also caja 191, leg. 495, no. 495, Teodoro Delgadillo (Managua) to Departmental Prefect (Granada), 29 May 1883, and no. 502, Teodoro Delgadillo (Managua) to Departmental Prefect (Granada), 6 June 1883.

19. AMPG, caja 156, leg. 435, "Asunto entre la municipalidad y el cura de Masatepe," 1880.

20. J. L. Gould, *To Die in This Way*, 33.

21. Nicaragua, Ministerio de Gobernación, *Memoria* (1860). For earlier efforts to reform the state's military practices, see Casanova Fuertes, "Orden o anarquía," 285–87; Burns, *Patriarch and Folk*, 68.

22. The state kept local police and political authorities abreast of regional political and military development, especially those related to William Walker and his seemingly never-ending plans for reinvasion. See, e.g., AMPG, caja 2, leg. 3, "Correspondencias oficial del prefecto," 1857.

23. Nicaragua, Ministerio de Gobernación, *Memoria* (1860), 7.

24. Cf. Rosalío Cortés in Nicaragua, Ministerio de Gobernación, *Memoria* (1859), and Jerónimo Pérez in the *Memoria* of 1860.

25. Teplitz, "Political and Economic Foundations," 107.

26. Nicaragua, Ministerio de Guerra, *Memoria* (1863), 9. This also reflects the calls toward the end of the National War for fairer recruitment and a more professional militia: "Proyecto para establecer provisionalmente en la república la milicia nacional," *Boletín Oficial* (León), 4 February 1857; "Articulación del Proyecto comenzado en el número 35," *Boletín Oficial* (León), 15 February 1857.

27. Cruz, *Nicaragua's Conservative Republic*, 55.

28. On this rebellion see Cruz, *Nicaragua's Conservative Republic*, 60–61; Belli Cortés, *Cincuenta años de vida republicana*, 71–75

29. AMPG, caja 76, leg. 244, Anselmo H. Rivas (Managua) to Prefect (Granada), 25 July 1870.

30. Nicaragua, Ministerio de Gobernación, *Memoria* (1869–70), 8.

31. AMPG, caja 29, leg. 85, Jerónimo Pérez (Managua) to Prefect (Granada), 4 January 1861.

32. See, e.g., AMPG, caja 216, leg. 3, "Escalafón de la oficialidad del departamento

de Granada," 1887; Anexo del Juzgado, Libro 5, "Escalafón militar de Granada," 1900.

33. Romero Vargas, *Estructuras sociales*, 324–42.

34. Romero Vargas, *Estructuras sociales*, 325, 335; Newson, *Indian Survival*, 330.

35. Burns, *Patriarch and Folk*, 68; Radell, "Historical Geography of Western Nicaragua," 176.

36. Lévy, *Notas geográficas*, 341.

37. Burns, *Patriarch and Folk*, 68.

38. See, e.g., Pérez, *Obras*, 215, 260–61, 282–83.

39. Lévy, *Notas geográficas*, 249, indicates that Indians and zambos formed the rank and file of the military. See also Herrera C., *Bongos, bogas, vapores y marinos*, 58–68.

40. AMPG, caja 62, leg. 203, Bernabé Portocarrero (Granada) to Prefect (Granada), 23 April 1868, and Bernabé Portocarrero (Rivas) to Prefect (Granada), 29 April 1868.

41. Cf. Nicaragua, Ministerio de Guerra, *Memoria* (1863), 9.

42. AMPG, caja 62, leg. 203, Teodoro Delgadillo (Granada) to Prefect (Granada), 27 May 1868.

43. A similar request from ladinos in Diriá was denied with even greater dispatch and much less courtesy. AMPG, caja 62, leg. 203, Bernabé Portocarrero (Managua) to Prefect (Granada), 12 May 1868.

44. AMPG, caja 156, leg. 435, "Asunto entre la municipalidad y el cura de Masatepe," 1880.

45. On Vijil's life and historiographic treatment see Vijil, *El Padre Vijil*; Burns, *Patriarch and Folk*, 201–2.

46. AMPG, caja 156, leg. 435, "Asunto entre la municipalidad y el cura de Masatepe," Ramon Navarro (Masatepe) to Subprefect (Masaya), 24 March 1880.

47. AMPG, caja 156, leg. 435, "Asunto entre la municipalidad y el cura de Masatepe," Roberto Lacayo (Granada) to Subprefect (Masaya), 18 March 1880.

48. Pérez, "Biografía de Don Manuel Antonio de la Cerda," 479, emphasis in the original.

49. Teplitz, "Political and Economic Foundations," 317–19.

50. Wortman, "Government Revenue," 264–65.

51. Eagleton, "The Ideology of the Aesthetic," 330.

52. "Discurso pronunciado por el Director Sr. D. José León Sandoval al entregar el mando supremo del estado en 10. de abril de 1.847," reprinted in Vega Bolaños, *Gobernantes de Nicaragua*, 125–26.

53. Nicaragua, *Código*, 219. Despite the provision for inspections of chicha production, local officials complained that indigenous alcaldes were responsible for the

difficulties they had in exterminating illegal chicha production. See AMPG, caja 129, leg. 371, 1877–1878.

54. Nicaragua, *Código*, 218.

55. Nicaragua, *Código*, 138–39.

56. Nicaragua, *Código*, 218–19.

57. Nicaragua, *Código*, 140.

58. AMPG, caja 224, unnumbered leg. (119 folios), Padilla (Managua) to Prefect (Granada), 30 May 1887, no. 890.

59. Nicaragua, *Código*, 140–41, 218.

60. AMPG, caja 224, unnumbered leg. (119 folios), Padilla (Managua) to Prefect (Granada), 16 May 1887, no. 276.

61. AMPG, caja 222, leg. 14, Lacayo (Managua) to Prefect (Granada), 25 November 1887, no. 1793.

62. AMPG, caja 175, leg. 464, García (Managua) to Prefect (Granada), 3 August 1882, no. 535.

63. See Dore, "One Step Forward."

64. The history of gender in nineteenth-century Nicaragua remains little studied. See, however, Dore, *Myths of Modernity*; Cobo del Arco, *Políticas de género*; González, "From Feminism to Somocismo."

65. Nicaragua, *Código*, 140.

66. The phrase "physically or morally deformed" was used as one of the column heads in the 1883 census.

67. Júdice, "Un decreto infundado," *El Porvenir de Nicaragua* (Valle Gottel), 22 March 1874.

68. "Sr. editor de El Porvenir," *El Porvenir de Nicaragua* (Valle Gottel), 29 March 1874.

69. AMPG, caja 222, leg. 14, Ortega (Managua) to Prefect (Granada), 9 March 1887, no. 174.

70. For examples of the law's use see AMPG, caja 2, leg. 4, "Queja de Francisco Hernandez contra el policia de San Rafael," 1857, and caja 46, leg. 179, "Máximo Sauzo se queja de abuso de autoridad del alcalde de Diriomo," 1865.

71. AMPG, caja 62, leg. 203, Anselmo H. Rivas (Managua) to Prefect (Granada), 22 September 1868.

72. See, e.g., AMPG, caja 38, leg. 116, "Diligencias por las que se comprueba el total abandono en que se encuentra la policia de esta ciudad, por los ajentes del ramo," 1863; caja 109, leg. 306, Lopez (Managua) to Prefect (Granada), 25 May 1874; caja 115, leg. 334, Rosalío Cortés (Managua) to Prefect (Granada), 8 November 1875; caja 196, leg. 1, Teodoro Delgadillo (Managua) to Prefect (Granada), 17 September 1884.

73. See, e.g., AMPG, caja 87, leg. 272, "Información de testigos instruidas para

averiguar la certeza de las fallas que Don Marcos Urbina denuncia en un impreso contra el Agente general de agricultura," 1872; caja 98, leg. 287, "Queja del Agente General de agricultura Don Ygnosente Fletes contra el Juez de agricultura de Granada," 1873; caja 108, leg. 319, "Don Agustín Lacayo acusa al Sr. Gobernador de Policia de Masaya, Don Marcelo Vega," 1874; caja 108, leg. 319, "El Señor Don Agustín Lacayo presente contestar demanda que pone contra el Señor Fernando Brenes," 1874; caja 201, leg. 18, José Chamorro (Managua) to Prefect (Granada), 29 Deember 1884, no. 408; caja 229, unnumbered leg. (171 folios), "Don Pedro José Chamorro se queja del Agente de Policia Rural Francisco Mora Castillo," 1888.

74. See Arnaiz Quintana, *Historia del pueblo de Dios*; Zúñiga C., *Historia eclesiástica de Nicaragua*; Arellano, *Breve historia.*

75. Wortman, *Government and Society*, 271.

76. Burns, *Patriarch and Folk*, 68.

77. Burns, *Patriarch and Folk*, 22–23, 70–71.

78. See Pérez, *Obras*, 140–41, 224. See also the defense offered by Vijil's grandson in Vijil, *El Padre Vijil.*

79. Burns, *Patriarch and Folk*, 201.

80. Pérez, *Obras*, 224.

81. See Wheelock Román, *Raíces indígenas*; Velázquez, *La formación del estado*; Teplitz, "Political and Economic Foundations."

82. AMPG, caja 21, leg. 65, Jerónimo Pérez (Managua) to Prefect (Granada), 12 December 1860.

83. Teplitz, "Political and Economic Foundations," 76; Bendaña et al., *América Central*, 263–64.

84. See, e.g., Sullivan-González, *Piety, Power, and Politics.*

85. See, e.g., AMPG, caja 28, leg. 84, "Expediente relativo a la reunión de los Yndígenas de Nindirí habida el 19 en la noche del mes de Octubre," 1861; caja 52, leg. 138, "Diligencias sobre lo ocurrido entre el cura y la municipalidad de Diriomo," 1866; caja 156, leg. 435, "Asunto entre la municipalidad y el cura de Masatepe," 1880.

86. AMPG, caja 68, leg. 219, Teodoro Delgadillo (Managua) to Prefect (Granada), 6 November 1869.

87. AMPG, caja 68, leg. 219, Teodoro Delgadillo (Managua) to Prefect (Granada), 12 November 1869.

88. Vicente Quadra, "Manifesto dirijido a los pueblos por el presidente de la republica" (1871), in *Colección de varios*, 2:8, Library of Congress, Washington DC.

89. J. L. Gould, "*¡Vana Ilusión!*"; Téllez Argüello, *Muera la gobierna*, 293–305.

90. See AMPG, caja 165, leg. 447, Joaquín Elizondo (Matagalpa) to Prefect (Granada), 4 May 1881, no. 25, García (Managua) to Prefect (Granada), 9 May 1881, no. 40, and García (Managua) to Prefect (Granada), 11 May 1881, no. 26.

91. AMPG, caja 168, leg. 457, "Para averiguar la perturbación del orden público que pretenden algunas personas a consecuencia del decreto de 8 de abril," 1881.

92. See J. L. Gould, *To Die in This Way*, 35; Cerutti, *Los Jesuitas en Nicaragua*; Guerrero C. and Soriano, *Caciques heróicos de Centroamérica*, 181; cf. Collado H., "Liberales y conservadores," 72.

93. Gobat, *Confronting the American Dream*, 51–53.

94. On the elections and the conspiracy see Cruz, *Nicaragua's Conservative Republic*, 98–109. See also the compelling argument for Nicaragua's post-Walker cosmopolitan spirit in Gobat, *Confronting the American Dream*, 42–71.

95. For evidence and testimony regarding the 1884 plot, see Nicaragua, *Documentos relativos a la rebelión*.

96. See Esgueva Gómez, *Constituciones políticas*, 1:371–92.

97. Bendaña et al., *América Central*, 324–29; Arnaiz Quintana, *Historia del pueblo de Dios*, 82–86.

98. Arnaiz Quintana, *Historia del pueblo de Dios*, 84. See also J. L. Gould, *To Die in This Way*, 39.

99. Adán Cárdenas, "Discurso pronunciado por el señor Doctor Don Adán Cárdenas al Soberano Congreso de Nicaragua, al tomar posesión de la presidencia de la república el 1 de marzo de 1883" (1883), in *Colección de varios*, 8:7–8 (my emphasis), Library of Congress.

100. On Sandoval see Casanova Fuertes, "Orden o anarquía."

101. Granada also levied taxes on business establishments, from the lowliest market stall to the largest merchant and banking houses. See, e.g., AMPG, caja 96, leg. 285, "Listas de almacenes, tiendas, estantes, billares, pulperias, etc.," 1873. These lists were updated on a yearly basis and indicated the monthly taxes to be paid by those listed.

102. An example from Jinotepe, listing all people with at least 500 pesos of capital can be found in AMPG, caja 120, leg. 342, 1876; see also caja 173, leg. 168, "Lista de los calificados por la Junta de desagravios, acerca del impuesto que se cobra, en beneficio de este [Granada] Hospital," 1882.

103. See, e.g., AMPG, caja 38, leg. 156, "Solicitud de varios vecinos de Catarina sobre emprestito," 1863, and "Solicitud de varios indigenas de Catarina sobre emprestito," 1863. Since the determination of wealth was made by the tax-collecting body, protests of poverty or reduced wealth were not infrequent.

104. AMPG, caja 156, leg. 435, "Asunto entre la municipalidad y el cura de Masatepe," 1880.

105. For this strategy see, e.g., AMPG, caja 167, leg. 456, "Queja entre San Marcos y Masatepe," 1881, and caja 175, leg. 478, "Queja de la municipalidad de la Victoria contra la municipalidad de Masatepe por haber hecho donaciones de terrenos," 1882.

106. AMPG, caja 62, leg. 203 (141 folios), Portocarrero (Managua) to Prefect (Granada), 24 December 1868.

107. AMPG, caja 60, leg. 192 bis, "Censo de El Rosario," 1867, and caja 13, leg. 10, "Censo de Jinotepe," 1858.

108. Nicaragua, *Decretos y leyes de 1881–1882*, 11.

109. In Diriamba, children of unmarried parents were always called "illegitimate," while in Diriomo both "illegitimate" and "natural" were used. See AMPG, caja 184, leg. x5, "Censo de Diriamba," 1883, and caja 191, leg. x7, "Censo de Diriomo," 1883. While the positivist-inspired census sought to define everyone as either legitimate or illegitimate, Iberian law had long also distinguished those "natural" children born out of wedlock to a couple who could legally marry.

110. See, e.g., AMPG, caja 120, leg. 342, "Carpeta de los ciudadanos inscritos en los cantones de los pueblos del departamento," 1876.

111. H. H. Leavitt to Secretary of State, no. 20, "Report on the Political Situation in Nicaragua," 18 March 1885, U.S. Department of State, Despatches from U.S. Consuls in Managua, 1884–1906, microfilm T-634, roll 2, National Archives, Washington DC.

112. On the diversity of complaints see, e.g., AMPG, caja 38, leg. 116, "Solicitud de Indalecio Quesada sobre que se declare que la elección de alcaldes natural por costumbre sea preferible a los constitutionales," 1863; caja 159, leg. 430, "Nulidad de la elección de José Quintania de Diriá," 1880; caja 175, leg. 478, "Queja contra el Alcalde de Catarina Nicolas Borge por delitos contra la libertad del sufragio de Máximo Guerrero y Francisco Acuña," 1882; caja 210, unnumbered leg. (115 folios), "Pruebas presentadas por el Sr. Cipriano Ruiz sosteniendo la validéz de las elecciones de A. A. L. L. del pueblo de Catarina," 1886. See also Avendaño Rojas, "Las características de la ciudadanía" and "El pactismo."

113. For example, in Costa Rica, which is often held up as the paragon of the "good" state, free and obligatory education was not mandated until the Constitution of 1869. Dengo de Vargas, *Educación costarricense*, 92–93.

114. Arellano, *Breve historia*, 39–44; Alvarez Lejarza, "El liberalismo en los 30 años." On university education in colonial Central America see Lanning, *Eighteenth-Century Enlightenment*.

115. Rodríguez Rosales, "Proyectos educativos"; Burns, *Patriarch and Folk*, 95–96.

116. Nicaragua, Ministerio de Instrucción Pública, *Memoria* (1859), 5.

117. Elizondo, "Infraestructura de Nicaragua en 1860," 56.

118. Nicaragua, Ministerio de Gobernación, *Memoria* (1860), 6.

119. Nicaragua, Ministerio de Gobernación, *Informe* (1871).

120. See AMPG, caja 118, leg. 336, 1875, in which the "padres de familia" of Jalteva petition against the removal of the teacher.

121. Lévy, *Notas geográficas*, 362; Niederlein, *State of Nicaragua*, 48.

122. Wolfe, "Rising from the Ashes," 112. See also Rodríguez Rosales, *Educación durante el liberalismo*, 21–49; Cruz, *Nicaragua's Conservative Republic*, 88–89.

123. Arellano, *Brevísima historia*, 38–51.

124. R. Contreras, "La ciencia de la educación," *El País* (Managua), 1 January 1888.

125. *Correo del Istmo* (León), 14 March 1850, quoted in Herrera C., "La hoja amarga," 300.

3. The Wealth of the Country

1. A. Guerra, J. Miguel Cárdenas, E. Carazo, P. Chamorro, J. Elizondo, and Ireneo Delgadillo, *Datos relativos a la proyectada inmigración al país, presentados por las comisiones nombradas con este fin por el supremo gobierno de la república de Nicaragua* (Managua: Imprenta del Gobierno, 1868), reprinted in *Revista de la Academía de Geografía e Historia de Nicaragua* 35 (January–June 1969): 47.

2. See Kaimowitz, "Nicaraguan Debates on Agrarian Structure."

3. The most prominent exponents of this theory are Wheelock Román, *Imperialismo y dictadura*, and Biderman, "Class Structure."

4. See in particular Baumeister, "Agrarian Reform"; Charlip, *Cultivating Coffee*; Dore, *Myths of Modernity*. On both the importance and relative neglect of studies on smallholders in Latin America, see Gudmundson, *Costa Rica before Coffee*; Roseberry, "Beyond the Agrarian Question."

5. The *manzana* continues to be the main unit of land size in Nicaragua. It is equivalent to 0.7 hectares or 1.73 acres. Smaller plots, especially urban ones, are often listed in *varas* (0.7 square meters). One manzana is 10,000 varas.

6. Charlip, *Cultivating Coffee*, 10–12.

7. On patterns of colonial land tenure see Romero Vargas, *Estructuras sociales*, 223–46, 307–16; Newson, *Indian Survival*, 131–38, 260–61; MacLeod, *Spanish Central America*, 302.

8. MacLeod, *Spanish Central America*; Newson, *Indian Survival*, 131–32; cf. Coronel Urtecho, *Reflexiones*, 85–86; Belli, "Luchas políticas," 51.

9. See, e.g., "Discurso pronunciado por el Director Sr. D. José León Sandoval al presentarse á la A. L. del Estado en la sesion del 22 del presente mes de Marzo de 847," and José Guerrero, "El Director Supremo del Estado á los habitantes del mismo," Managua, 6 April 1847, both reprinted in Vega Bolaños, *Gobernantes de Nicaragua*, 119–20, 431. See also Kinloch Tijerino, "Canal interoceánico."

10. José Guerrero, "Contestación del president del Congreso," 3 September 1847, reprinted in Vega Bolaños, *Gobernantes de Nicaragua*, 134–35.

11. Kinloch Tijerino, "Canal interoceánico," 42.

12. José Guerrero, "El director supremo del estado de Nicaragua á los habitantes del mismo," 1 January 1848, reprinted in Vega Bolaños, *Gobernantes de Nicaragua*, 135–36.

13. Folkman, *The Nicaragua Route*; Kinloch Tijerino, "Canal interoceánico"; Herrera C., *Bongos, bogas, vapores y marinos*.

14. Clayton, "Nicaragua Canal," 326–27.

15. The discussion in this paragraph is drawn largely from Gobat, *Confronting the American Dream*, ch. 1.

16. Gobat, *Confronting the American Dream*, 30.

17. The Walker episode was but one of many chapters in U.S. and British imperial activity in Nicaragua. See Bermann, *Under the Big Stick*; Dozier, *Nicaragua's Mosquito Coast*; LaFeber, *Inevitable Revolutions*; May, *Southern Dream*; Schoonover, *United States in Central America*.

18. Crowell, "Central American Canal"; Clayton, "Nicaragua Canal." On European interest in the canal, see, e.g., Pim, *Gate to the Pacific*; Belly, *A travers l'Amerique Centrale*.

19. "El desarrollo de este departamento," *El Porvenir de Nicaragua* (Rivas), 20 June 1868.

20. *El Porvenir de Nicaragua* (Rivas) began publishing Walker's book on 6 June 1868. See "Nicaragua y los EE.UU," *El Porvenir de Nicaragua* (Rivas), 13 February 1869, regarding the "weakness" and "smallness" of Nicaragua in the face of "the powerful North American Government."

21. Charlip, "Cultivating Coffee," 82; Burns, *Patriarch and Folk*, 220.

22. Cruz, *Nicaragua's Conservative Republic*, 43–44.

23. Charlip, "Cultivating Coffee," 83–90, offers an excellent survey of these measures.

24. Nicaragua, Ministerio de Fomento y Obras Públicas, *Memoria* (1867), 4. See also R. G. Williams, *States and Social Evolution*, 35.

25. Schoonover and Schoonover, "Statistics," 108.

26. Lévy, *Notas geográficas*, 477.

27. Biderman, "Class Structure," 52–53.

28. Cruz, *Nicaragua's Conservative Republic*, 81–84, 150.

29. R. G. Williams, *States and Social Evolution*, 175–76, 208–9, 19; Dunkerley, *Power in the Isthmus*, 40–41.

30. R. G. Williams, *States and Social Evolution*, 212–19, table 6.1.

31. In a study of economic growth in nineteenth-century Latin America, Victor Bulmer-Thomas offers a means of comparing the growth of economies, absent sufficient data to calculate GDP figures. In his own assessment of Nicaragua, he places it within the slow-growth category based on export figures from 1851, 1870, and 1900,

years chosen because the data were easily available. A broader look at Nicaraguan exports between 1851 and 1900, however, shows phenomenal growth that would place it in the high-growth category. See Bulmer-Thomas, *Economic History of Latin America*, 131.

32. These figures were calculated based on data in table 4.

33. See, e.g., Squier, *Nicaragua*, 441, 649; Stout, *Nicaragua*, 89; Ortega Arancibia, *Cuarenta años*.

34. Romero Vargas, *Estructuras sociales*; MacLeod, *Spanish Central America*; Fernández Molina, "Colouring the World in Blue."

35. Burns, *Patriarch and Folk*, 133. See also Pérez Estrada, "Comunidades indígenas en Nicaragua."

36. See AMPG, caja 51, leg. 177, "El Ldo. Jimenes, como representante de la municipalidad de Jinotepe, solicita el señalamiento de ejidos," 1866.

37. Charlip, *Cultivating Coffee*, 40–44, 59–61; Pérez Estrada, "Breve historia."

38. Charlip, *Cultivating Coffee*, 64.

39. Mendoza, *Historia de Diriamba*, 28.

40. Squier, *Nicaragua*, 649.

41. Lévy, *Notas geográficas*, 441, cited in Charlip, *Cultivating Coffee*, 40.

42. R. G. Williams, *States and Social Evolution*, 74; Burns, *Patriarch and Folk*, 132.

43. Romero Vargas, *Estructuras sociales*, 92–93.

44. Charlip, "Cultivating Coffee," 118.

45. AMPG, caja 122, leg. 341, "Don José Antonio Argüello denuncia unas caballerías de tierra en jurisdicción de Masaya," 1876. On Masaya's Indian lands see Romero Vargas, *Estructuras sociales*, 101, 110. Clearly, the lands that the municipality of Masaya claimed did not represent all of the Indian community's lands. In 1914 the indigenous community of Masaya paid Dr. José León Sandino, a Granadino lawyer, for his services in defending the community's more than 15,000 manzanas of land by giving him 1,500 hectares of land, valued at 160 córdobas. See Archivo de Protocolos Notariales de Granada, Ignacio Moreira, folios 93–96, 1914. Special thanks to Michel Gobat for providing this information.

46. Dore, "Land Privatization," 307.

47. See Casanova Fuertes, "¿Héroes o bandidos?" 24.

48. On the cajas in Nicaragua see Romero Vargas, *Estructuras sociales*, 98–100.

49. These values are found in AGCA, A3(5).40, leg. 168, exp. 1176, which provide accounts of indigenous community treasures for the years 1790, 1795, 1801, 1803–6, 1808–10, 1812, and 1814–19.

50. AMPG, caja 160, leg. 451, "Notas de varios empleados," 1881. Although, as J. L. Gould, "*¡Vana Ilusión!,*" points out that harsh state-sponsored labor drafts to

complete the telegraph and rumors of forced labor in far-off coffee haciendas were at the root of the 1881 Matagalpa rebellion, the proximity of the prefect's circular to these events should be examined. The circular was sent by prefects to municipalities throughout Nicaragua in early March, just one month before the uprisings. A similar request was made regarding cofradía holdings and leadership.

51. On cofradías in nineteenth-century Nicaragua see Peña and Castillo, "Estado-iglesia y cofradías." For discussions of the eighteenth century see Romero Vargas, *Estructuras sociales*, 100–105.

52. Romero Vargas, *Estructuras sociales*, 101.

53. See, e.g., AMPG, caja 28, leg. 84, "Expediente relativo a la reunion de los yndígenas de Nindirí habida el 19 en la noche del mes de Octubre," 1861, and caja 36, leg. 117, "El alcalde indíjena de Jinotepe se queja del alcalde 2° de su vecindario," 1863.

54. See AMPG, caja 166, leg. 450, "Notas de varios alcaldes": [Aldon Borges] (Catarina) to Departmental Prefect (Granada), 17 October 1881; Francisco Gonzales (Diriamba[?]) to Departmental Prefect (Granada), 17 October 1881; J. Antonio Alvarado (La Victoria [Niquinohomo]) to Departmental Prefect (Granada), 27 October 1881. In the case of Nandaime, Procopio Aragon (Nandaime) to Departmental Prefect (Granada), 18 October 1881, explicitly denies the existence of cofradías within the community. Caja 158, leg. 441, "Censo agropecuaria de Jinotepe," 1880, lists the Cofradía de la Victoria (500 manzanas in area, with an estimated value of 6,000 pesos and 100 head of cattle) and the Cofradía de San Juan (300 manzanas in area and valued at 1,000 pesos, but without agricultural assets).

55. To trace the breakup of the cofradía, see RPPG-RC, 1883, no. 318; 1884, nos. 57, 135, 299, 315, 331, 462, 478; 1885, nos. 77, 380, 398; 1890, nos. 342, 359, 387, 388, 389, 441, 618, 619, 651, 652, 690. A copy of the original donation from the king of Spain can be found in RPPG-RC, 1890, no. 39.

56. See AMPG, caja 158, leg. 441, "Censo agropecuaria de La Victoria [Niquinohomo]," 1880. Although the arroba was a standard unit of measurement, equivalent to 25 pounds, the fanega and medio were volume measurements and weight varied from product to product. Charlip, *Cultivating Coffee*, 71, cites Gulden, *Vocabulario nicaragüense*, on the weight equivalent for a medio of corn (13 pounds) and beans (14 pounds). One fanega equals 24 medios.

57. On the leadership of the cofradía in Niquinohomo see AMPG, caja 166, leg. 450, "Notas de varias alcaldes," J. Antonio Alvarado (La Victoria [Niquinohomo]) to Departmental Prefect (Granada), 27 October 1881. The complaint against Muños is found in caja 124, leg. 346, "Guillermo Conto y otros ocurren de queja contra la municipalidad de La Victoria [Niquinohomo]," 1876. See also caja 190, leg. 494, Delgadillo (Managua) to Prefect (Granada), 23 May 1883, which refers to a complaint made by indigenous members of Diriamba complaining against ladino abuses of local cofradía lands and assets.

58. Watanabe, "Enduring Yet Ineffable Community," makes a similar argument for the survival of some Mayan communities despite their loss of "traditional" symbols of community identity like communal land and distinctive dress.

59. AMPG, caja 2, leg. 4, "Información instruida por el Sr. alcalde constitucional de Nindirí contra Encarnación Vicente de aquel vecindario," testimony of Rosario Garcias, 7 July 1857.

60. AMPG, caja 2, leg. 4, "Información instruida por el Sr. alcalde constitucional de Nindirí contra Encarnación Vicente de aquel vecindario," testimony of Cecilio Martínez, 7 July 1857.

61. AMPG, caja 2, leg. 4, "Información instruida por el Sr. alcalde constitucional de Nindirí contra Encarnación Vicente de aquel vecindario," Gabriel Membreño, Alcalde Constitutional (Nindirí), to Departmental Prefect (San Fernando [Masaya]), 9 July 1857.

62. AMPG, caja 2, leg. 4, "Información instruida por el Sr. alcalde constitucional de Nindirí contra Encarnación Vicente de aquel vecindario," Encarnación Vicente (Nindirí) to Departmental Prefect (Masaya), 14 July 1857.

63. AMPG, caja 2, leg. 4, "Información instruida por el Sr. alcalde constitucional de Nindirí contra Encarnación Vicente de aquel vecindario," decision of Santiago Vega, Departmental Prefect of Masaya, 15 July 1857.

64. While the circumstances were different, other cases frequently involved the same core issues. See, e.g., AMPG, caja 2, leg. 4, "Queja de Francisco Hernandez contra el policia de San Rafael," 1857, and caja 46, leg. 179, "Máximo Sauzo se queja de abuso de autoridad del alcalde de Diriomo," 1865.

65. See also Rojas, Tórrez, and Fernández, "Acceso a la tierra."

66. The entirety of this case is drawn from AMPG, caja 51, leg. 177, "Asuntos de egidos de San Marcos," German Marquez, Francisco García, Benancio García, Felipe Campos, Cando Sanches, Juan Feliz Mercado, and Sirilo Campos to the Corporación Municipal, 10 April 1866.

67. On this area's subsequent history see Charlip, "Cultivating Coffee," 211–21.

68. See, e.g., AMPG, caja 122, leg. 341, "Don José Antonio Argüello denuncia unas caballerías de tierra en jurisdicción de Masaya," 1876, and caja 247, unnumbered leg. (200 folios), "Sisto Obando y Francisca Menocal Barbarena piden la destrucción de una cerca en el que se encuentra en el punto llamada 'El Charco,'" 1890.

69. AMPG, caja 51, leg. 177, "El Ldo. Jimenes, como representante de la municipalidad de Jinotepe, solicita el señalamiento de ejidos," 1866.

70. AMPG, caja 51, leg. 177, "El Ldo. Jimenes, como representante de la municipalidad de Jinotepe, solicita el señalamiento de ejidos," petition of Luciano Gonzales (alcalde indígena), Indalecio Lopez, Juan Chamorro, Timoteo Vivas, Ylario Guevara (all regidores), and seventy-nine *reformados* to the municipality of Jinotepe, 1 September 1866.

71. Dore, "Land Privatization," 308.

72. AMPG, caja 51, leg. 177, "El Ldo. Jimenes, como representante de la municipalidad de Jinotepe, solicita el señalamiento de ejidos," Francisco Jimenes (Jinotepe) to Departmental Prefect (Granada), 6 September 1866.

73. Charlip, "Cultivating Coffee," 139–40.

74. The original request for ejidal measurement and the subsequent mapping are found in AMPG, caja 51, leg. 177, "Esposición documentada relativo a los ejidos del pueblo de La Paz," 1867, and caja 107, leg. 318, "Mapa de los ejidos de La Paz," 1874. The 1889 solicitation is found in caja 241, unnumbered leg. (126 folios), "Los vecinos de La Paz, departamento de Granada, solicitan ejidos," 1889. For La Paz's additional ejidos in 1881 and its success with its 1889 request, see Charlip, "Cultivating Coffee," 139. For a similar example in Nandaime, see AMPG, caja 252, unnumbered leg. (108 folios), "Solicitud hecha por los vecinos de la villa de Nandaime," 1890.

75. See RPPG-RC, 1883, no. 716 (Diriomo); 1884, no. 111 (Niquinohomo); 1888, no. 123 (El Rosario); 1888, no. 124 (Jinotepe). For references to the land donations in San Marcos, Diriamba, Santa Teresa, and the 1892 and 1900 donations to Jinotepe, see Charlip, "Cultivating Coffee," 139–40. See also, for Diriamba, AMPG, caja 107, leg. 318, "Mapa de los ejidos de labranza del pueblo de Diriamba. Contiene nueve caballerías y tres cuartos de otra," 1874.

76. These figures are calculated from table 5. The public land registry contains no records of ejidal transactions for Masaya for 1888 to 1897, but this could also indicate that these records are to be found in Masaya's land registry rather than in Granada's.

77. Charlip, "Cultivating Coffee," 127–28.

78. AMPG, caja 124, leg. 346, "Guillermo Conto y otros occurren de queja contra la municipalidad de la Victoria [Niquinohomo]," Guillermo Conto, Agapito Campos, Segundo Canelo, Pedro Hernandes, Cesilio Baltodano and Beltran Muños (Granada) to Departmental Prefect (Granada), 4 March 1876.

79. AMPG, caja 124, leg. 346, "Guillermo Conto y otros occurren de queja contra la municipalidad de la Victoria [Niquinohomo]," Guillermo Conto to Departmental Prefect (Granada), 4 March 1876.

80. AMPG, caja 124, leg. 346, "Guillermo Conto y otros occurren de queja contra la municipalidad de la Victoria [Niquinohomo]," Junta Municipal (La Victoria) to Departmental Prefect (Granada), 18 March 1876.

81. AMPG, caja 124, leg. 346, "Guillermo Conto y otros occurren de queja contra la municipalidad de la Victoria [Niquinohomo]," Departmental Prefect (Granada), 29 March 1876.

82. See note 56 above.

83. AMPG, caja 158, leg. 441, "Censo agropecuaria de La Victoria [Niquinohomo]," 1880.

84. The conflict between Aguirre and Borge is recounted and analyzed in greater detail in Dore, "Land Privatization," 313–15.

85. These figures are calculated from RPPG-RC, 1877–97. For detailed breakdowns see Wolfe, "Rising from the Ashes," 170–71.

86. AMPG, caja 159, leg. 431, "Juan Lopez queja contra el alcalde de Diriomo," 1880.

87. AMPG, caja 118, leg. 339 bis, "Don Nilo Ortega se queja contra el gobernador de policia de este districto," 1875.

88. Dore, "Land Privatization," 311.

89. Archivo Municipal de Diriomo, Libro de Actas Municipales, 13 October 1875, cited in Dore, "Land Privatization," 311.

90. See, however, the following important counterexamples: AMPG, caja 156, leg. 438, "Asunto entre la municipalidad y el cura de Masatepe," 1880; caja 159, leg. 431, "Varios vecinos del pueblo de Catarina se quejan de la municipalidad de dicho pueblo," 1880; caja 175, leg. 478, "Queja de la municipalidad de la Victoria [Niquinohomo] contra la municipalidad de Masatepe por haber hecho donaciones de terrenos," 1882.

91. Dore, *Myths of Modernity*.

92. Charlip, *Cultivating Coffee*, 9.

93. Charlip, *Cultivating Coffee*, 219.

94. For a fuller discussion of regional land tenure and a more detailed statistical analysis, see Wolfe, "Rising from the Ashes," ch. 3.

95. Charlip, *Cultivating Coffee*, 9.

96. Edelman and Seligson, "Land Inequality," 453–54.

97. Dore, "Land Privatization."

98. In this case, "farmers" include agricultores, hacendados, and labradores. The summary values for the prefecture of Granada are calculated from Nicaragua, Ministerio de Gobernación, *Memoria* (1885).

99. Calcualted from RPPG-RC, 1877–97. For detailed breakdowns see Wolfe, "Rising from the Ashes," 177–78.

100. Elizabeth Dore's pathbreaking work on gender and class during Nicaragua's coffee boom makes it clear how limited our understanding of community change in Nicaragua has been. On this complexity and as a call to further research, see, e.g., Dore, "Property, Households, and Public Regulation" and "Patriarchy from Above."

101. Charlip, *Cultivating Coffee*, 183.

102. RPPG-RC, 1889, no. 74.

103. RPPG-RC, 1883, no. 303; 1884, no. 371; 1885, no. 277; 1887, no. 579; 1889, nos. 376 and 494.

104. RPPG-LH, 1883, no. 40; 1884, no. 54.

105. For a discussion of a similar process in Diriomo at the same time, see Dore, "Land Privatization."

106. Geertz, "Integrative Revolution," 276.

107. Nicaragua, Ministerio de Fomento y Obras Públicas, *Memoria* (1867), 3–4, my emphasis.

4. The Work of Their Hands

1. Liberato Dubón, *Gaceta de Nicaragua* (Managua), 5 March 1864.

2. Romero Vargas, *Estructuras sociales*, 158; MacLeod, *Spanish Central America*, 204–31, 288–309; Burns, *Patriarch and Folk*, 8–9, 31.

3. Lanuza, "Nicaragua, territorio y población," 9–11.

4. Guerrero C. and Soriano, *Carazo (monografía)*, 68–71, 80–81, 85–87; Romero Vargas, *Estructuras sociales*, 187.

5. Lanuza, "Nicaragua, territorio y población," 7.

6. AMPG, caja 21, leg. 65, circular from Zepeda (Managua) to Prefects, 24 October 1860.

7. Calculations are based on data from RPPG-RC, 1878–97, and from agricultural censuses found in AMPG, caja 158, leg. 441.

8. Lévy, *Notas geográficas*, 446. American diplomat E. George Squier made a similar observation a decade earlier (*Nicaragua*).

9. See Elizondo, "Infraestructura de Nicaragua en 1860," 55–56; and Nicaragua, Ministerio de Gobernación, *Memoria* (1860), 5, for Jerónimo Pérez's words.

10. See Romero Vargas, *Estructuras sociales*, 129–68; Newson, *Indian Survival*, 277–78. See also the compelling examination of the relationship between power (and class) inequalities and the changing meanings of ethnicity in Comaroff, "Of Totemism and Ethnicity."

11. Hobsbawm, *Primitive Rebels*.

12. Central to the historiography of the Zelaya regime and to claims of its novelty are Teplitz, "Political and Economic Foundations"; Wheelock Román, *Imperialismo y dictadura*; Barahona, *Estudio sobre la historia de Nicaragua*; Vargas, *La revolución que inició el progreso*; Stansifer, "José Santos Zelaya," 469, 474, 476. More recent works have repeated these assertions: Paige, *Coffee and Power*; R. G. Williams, *States and Social Evolution*; Mahoney, *The Legacies of Liberalism*.

13. Nicaragua, *Colección de leyes y acuerdos* (1859), 79–87.

14. *Ley de agricultura*, 18 February 1862, printed in *Boletín Oficial* (Managua), 22 February 1862.

15. Nicaragua, *Decretos y leyes de 1869–1870*, 68–71.

16. Nicaragua, *Decretos y leyes de 1867–1868*, 45–49.

17. Nicaragua, *Ley sobre persecución de operarios prófugos*, article 1. A copy of the law is located in AMPG, caja 184, leg. x3. Two years earlier the legislature had passed a new agricultural law, but it did not substantially modify its predecessors. See Nicaragua, *Decretos y leyes de 1881–1882*, 47–59.

18. Nicaragua, *Ley sobre persecución de operarios prófugos*, article 5.

19. AMPG, caja 201, leg. 18, no. 408, Ministro de Hacienda, José Chamorro (Managua), to Departmental Prefect (Granada), 29 December 1884. Personal rivalries and disputes were not unknown (see, e.g., caja 167, leg. 456, "Acusación contra el juez de agricultura del Diriá," 1881), of course, just relatively rare.

20. Nicaragua, *Decretos y leyes de 1881–1882*, 47–59; Nicaragua, *Decretos y leyes de 1885–1886*, 102–4.

21. R. G. Williams, *States and Social Evolution*, 197. See also Barahona, *Estudio sobre la historia de Nicaragua*, 13–32; Vargas, *La revolución que inició el progreso*; Velázquez, *La formación del estado*. Although these authors tend to agree on the substance of the changes during the Zelaya period, there is little coincidence in the meanings they assign to them.

22. Teplitz, "Political and Economic Foundations," 200.

23. See chapter 2 for a discussion of the trends in Nicaraguan trade.

24. An excellent synthesis of the emerging challenges to this historiography is Gudmundson and Lindo-Fuentes, *Central America, 1821–1871*.

25. Teplitz, "Political and Economic Foundations," 195–98; R. G. Williams, *States and Social Evolution*, 137–38.

26. Both characterizations are from Nicaragua, Ministerio de Fomento, *Memoria del Ministerio de Fomento, 1888–1890* (Managua: Imprenta Nacional, 1891), cited in Teplitz, "Political and Economic Foundations," 182, 184.

27. J. L. Gould, *To Die in This Way*, 41–42.

28. Fernando Guzmán, "Manifiesto de S. E. el Presidente D. Fernando Guzmán a los pueblos de la república," *Gaceta de Nicaragua* (Managua), 9 March 1867, reprinted in Pérez, *Obras*, 791–92. Guzmán's discourse mirrors much of the "natural rights" doctrine prevalent in nineteenth-century Central America. See M. Rodríguez, *Cádiz Experiment*, 53–74.

29. *Ley de agricultura*, 18 February 1862. The remaining articles are more or less divided between those that pertain to the qualities, duties, and limitations of the juez de agricultura and those concerning laborers.

30. *Ley de agricultura*, 18 February 1862, articles 25–26.

31. Decreto no. 47, 18 April 1859, article 39, in Nicaragua, *Decretos y leyes, 1859*, 79–89.

32. AMPG, caja 82, leg. 260, "Urbano Tifer acusa al juez de agricultura de Diriomo," 1871.

33. See, e.g., AMPG, caja 21, leg. 64, "El Señor Sebastian Ramírez, vecino de Santa Teresa, se queja de los hechos que convertió el señor gobernador de policia de este distrito," 1860; caja 37, leg. 119, "Denuncia de Don Rafael Bermudez contra el Gobernador de Policia Don Guadalupe Montiel," 1873; caja 119, leg. 332, "Carpeta de varios escritos sobre queja," 1875; caja 240, unnumbered leg. (128 folios), "Diligencias seguidas en averiguación de varios hechos que se atribuyen al Comandante del Presidio Don Celedonio Borge," 1889. McCreery notes the same raft of problems among Guatemalan landowners. See McCreery, *Rural Guatemala*, 219–20, 223–32.

34. AMPG, caja 87, leg. 272, "Información de testigos instruida para averiguar la certeza de la fallas que Don Marcos Urbina denuncia en un impreso contra el agente general de agricultura del distrito Don Inocente Fletes," 1872. The leaflet, titled "Al publico," was printed by the Imprenta de José de J. Cuadra. Given that Cuadra's brother, Vicente, was then president of Nicaragua, the charges were thoroughly investigated. See also Libro 19, Departmental Prefect (Granada) to Inocente Fletes (Granada), 18 July 1872.

35. Burns, *Patriarch and Folk*, 138.

36. AMPG, caja 229, unnumbered leg. (171 folios), "Don Pedro José Chamorro se queja del Agente de Policia Rural Francisco Mora Castillo," 1888; United Kingdom, Parliament, "Report for the Year 1897 on the Trade of Nicaragua," C. 8648-158 (1898), Parliamentary Papers, microfiche, vol. 6, Nicaragua, fiche 5; H. H. Leavitt to Secretary of State, no. 20, "Report on the Political Situation of Nicaragua," 18 March 1885, in *Despatches from U.S. Consuls in Managua, 1884–1906*, microfilm T-634, National Archives, Washington DC.

37. R. G. Williams, *States and Social Evolution*, 135.

38. J. L. Gould, *To Die in This Way*, 50.

39. The latter figure is corroborated in Le Baron, "Nicaragua," 351, which states that "agricultural laborers are paid from $12 to $14 per month, in Nicaraguan money, and board." This rise in wages is nearly as rapid as that found in mid-nineteenth-century Costa Rica. See Cardoso, "Historia económica," 25, table 2.

40. Charlip, *Cultivating Coffee*, 147.

41. This diet calculated based on figures from Palacios, *Coffee in Colombia*, 103.

42. R. G. Williams, *States and Social Evolution*, 265–74, table A-1. The price set for coffee used in Lindo-Fuentes, *Weak Foundations*, 112–13, table 19, suggests significantly less pronounced price disparities for this same time period, but the trends remain the same.

43. AMPG, caja 119, leg. 332, "Bartolomé Lara Rodriguez se queja del ajente de agricultura de Nandaime," 1875.

44. AMPG, caja 2, leg. 3, Pio Echaverri, Alcalde Constitucional (Masatepe), to Departmental Prefect (Granada), 12 February 1857.

45. See, e.g., AMPG, caja 21, leg. 65, Rosalío Cortés, Ministro de Gobernación (Managua), to Departmental Prefect (Granada), 25 April 1860; caja 29, leg. 85, Jerónimo Pérez, Ministro de Gobernación (Managua), to Departmental Prefect (Granada), 17 September 1861.

46. AMPG, caja 98, leg. 287, "Queja del agente general de agricultura Don Ygnosente Fletes contra el juez de agricultura de Granada." This was not Fletes's first conflict with the jueces de agricultura of Granada. See AMPG, caja 87, leg. 272, "Información de testigos instruidas para averiguar la certeza de las fallas que Don Marcos Urbina denuncia en un impreso contra el agente general de agricultura del districto Don Inocente Fletes," 1872.

47. For an exception, see the discussion in chapter 1 of how the state's inability to exert control over local officials led to the failure of its efforts to eradicate contraband aguardiente.

48. Calculated from figures cited in Teplitz, "Political and Economic Foundations," 199–200.

49. AMPG, caja 129, leg. 371, "Narciso Arévalo contra el juez de agricultura de la Victoria [Niquinohomo]," 1882. Compare this with caja 167, leg. 456, "Acusación contra el juez de agricultura del Diriá," 1881.

50. AMPG, caja 129, leg. 371, "Narciso Arévalo contra el juez de agricultura de la Victoria [Niquinohomo]," Rumualdo Espinoza and Agustín Vega (Niquinohomo) to Nicolas Borges, Municipal Secretary (Niquinohomo), 6 November 1882.

51. AMPG, caja 129, leg. 371, "Narciso Arévalo contra el juez de agricultura de la Victoria [Niquinohomo]," Narciso Arévalo (Niquinohomo) to Nicolas Borges, Municipal Secretary (Niquinohomo), 6 November 1882.

52. McCreery, *Rural Guatemala*, 284.

53. Teplitz, "Political and Economic Foundations," 198–200.

54. *Ley de agricultura*, 18 February 1862.

55. Charlip, *Cultivating Coffee*, 147.

56. On the mandamiento system in Guatemala see McCreery, "Debt Servitude in Rural Guatemala"; McCreery, "An Odious Feudalism"; McCreery, *Rural Guatemala*, 220–23, 266–68.

57. Dore, "Debt Peonage in Granada," 554.

58. AMPG, caja 63, leg. 212, "Señor juez de agricultura de Masatepe," 1868.

59. In an 1880 petition, Masatepe's indigenous community complained that only Indians were forced into military service. Although the ladino alcalde denied this charge, it was later confirmed. See AMPG, caja 156, leg. 435, "Asunto entre la municipalidad y el cura de Masatepe," 1880.

60. AMPG, caja 63, leg. 212, "Señor juez de agricultura de Masatepe," Pedro Calero, Alcalde Indígena (Masatepe), to Juez de Agricultura (Masatepe), 5 May 1868.

61. Charlip, *Cultivating Coffee*, 196–97.

62. AMPG, caja 63, leg. 212, "Señor juez de agricultura de Masatepe," petition of Francisco Noguera (Granada) to the Departmental Prefect (Granada), 10 July 1868.

63. AMPG, caja 126, leg. 358, "El alcalde indígena de Masatepe se queja del juez de agricultura de aquella villa," Cornelio Lopez to President of Nicaragua, 10 October 1871.

64. AMPG, caja 63, leg. 212, "El alcalde indígena se queja del juez de agricultura de aquella villa," Rafael Zurita (Managua) to Departmental Prefect (Granada), 11 October 1871.

65. On the importance of the military and military service to the nation-state, see two very different but congruent theoretical views in Tilly, *Coercion, Capital, and European States*, 28–33, and Anderson, *Imagined Communities*, 144.

66. Evidence from the 1880 agricultural census suggests that holdings of five manzanas could produce more than ten times the amount required by 1853 decree. See, e.g., AMPG, caja 158, leg. 41, "Censo agropecuaria de Nandaime," 1880.

67. Teplitz, "Political and Economic Foundations," 203.

68. On municipal and indigenous community cooperation, see, e.g., AMPG, caja 51, leg. 177, "Asuntos de egidos de S^n Marcos," 1866; caja 51, leg. 177, "El Ldo. Jimenes, como representante de la municipalidad de Jinotepe, solicita el señalam^{to} de ejidos," 1866; caja 118, leg. 339 bis, "Don Nilo Ortega se queja contra el gobernador de policia de este districto," 1875. Cooperation, however, frequently disintegrated into conflict: caja 119, leg. 332, "Queja de Juan Zuniga contral el juez de agricultura de San Marcos," 1875; caja 156, leg. 435, "Asunto entre la municipalidad y el cura de Masatepe," 1880. See also Dore, "Land Privatization," 311.

69. AMPG, caja 179, leg. 477, "Solicitud que hace el Señor Nieves Ramírez de Diriomo," 1882, my emphasis. See J. L. Gould, *To Die in This Way*, 48–50.

70. These figures, based on men age fifteen and above, are calculated from AMPG, caja 191, leg. x7, "Censo de Diriomo," 1883. In the nearby towns of San Marcos and Diriamba, where coffee production had grown more aggressively, Indians were even more likely to be listed as laborers. By contrast, in the subsistence-oriented town of Santa Catarina nearly 70 percent of Indians were farmers, and Indians outnumbered ladinos in every occupation.

71. For more on Indian-ladino labor relations in Diriomo see Dore, "Patriarchy from Above," 554–55.

72. For an interesting contrast see AMPG, caja 159, leg. 431, "Juan Lopez queja contra el alcalde de Diriomo," 1880. Ramírez and Lopez mirror each other in many ways, struggling between past and future. But where Ramírez has left the indigenous community, Lopez remains, defending it against state and municipal intervention.

73. J. L. Gould, *To Die in This Way*, 86.

74. See Romero Vargas et al., *Persistencia indígena en Nicaragua*; Téllez Argüello, *Muera la gobierna*; J. L. Gould, *To Die in This Way*.

75. See Grandin, *Blood of Guatemala*, for an important and contrasting trajectory of indigenous history.

76. "El artesano," *El País* (Managua), 13 June 1888.

5. Customs of the Nicaraguan Family

1. Lévy, "Notes ethnologiques." Lévy's fascination stemmed from his efforts to prove racist "scientific" theories on the relationship between "half-breed races" (*races métisses*) and society. Regarding such theories and their history see S. J. Gould, *The Mismeasure of Man*. For their relationship to Latin America see Mörner, *Race Mixture*, 139–42; Nancy Stepan, *The Hour of Eugenics*; Lomnitz-Adler, *Exits from the Labyrinth*, 274–77.

2. Lévy, *Notas geográficas*, 241.

3. Romero Vargas, *Estructuras sociales*, 287–360. See also AGCA, A1.1, leg. 21, exp. 599, 1801; A1.1(5), leg. 76, exp. 613, 1808; B2.7, leg. 36, exp. 817, 1817.

4. De la Rocha, *Revista política*, 49.

5. Fruto Chamorro, "Mensaje de S. E. el general director supremo Don Fruto Chamorro a la Asamblea Constituyente del Estado de Nicaragua, instalada el 24 de enero del año de 1854," reprinted in Alvarez Lejarza, *Las constituciones de Nicaragua*, 109.

6. Naylor, *Penny Ante Imperialism*, 148–76.

7. Sebastián Salinas (León) to Frederick Chatfield, September 1847, quoted in Tompson, "Frontiers of Identity," 179.

8. "Convenio celebrado entre el Comisionado del Estado Soberano de Nicaragua y el jefe principal de la Costa de Mosquitos en 1847"; Sebastián Salinas (León) to Princess Agnes Anne Frederick (Cabo Gracias a Dios), 8 December 1847, both reprinted in Nicaragua, Ministerio de Relaciones Exteriores, *Memoria* (1920), 1:397, 401. Emphasis in the original. Tompson, "Frontiers of Identity," 191–95, provides a more detailed exploration of this treaty and its place in Nicaraguan-Miskitu relations.

9. Pablo Buitrago (León) to Frederick Chatfield, 24 October 1849, quoted in Kinloch Tijerino, *Nicaragua*, 187. The question of Miskitu kingship has been a source of debate, and until recently scholars have tended to follow Nicaraguan nationalists in viewing it as a British invention to manage coast politics. Recent rebuttals include Dennis and Olien, "Kingship among the Miskito," and Offen, "The Sambo and Tawira Miskitu"; cf. Helms, "Of Kings and Contexts."

10. Gámez, *Historia de Nicaragua*, 361.

11. Kinloch Tijerino, *Nicaragua*, 185.

12. Sebastián Salinas (León) to Frederick Chatfield, September 1847, quoted in Tompson, "Frontiers of Identity," 179.

13. Naylor, *Penny Ante Imperialism*, 89, 136–37.

14. J. L. Gould, *To Die in This Way*.

15. For nineteenth-century Nicaragua see, e.g., Dore, "Debt Peonage in Granada"; and J. L. Gould, *To Die in This Way*. More broadly this trend is evident in Urban and Sherzer, *Nation-States and Indians in Latin America*; and C. A. Smith, *Guatemalan Indians*.

16. Anderson, *Imagined Communities*, 166.

17. On the importance of both discursive and quantitative analysis of census data see Nobles, *Shades of Citizenship*; Hirschman, "Meaning and Measurement of Ethnicity"; J. W. Scott, "A Statistical Representation of Work."

18. The 1846 and 1867 censuses were considered notoriously flawed in their own times. See, e.g., Squier, *States of Central America*, 348; and B., "Estadística," *El Porvenir de Nicaragua* (Valle Gottel), 18 January 1874.

19. Niederlein, *State of Nicaragua*, 45. J. L. Gould, *To Die in This Way*, 17, examined late-nineteenth-century birth registries in the central Nicaraguan town of Boaco and found they separated Indians and non-Indians.

20. According to Newson, *Indian Survival*, 318, the expense of purchasing indulgences meant that those who were too poor to afford them, especially Indians, were not counted, and thus this listing underrepresents the indigenous population. See also Romero Vargas, *Estructuras sociales*, 45–46. Nonetheless, both authors note that these are the most complete figures available for this period.

21. AGCA, A3.29, leg. 1749, exp. 28130, "Extracto del número de personas . . . capaces de tomar bulas de Santa Cruzada," 1778. In the rest of Central America, most of the census takers lumped all non-Indians together as ladinos. Exceptions included Petén, a frontier region in Guatemala, and the island fort of Omoa, which had large slave and free black populations. In a survey of more than three hundred local censual enumerations in Guatemala from 1750 to 1820, Little-Siebold ("Where Have All the Spaniards Gone," 114) shows clearly that at the local level, racial categorization was both more diverse and less uniform.

22. See Romero Vargas, *Estructuras sociales*, 470–73. By comparison, Seed, "Social Dimensions," 572–73, argues that the "zambo" category "never gained widespread currency in colonial Mexico and [was] seldom used by the end of the sixteenth century."

23. Squier, "Nicaragua," 757.

24. AMPG, caja 184, leg. x5, M. Bravo (Managua) to Jefe Departamental de Estadística, Granada, "Circular no. 4," 18 May 1883.

25. See AMPG, caja 184, leg. x5, "Estadísticas"; caja 188, unnumbered leg. (100 folios); caja 191, leg. x7; and caja 192, unnumbered leg. (192 folios). These account for nine towns and more than eleven thousand people.

26. Lévy, *Notas geográficas*.

27. Romero Vargas, *Estructuras sociales*; Lanuza, "Nicaragua, territorio y población."

28. AMPG, caja 184, leg. x5, M. Bravo (Managua) to Jefe Departamental de Estadística, Granada, "Circular no. 4," 18 May 1883.

29. Niederlein, *State of Nicaragua*, 85.

30. According to the 1920 census, Nicaraguans were distributed as 16.8 percent white, 69.0 percent trigueño, 4.6 percent cobrizo, 9.5 percent black, and 0.1 percent yellow. See Nicaragua, Dirección General de Estadística, *Censo general de 1920*, 11.

31. In the southern Pacific department of Rivas, 141 cobrizos accounted for less than one-half of 1 percent of the area's 31,090 people.

32. New "white" populations appeared in all of these communities in 1920, apparently carved out of the mostly mixed populations.

33. J. L. Gould, *To Die in This Way*, 17, also notes that in late-nineteenth-century birth registries in the central department of Boaco, some indigenous peoples were noted as being "color trigueño."

34. See Roger N. Lancaster, "Skin Color, Race, and Racism"; J. L. Gould, "*¡Vana Ilusión!*"; Téllez Argüello, *Muera la gobierna*

35. Adams, *Cultural Surveys*, 232.

36. Adams, *Cultural Surveys*, 197.

37. On the colonial history of the Atlantic coast region see Romero Vargas, *Sociedades del Atlántico*; Troy, *Anglo-Spanish Struggle for Mosquitia*; Dozier, *Nicaragua's Mosquito Coast*; Naylor, *Penny Ante Imperialism*; Offen, "The Miskitu Kingdom."

38. The text of the Treaty of Managua, signed on 28 January 1860, is reprinted in Wünderich, von Oertzen, and Rossbach, *The Nicaraguan Mosquitia*, 315–17.

39. Offen, "Geographical Imagination," 64–65.

40. Offen, "Geographical Imagination," 58.

41. Gordon, *Disparate Diasporas*, 57–60.

42. Gámez, *Historia de Nicaragua*, 369.

43. Gámez, *Historia de Nicaragua*, 168–69.

44. Offen, "Geographical Imagination," 58.

45. "La Mosquitia," *El Cronista* (Granada), 22 July 1894.

46. Quoted in Hale, *Resistance and Contradiction*, 37. On anti-black discourse see Gordon, *Disparate Diasporas*, 59.

47. "Problema Nacional," *El Cronista* (Granada), 2 August 1894. On this rebellion see Hale, *Resistance and Contradiction*, 42–43.

48. Alemán Bolaños, *El pueblo de Nicaragua*, 51. This discourse's most famous proponent was the revolutionary Augusto Sandino. On Sandino's use of the term and Nicaraguan *mestizaje*, see J. L. Gould, *To Die in This Way*, 155–61.

49. Alemán Bolaños, *El pueblo de Nicaragua*, 53.

50. Ruiz y Ruiz, *Costa Atlántica de Nicaragua*, 115.

51. Cuadra Pasos, *Obras*, 2:666–69.

52. Adams, *Cultural Surveys*, 229.

53. Adams, *Cultural Surveys*, 229. In a footnote to this discussion (n. 23), Adams related that Doris Stone indicated her belief "that this negroid component derives from the slaves formerly used on large *haciendas*." Evidence from the colonial period certainly points to Stone's hypothesis. See, e.g., AGCA, AI(5), leg. 21, exp. 145, 1726. See also Romero Vargas, "Presencia africana."

54. Helms, "The Society and Its Environment," 72.

55. Cuadra, "Los hijos de Septiembre," in *El nicaragüense*, 17.

56. On these terms see, e.g., Taracena Arriola, "El vocabulo 'Ladino' en Guatemala"; Knight, "Racism, Revolution, and *Indigenismo*," esp. 74–78.

57. Fernández Figueroa, *Historia*, 18.

58. Forbes, *Africans and Native Americnas*, 182.

59. J. L. Gould, *To Die in This Way*, 136; Wade, *Race and Ethnicity*, 28.

60. Gilroy, *"There Ain't No Black in the Union Jack,"* 38.

61. See Mörner, *Race Mixture*.

62. For these trends in colonial Guatemala and Mexico, respectively, see Lutz, *Santiago de Guatemala*; and Cope, *Limits of Racial Domination*.

63. Katzew, "Casta Painting"; Seed, "Social Dimensions," 572–73; see also Cahill, "Colour by Numbers."

64. See, e.g., J. L. Gould, *To Die in This Way*; Grandin, *Blood of Guatemala*; Thurner, *From Two Republics to One Divided*; Wade, *Blackness and Race Mixture*.

65. Kinloch Tijerino, *Nicaragua*, 41.

66. By contrast, see J. L. Gould, *To Die in This Way*, on Indian communal lands in Matagalpa, Chinandega, Jinotega, Nueva Segovia, and Chontales.

67. Barth, introduction; see also Adams, "Strategies of Ethnic Survival," 200.

68. Comaroff, "Of Totemism and Ethnicity," 63.

69. Newson, *Indian Survival*, 330; J. L. Gould, *To Die in This Way*; Romero Vargas et al., *Persistencia indígena en Nicaragua*. See also AGCA, A3(5).40, leg. 168, exp. 1176, for disparities in indigenous community wealth.

70. See Alvarez Lejarza, *Ensayo histórico*, 231; Buitrago, "El municipio en Nicaragua."

71. For Matagalpa see J. L. Gould, *"¡Vana Ilusión!"* 397–400. Compare Masatepe's history in AMPG, caja 28, leg. 84, "Los yndígenas del barrio de Jalata en Masatepe

solicitan que se los preservan sus usos y costumbres ignocentes, en conforme á las leyes," 1861, and caja 156, leg. 435, "Asunto entre la municipalidad y el cura de Masatepe," 1880.

72. Newson, *Indian Survival*, 131, 300. In 1740 only twenty-seven towns in all of Nicaragua had entirely Indian populations; by 1776 just sixteen of these remained so (Romero Vargas, *Estructuras sociales*, 298).

73. Nicaragua, Constitution of 1858, articles 75 and 76, reprinted in Esgueva Gómez, *Constituciones políticas*, 1:346.

74. AMPG, caja 28, leg. 84, "Los yndígenas del barrio de Jalata en Masatepe solicitan que se los preservan sus usos y costumbres ignocentes, en conforme á las leyes," Celedón Ampie (Masatepe) to Prefect (Granada), 1 January 1861.

75. AMPG, caja 28, leg. 84, "Los yndígenas del barrio de Jalata en Masatepe solicitan que se los preservan sus usos y costumbres ignocentes, en conforme á las leyes," Juan Gutiérrez (Masatepe), Juzgado 1o Constitucional, 22 January 1861.

76. See, e.g., Charlip, *Cultivating Coffee*, 195–97; Dore, "Land Privatization," 306–7.

77. AMPG, caja 29, leg. 85 (282ff), Miguel Cárdenas (Managua) to Prefect (Granada), 20 February 1861; caja 28, leg. 84, "Los yndígenas del barrio de Jalata en Masatepe solicitan que se los preservan sus usos y costumbres ignocentes, en conforme á las leyes," 1861.

78. AMPG, caja 38, leg. 116, "Solicitud de Indalecio Quesada sobre que se declare que la elección de alcaldes naturales por costumbre sea preferible á la de los jefes de canton," 1863.

79. All of Nicaragua's constitutions from 1838 to 1893 have provided both rights and responsibility of citizenship. Thus, for example, along with the right to vote came the responsibility to hold office if elected. See Alvarez Lejarza, *Ensayo histórico*, 145–47, 171–72, 198–99, 218, 238. The belief that being Nicaraguan did not necessarily entitle one to the exercise of political rights formed a foundational block of the elite's state ideology that was still being propagated as late as the 1920s. See, e.g., the children's textbook of Liberal José María Moncada, *El ideal ciudadano*.

80. Comaroff and Comaroff, "Ethnography," 4–5, 32.

81. State vigilance over municipal taxation, public works requirements, and similar obligations served as similar mechanisms. Ostensibly to promote liberal reform, but also in recognition of the role that Liberal party victories in municipal elections played in fracturing Conservative unity, the Zelaya regime's 1893 Constitution loosened the state's grip on municipalities. Zelaya's desire to tighten his grip on power, however, led to the constitutional reforms of 1896, which reinstated state intervention in municipal power. See Alvarez Lejarza, *Ensayo histórico*, 253–54, 62.

82. Geertz, "Integrative Revolution," 277; cf. Chatterjee, *The Nation and Its Fragments*, 220–39.

83. AMPG, caja 184, leg. x6, "Protesta de la elección del alcalde indio de la villa de Masatepe," Eduardo Córdoba (Masatepe) to Ascención Rivas (Granada), 24 December 1883.

84. See, e.g., AMPG, caja 36, leg. 117, "El alcalde indíjena de Jinotepe se queja del alcalde 2° de su vecindario," 1863; caja 28, leg. 84, "Los yndígenas del barrio de Jalata en Masatepe solitican que se los preservan sus usos y costumbres ignocentes, en conforme a las leyes," 1861; caja 52, leg. 138, "Diligencias sobre lo ocurrido entre el cura y la municipalidad de Diriomo," 1866.

85. For a broader discussion of this issue in Latin America see Stutzman, "*El Mestizaje*"; Wade, *Blackness and Race Mixture*, 3–28. See also Paul Gilroy's fascinating analysis of the complex relationship of race, nation, racism, and Enlightenment reason, *The Black Atlantic*, esp. chs. 1–2.

86. Comaroff, "Of Totemism and Ethnicity," 62–63. J. L. Gould, *To Die in This Way*, 75–76, notes how mestizos dismissed the "authenticity" of Boaqueño Indians who were literate and urban-dwelling.

87. "Ladino" is frequently noted by its discursive absence, just as whiteness is in the United States. See Frankenberg, *White Women, Race Matters*; Roediger, *The Wages of Whiteness*.

88. *Gaceta de Nicaragua* (Managua), 22 September 1866.

89. Comaroff, "Of Totemism and Ethnicity," 52–53.

90. "Discurso pronunciado por el ex-Ministro de Relaciones exteriores y diputado al Congreso de la Republica, Dr. Don Rosalío Cortez, en la inauguracion de la media Universidad de San Fernando," *Gaceta de Nicaragua*, 13 July 1867.

91. The discussion of this case is drawn from AMPG, caja 28, leg. 84, "Expediente relativo a la reunión de los yndígenas de Nindirí habida el 19 en la noche del mes de Octubre," 1861.

92. Dore, "Land Privatization," 311–12.

93. Burns, *Patriarch and Folk*, 145–59; Casanova Fuertes, "¿Héroes o bandidos?"; Coronel Urtecho, "Introducción," 42–44, 47–48; Wheelock Román, *Raíces indígenas*, 94–97.

94. Besides their opposing political views, Ayón (1821–87) and Gámez (1851–1918) differ in generational experience; Ayón had lived through the horrors of the National War, while Gámez was only five or six years old during wartime.

95. J. L. Gould, "*¡Vana Ilusión!*"; Téllez Argüello, *Muera la gobierna*.

96. Gámez, *Historia de Nicaragua*, 351, my emphasis.

97. For nearly identical claims, see AMPG, caja 184, leg. x6, "Ynformación de testigos practicada a favór de Felipe Hernández sobre elección de alc^de yndígena," 1883, and "Protesta de la elección del alc. indio de la villa de Masatepe," 1883.

98. J. L. Gould, *To Die in This Way*, 47–56.

99. Ayón, *Historia de Nicaragua*, 1:prologue.

100. Ayón, *Historia de Nicaragua*, 2:239–56.

101. See, e.g., AGCA, A1.15(5), leg. 97, exp. 746, 1730.

102. Ayón, *Historia de Nicaragua*, 2:244.

103. Ayón, *Historia de Nicaragua*, 2:248.

104. Ayón, *Historia de Nicaragua*, 2:252–54. Ayón emphasizes that one of Padilla's legs was specifically placed in the plaza of San Felipe, the mulatto barrio of León.

105. Ayón, *Historia de Nicaragua*, 2:255.

106. Ayón, *Historia de Nicaragua*, 2:275–90. See also AGCA, A1.15(5), leg. 101, exp. 780, 1748, and A1.15 (5), leg. 106, exp. 802, 1757.

107. AMPG, caja 156, leg. 435, "Asunto entre la municipalidad y el cura de Masatepe," Navarro (Masatepe) to Rafael Blandino (Masaya), 24 March 1880, my emphasis.

108. Cf. Anderson, *Imagined Communities*, 145.

109. AMPG, caja 156, leg. 435, "Asunto entre la municipalidad y el cura de Masatepe," Navarro to Blandino, 24 March 1880, my emphasis.

110. In AMPG, caja 184, leg. x6, "Protesta de la elección del alc indio de la villa de Masatepe," 1883, the subprefect, Eduardo Córdoba, makes similar claims.

111. AMPG, caja 156, leg. 435, "Asunto entre la municipalidad y el cura de Masatepe," Navarro to Blandino, 24 March 1880.

112. I take these terms from Gilroy, *The Black Atlantic*, 37–38. Gilroy sees the "politics of transfiguration" as something covert and secret, imbricated with unspoken, radical constructions of cultural difference. I, however, will be using the term to refer to more openly constructed, but no less radical, counterideologies.

113. AMPG, caja 28, leg. 84, "Los yndígenas del barrio de Jalata en Masatepe solicitan que se los preserven sus usos y costumbres ignocentes, en conforme á las leyes," Ampie to Prefect, 9 January 1861.

114. I have found Gilroy's analysis of black cultures and their confrontations with discourses of modernity and the Enlightenment particularly inspiring. See, e.g., Gilroy, *The Black Atlantic*. See also B. F. Williams, *Stains on My Name*, 267–68; cf. Anderson, *Imagined Communities*, ch. 2.

115. AMPG, caja 28, leg. 84, "Los yndígenas del barrio de Jalata en Masatepe solicitan que se los preserven sus usos y costumbres ignocentes, en conforme á las leyes," Ampie to Prefect, 9 January 1861.

116. See, e.g., AMPG, caja 28, leg. 84, "Expediente relativo a la reunión de los yndígenas de Nindirí habida el 19 en la noche del mes de Octubre," 1861; caja 36, leg. 117, "El alcalde indíjena de Jinotepe se queja del alcalde 2° de su vecindario," 1863; caja 156, leg. 434, "Asunto entre la municipalidad y el cura de Masatepe," 1880.

117. AMPG, caja 52, leg. 138, "Diligencias sobre lo ocurrido entre el cura y la municipalidad de Diriomo," 1866.

118. AMPG, caja 37, leg. 119, "Los yndígenas del pueblo de Diriomo denuncian al Señor Urbano Morales como cuestor fraudulante," 1864. Morales testified as one of the principal ladino witnesses in the 1866 complaint discussed above.

119. On the importance of cofradías to Indian communities, see, e.g., AMPG, caja 36, leg. 117, "El alcalde indíjena de Jinotepe se queja del alcalde 2° de su vecindario," 1863.

120. AMPG, caja 156, leg. 434, "Asunto entre la municipalidad y el cura de Masatepe," 1880.

121. AMPG, caja 156, leg. 434, "Asunto entre la municipalidad y el cura de Masatepe," 1880.

122. AMPG, caja 156, leg. 434, "Asunto entre la municipalidad y el cura de Masatepe," 1880.

123. "Ecos de Masatepe," *El Diarito* (Granada), 10 November 1895.

124. Teplitz, "Political and Economic Foundations," 83–101. On Indian-church conflict see J. L. Gould, *To Die in This Way*, 38–40.

125. J. L. Gould, *To Die in This Way*, 92, notes similar practices, albeit for different reasons, in the 1920s: "Typically, the coalition government forces imprisoned or recruited Indians into the army so that they would be ineligible to vote in the elections."

126. AMPG, caja 156, leg. 434, "Asunto entre la municipalidad y el cura de Masatepe," 1880.

127. AMPG, caja 158, leg. 441, "Censos agropecuarias," 1880.

128. No agricultural census for San Marcos was found, but its early adoption of coffee production and its importance to the coffee boom of the 1880s suggest that its economy would have been similar to Diriamba's. In his survey of Nicaragua at the end of the nineteenth century, Niederlein, *State of Nicaragua*, 51, lists San Marcos alongside Diriamba and Jinotepe in his discussion of "coffee-finca owners." See also the rich and thorough study of this region in Charlip, *Cultivating Coffee*.

129. Newson, *Indian Survival*, 179.

130. Dore, *Myths of Modernity*.

131. In his prickly history of the region, Mendoza, *Historia de Diriamba*, 372–75, blasts some of the most prominent families for what he saw as preposterous claims to whiteness or pure Spanish descent.

132. AMPG, caja 191, leg. 495, Navas (Managua) to Prefect (Granada), 10 March 1883.

133. Charlip, *Cultivating Coffee*, 195. Lauria-Santiago, "Land, Community, and Revolt," 529–30, notes a similar pattern.

134. AMPG, caja 159, leg. 431, "Juan Lopez queja contra el alcalde de Diriomo," 1880.

135. Hernández Somoza, *Catecismo político*, 15.

136. For ladino refusals to accept governmental positions, see, e.g., AMPG, caja 6, leg. 22, "Renuncias de cargos consejiles," 1858; caja 51, leg. 171, "Renuncias de registros, jueces de agricultura y alcaldía municipales," 1866; caja 76, leg. 241, "Renuncias, excusas y recursos de nulidad en material electoral," 1870; caja 87, leg. 275, "Nombramientos, renuncias de varías autoridades y multas impuestas," 1872; caja 203, unnumbered leg. (84 folios) "Renuncias de varias autoridades y otras cosas," 1884. Similar documents for almost every year are available in the AMPG.

137. AMPG, caja 184, leg. X6, "Ynformación de testigos practicada a favór de Felipe Hernández sobre elección de alcalde indígena," 1883.

138. AMPG, caja 184, leg. X6, "Protesta de la elección del alcalde indio de la villa de Masatepe," 1883.

139. AMPG, caja 184, leg. X6, "Ynformación de testigos practicada a favór de Felipe Hernández sobre elección de alcalde indígena," 1883.

140. AMPG, caja 184, leg. X6, "Protesta de la elección del alcalde indio de la villa de Masatepe," 1883.

141. *Gaceta de Nicaragua* (Managua), August 1865.

142. AMPG, caja 184, leg. X6, "Protesta de la elección del alcalde indio de la villa de Masatepe," 1883.

143. AMPG, caja 184, leg. X6, "Ynformación de testigos practicada a favór de Felipe Hernández sobre elección del alcalde indígena," 22 February 1883. See also the 1858 Constitution reprinted in Alvarez Lejarza, *Ensayo histórico*, 216–35.

144. Contemporary indigenous movements may lay claim to legal protection or acceptance, but without compromising their complains to originary status. See, e.g., Warren, *Indigenous Movements and Their Critics*, and Hale, *Resistance and Contradiction*. Although it was inconceivable until very recently, some Latin American legal systems are exploring ways to incorporate indigenous customary practices. Still, as noted in Van Cott, "Political Analysis of Legal Pluralism," these projects remain fraught.

145. AMPG, caja 190, leg. 494, Delgadillo (Managua) to Prefect (Granada), 23 May 1883.

146. AMPG, caja 190, leg. 494, Delgadillo (Managua) to Prefect (Granada), 23 May 1883.

147. Dore, "Debt Peonage in Granada," 554.

148. Garrard-Burnett, "Liberalism, Protestantism, and Indigenous Resistance," 37.

149. Peña and Castillo, "Estado-iglesia y cofradías," 484–92.

150. Charlip, *Cultivating Coffee*, 57. Once titled, the cofradía listed its holdings at 400 caballerías (25,600 manzanas).

151. Quoted in J. L. Gould, *To Die in This Way*, 39.

152. J. Scott, *Weapons of the Weak*; Wolf, "Closed Corporate Communities."

153. Mendoza, *Historia de Diriamba*, 188.

154. J. L. Gould, *To Die in This Way*, 273.

155. Cuadra, "El primer personaje de la literatura nicaragüense: El Güegüense: La lengua y los mitos," in *El nicaragüense*, 67. These essays, most of which were first printed in *La Prensa Literaria* (Managua) in 1959, were originally collected and published in 1963.

156. See, e.g., Niederlein, *State of Nicaragua*, 84; Mendoza, *Historia de Diriamba*, 4. To the extent that an "Indian problem" persisted, it was widely perceived to be only an Atlantic coast issue. See Alvarez Lejarza, *El problema del indio*.

Conclusion

1. On Costeño history, identities, and Costeño-Nicaraguan relations and struggles, see Gordon, *Disparate Diasporas*; Hale, *Resistance and Contradiction*.

2. See, e.g., Wheelock Román, *Imperialismo y dictadura*; Barahona, *Estudio sobre la historia de Nicaragua*; Vargas, *La revolución que inició el progreso*; Velázquez, *La formación del estado*; Torres-Rivas, *History and Society*; Walter, *Regime of Anastasio Somoza*; Paige, *Coffee and Power*.

3. Guzmán, "La Torre de Babel."

4. These three were José León Sandoval (1845–47), José Laureano Pineda (1851–53), and Vicente Quadra (1871–75).

5. See Cruz, *Nicaragua's Conservative Republic*, 163.

6. Stone, *Heritage of the Conquistadors*, 38. On the complexities of Nicaraguan families and politics, especially during the twentieth century, see Vilas, "Family Affairs."

7. Cruz, *Nicaragua's Conservative Republic*.

8. Calculated from Nicaragua, Ministerio de Gobernación, *Memoria* (1885). Cruz, *Nicaragua's Conservative Republic*, 102, makes a similar point but inflates these figures in claiming that "jornaleros" (day laborers) were "journeymen."

9. Gobat, *Confronting the American Dream*, 79–80. According to "Instalación de la Sociedad de Artesanos en Managua," *El País* (Managua), 9 February 1888, the subsecretaries of government, foreign relations, and development all attended the society's opening party in 1888.

10. Cruz, *Nicaragua's Conservative Republic*, 154–55.

11. See Mendoza, *Historia de Diriamba*, 70–71, for nineteenth-century local parties. On the more defined parties see Cruz, *Nicaragua's Conservative Republic*, 92–121.

12. "Tres fantasmas," *El Diarito* (Granada), 22 October 1893.

13. "El espíritu de partido," *La Avispas* (Granada), 20 December 1854.

14. On Zelaya's use of physical violence, including executions of opponents, see Juárez, *Por Nicaragua* 33, 82–83, 105; Belli Cortés, *Cincuenta años de vida republicana*, 325. On the economic field, R. G. Williams, *States and Social Evolution*, 178, noted that "not one sale was recorded to a member of the Conservative Chamorro clan, and only one member from each of the Conservative Zavala, Sacasa, Carazo, Argüello, and Solórzano families was sold a piece of land by the Zelaya government."

15. On some manifestations of post-Zelaya political violence see Gobat, *Confronting the American Dream*, 77–80, 100–110.

16. The most thorough analysis of institutional changes is Teplitz, "Political and Economic Foundations." Typical of the historiography that posits 1893 as a radical break is Vargas, *La revolución que inició el progreso*. Cf. the revisionist political history, Cruz, *Nicaragua's Conservative Republic*.

17. Paige, *Coffee and Power*, 158.

18. Gobat, *Confronting the American Dream*, 76.

19. Cuadra Pasos, *Obras*, 1:601.

20. Schroeder, "Horse Thieves," 429. For a fuller exposition of this argument see Schroeder, "To Defend Our Nation's Honor." The literature on Sandino has grown immensely in recent years. See especially Vargas, *Floreció al filo de la espada*; Wünderich, *Sandino*; Dospital, *Siempre más allá*; Grossman, *"Hermanos en la Patria"*; Navarro-Genie, *Augusto "Cesar" Sandino*.

21. See Charlip, *Cultivating Coffee*; and Gobat, *Confronting the American Dream*, 150–74.

22. Gobat, *Confronting the American Dream*, 150.

23. J. L. Gould, *To Lead as Equals*, 29.

24. "El artesano," *El País* (Managua), 13 June 1888.

25. J. L. Gould, *To Lead as Equals*, 32–33; Gobat, *Confronting the American Dream*, ch. 4; Rice, "Nicaragua and the U.S.," 340–50.

26. Gobat, *Confronting the American Dream*, 80.

27. J. L. Gould, *El mito*, 122; Rice, "Nicaragua and the U.S.," 111–15.

28. J. L. Gould, *To Lead as Equals*, esp. ch. 3.

29. J. L. Gould, *To Die in This Way*, 43–47.

30. J. L. Gould, *To Die in This Way*, 189–92.

31. J. L. Gould, *El mito*, 136. My translation.

32. Ramírez, "The Kid from Niquinohomo," 61.

33. See, e.g., Vargas, *La revolución que inició el progreso*; Velázquez, *La formación del estado*; Paige, *Coffee and Power*; Mahoney, *The Legacies of Liberalism*; Cruz, *Nicaragua's Conservative Republic*.

34. Charlip, *Cultivating Coffee*, 187–90, offers an excellent discussion of this often profound social mobility in the part of the prefecture that became the department of Carazo.

35. See Vilas, "El sujeto social," 130–37.

36. Vilas, "El sujeto social," 135.

37. On the "minifundization" of Carazo, see Enriquez and Llanes, "Back to the Land," 254–55.

38. J. L. Gould, *To Lead as Equals*, 292–305.

39. Despite the FSLN's early organizing of Carazo's rural laborers, the region's agrarian reform efforts met resistance to both collective projects and state management of domestic agricultural production. Enriquez and Llanes, "Back to the Land," 261.

40. Vilas, "El sujeto social," table 7.

Bibliography

Primary Sources

Alemán Bolaños, Gustavo. *El pueblo de Nicaragua y los Estado Unidos*. Managua: Tipografía Alemana de Carlos Heuberger, 1923.

Alvarez Lejarza, Emilio. *Las constituciones de Nicaragua*. Madrid: Ediciones Cultura Hispanica, 1958.

Ayón, Tomás. "Apuntes sobre algunos de los acontecimientos políticos de Nicaragua en los Años de 1811 á 1824." In *Historia de Nicaragua: Desde los tiempos más remotos hasta el año de 1852*, 3:405–32. Managua: Fondo de Promoción Cultural–BANIC, 1993.

———. *Historia de Nicaragua desde los tiempos más remotos hasta el año de 1852*. 2nd ed. 3 vols. Managua: Fondo de Promoción Cultural–BANIC, 1993.

Bureau of the American Republics. *Nicaragua*. Washington DC: Government Printing Office, 1893.

de la Rocha, Pedro Francisco. *Revista política sobre la historia de la Revolución de Nicaragua en defensa de la administración del ex-director Don José León Sandoval*. Granada: Imprenta de la Concepción, 1847. Reprinted in *Revista del Pensamiento Centroamericano*, no. 180 (July–September 1983): 24–76.

Elizondo, Joaquín. "La infraestructura de Nicaragua en 1860." *Revista Conservadora del Pensamiento Centroamericano*, no. 57 (1965): 55–56.

Esgueva Gómez, Antonio, ed. *Las constituciones políticas y sus reformas en la historia de Nicaragua*. 2 vols. Managua: IHNCA-UCA, 2000.

———, ed. *Documentos de la historia de Nicaragua, 1523–1857*. Managua: Universidad Centroamericano, 1993.

Fernández Figueroa, Enrique Juan de Dios. *La historia como condicionante de la ordenación del territorio—Nicaragua: desde su conquista y colonización española a la situación actual*. [Spain]: Principado de Asturias Consejería de Medio Ambiente y Urbanismo, 1993.

Gámez, José Dolores. *Apuntamientos para la biografía de Máximo Jerez*. Managua: n.p., 1910.

———. *Historia de Nicaragua: Desde los tiempos prehistóricos hasta 1860, en sus relaciones con España, México y Centro-América*. 2nd ed. Managua: Fondo de Promoción Cultural–BANIC, 1993.

———. *Historia moderna de Nicaragua: Complemento a mi historia de Nicaragua*. Managua: Fondo de Promoción Cultural–BANIC, 1993.

Guzmán, Enrique. *Editoriales de La prensa, 1878*. Ed. Franco Cerutti. Managua: Fondo de Promoción Cultural, Banco de América, 1977.

247

————. "La Torre de Babel: La agonía de los partidos políticos en Nicaragua (1888)." *Revista Conservadora del Pensamiento Centroamericano* 26, no. 130 (1971): 31–35.

Hernández Somoza, Jesús. *Catecismo político.* Managua: Tiopgrafía de Managua, 1887.

Le Baron, J. Francis. "Nicaragua: Industrial and Agricultural Resources." *Monthly Bulletin of the Bureau of the American Republics* 5, no. 3 (1897): 346–51.

Mendoza, Juan. *Historia de Diriamba.* Guatemala: Staebler, 1920.

Moncada, José María. *El ideal ciudadano.* Managua: Tipografía Alemana de Carlos Heuberger, 1929.

Nicaragua. *Código de la legislación de la república de Nicaragua.* Vol. 8. Managua: El Centro-Americano, 1873.

————. *Colección de leyes y acuerdos.* Managua: Imprenta Nacional, 1857–89.

————. *Decretos y leyes.* Managua: Imprenta Nacional, 1857–89.

————. *Documentos relativos a la rebelión frustrada en Granada a mediados de Agosto de 1884.* Managua: Tipografía Nacional, 1885.

————. *Ley sobre persecución de operarios profugos.* Managua: Tipografía Nacional, 1883.

Nicaragua. Dirección General de Estadistica. *Censo general de 1920.* Managua: Tipografía Nacional, 1920.

Nicaragua. Ministerio de Fomento y Obras Públicas. *Memoria,* 1867, 1869, 1888–90.

Nicaragua. Ministerio de Gobernación. *Informe,* 1871.

————. *Memoria,* 1859, 1860, 1869–70, 1884–85.

Nicaragua. Ministerio de Guerra. *Memoria,* 1863, 1873, 1874.

Nicaragua. Ministerio de Hacienda Pública. *Informe,* 1863, 1873–74.

————. *Memoria,* 1861–62, 1865–66, 1869–70, 1878, 1897, 1903.

Nicaragua. Ministerio de Instrucción Pública. *Memoria,* 1859.

Nicaragua. Ministerio de Relaciones Exteriores. *Memoria.* 2 vols. Managua: Tipografía Nacional, 1920.

Niederlein, Gustavo. *The State of Nicaragua.* Philadelphia: Philadelphia Commercial Museum, 1898.

Ortega Arancibia, Francisco. *Cuarenta años (1838–1878) de historia de Nicaragua.* 4th ed. Managua: Fondo de Promoción Cultural–BANIC, 1993.

Pérez, Jerónimo. "Biografía de Don Manuel Antonio de la Cerda." In *Obras históricas completas,* 461–93. Managua: Fondo de Promoción Cultural–BANIC, 1993.

————. "Memorias para la historia de la campaña nacional contra el filibusterismo en 1856 y 1857." In *Obras históricas completas,* 173–420. Managua: Fondo de Promoción Cultural–BANIC, 1993.

————. "Memorias para la historia de la Revolución de Nicaragua en 1854." In *Obras históricas completas*, 19–170. Managua: Fondo de Promoción Cultural– BANIC, 1993.

————. *Obras históricas completas*. Ed. Pedro Joaquín Chamorro Zelaya. 2nd ed. Managua: Fondo de Promoción Cultural–BANIC, 1993.

Pim, Bedford. *The Gate to the Pacific*. London: L. Reeve, 1863.

Ruiz y Ruiz, Frutos. *Costa Atlántica de Nicaragua*. Managua: Tipografía Alemana de Carlos Heuberger, 1927.

Squier, E. G. "Nicaragua." *Harper's New Monthly Magazine*, November 1855, 744–63.

————. *Nicaragua: Its People, Scenery, Monuments, Resources, Condition, and Proposed Canal*. New York: Harper & Brothers, 1860.

————. *The States of Central America*. New York: Harper & Brothers, 1858.

————. *Travels in Central America, Particularly in Nicaragua*. New York: D. Appleton, 1853.

Stout, Peter F. *Nicaragua: Past, Present, and Future*. Philadelphia: Potter, 1859.

Vega Bolaños, Andrés. *Gobernantes de Nicaragua: Notas y documentos*. Managua, 1944.

Walker, William. *The War in Nicaragua*. Mobile AL: S. H. Goetzel, 1860. Reprint, Tucson: University of Arizona Press, 1985.

Wünderich, Volker, Elenor von Oertzen, and Lioba Rossbach, eds. *The Nicaraguan Mosquitia in Historical Documents, 1844–1927*. Berlin: Dietrich Reimer Verlag, 1990.

Secondary Sources

Adams, Richard N. *Cultural Surveys of Panama, Nicaragua, Guatemala, El Salvador, Honduras*. Washington DC: Pan American Sanitary Bureau Regional Office of the World Health Organization, 1957.

————. "Strategies of Ethnic Survival in Central America." In *Nation-States and Indians in Latin America*, ed. Greg Urban and Joel Sherzer, 181–206. Austin: University of Texas Press, 1991.

Alonso, Ana María. "The Politics of Space, Time, and Substance: State Formation, Nationalism, and Ethnicity." *Annual Review of Anthropology* 23 (1994): 379–405.

Van Alstyne, Richard W. "The Central American Policy of Lord Palmerston, 1846– 1848." *Hispanic American Historical Review* 16, no. 3 (1936): 339–59.

Alvarez Lejarza, Emilio. *Ensayo histórico sobre el derecho constitucional de Nicaragua*. Managua: Tip. La Prensa, 1936.

————. "El liberalismo en los 30 años." *Revista Conservadora del Pensamiento Centroamericano* II, no. 51 (1964): 23–33.

———. *El problema del indio en Nicaragua*. Managua: Editorial Nuevos Horizontes, 1943.

Anderson, Benedict. *Imagined Communities: Reflections on the Origin and Spread of Nationalism*. Rev. ed. London: Verso, 1991.

Arellano, Jorge Eduardo. *Breve historia de la iglesia en Nicaragua (1523–1979)*. Managua: Editorial Manolo Morales, 1986.

———. *Brevísima historia de la educación en Nicaragua (de la colonia a los anos '70 del siglo XX)*. Managua: Instituto Nicaragüense de Cultura Hispanica, 1997.

———. *Panorama de la literatura nicaragüense*. 3rd ed. Managua: Ediciones Nacionales, 1977.

Arnaiz Quintana, Angel. *Historia del pueblo de Dios en Nicaragua*. Managua: Centro Ecuménico Antonio Valdivieso, 1990.

Avendaño Rojas, Xiomara. "Las características de la ciudadanía en Centroamérica durante el siglo XIX: Estudio de los distritos electorales de Quezaltenango y Granada." *Revista de Historia* (Nicaragua), nos. 5–6 (1995): 20–29.

———. "El pactismo: El mecanismo de ascenso de los notables, 1858–1893." *Revista de Historia* (Nicaragua), no. 7 (1996): 26–41.

Barahona, Amaru. *Estudio sobre la historia de Nicaragua: Del auge cafetalero al auge de la revolución*. Managua: INIES, 1989.

Barquero, Sara L. *Gobernantes de Nicaragua: 1825–1947*. 2nd ed. Managua: Ministerio de Instrucción Pública, 1945.

Barth, Fredrik. Introduction. In *Ethnic Groups and Boundaries: The Social Organization of Culture Difference*, ed. Fredrik Barth, 9–38. Boston: Little Brown, 1969.

Baumeister, Eduardo. "Agrarian Reform." In *Revolution and Counterrevolution in Nicaragua*, ed. Thomas W. Walker, 229–47. Boulder CO: Westview Press, 1991.

Belli, Humberto. "Un ensayo de interpretación sobre las luchas políticas nicaragüenses: De la independencia hasta la revolución cubana." *Revista del Pensamiento Centroamericano* 32, no. 157 (1977): 50–59.

Belli Cortés, Enrique. *Cincuenta años de vida republicana, 1859–1909*. Managua: n.p., 1998.

Belly, Felix. *A travers l'Amerique Centrale: Le Nicaragua et le canal interoceanique*. 2 vols. Paris: Librarie de la Suisse romande, 1867.

Bendaña, Ricardo, Rodolfo Cardenal, Marcos Carías, Miguel Picado, Jorge Eduardo Arellano, and Wilton Nelson. *América Central*. Vol. 6 of *Historia general de la iglesia en América Latina*. Ed. Enrique D. Dussel. 10 vols. Salamanca: Ediciones Sígueme, 1985.

Bermann, Karl. *Under the Big Stick: Nicaragua and the United States since 1848*. Boston: South End Press, 1986.

Biderman, Jaime M. "Class Structure, the State, and Capitalist Development in Nicaraguan Agriculture." PhD diss., University of California, Berkeley, 1982.

Bolaños Geyer, Alejandro. *William Walker: The Gray-eyed Man of Destiny*. 5 vols. Lake Saint Louis MO: A. Bolaños-Geyer, 1988.

Brass, Paul R. *Ethnicity and Nationalism: Theory and Comparison*. New Delhi: Sage, 1991.

Breuilly, John. *Nationalism and the State*. Chicago: University of Chicago Press, 1993.

Buitrago, Edgardo. "El municipio en Nicaragua." León, Nicaragua, 1987. Mimeograph.

Bulmer-Thomas, Victor. *The Economic History of Latin America since Independence*. Cambridge: Cambridge University Press, 1994.

Burns, E. Bradford. *Patriarch and Folk: The Emergence of Nicaragua, 1798–1858*. Cambridge: Harvard University Press, 1991.

Cahill, David. "Colour by Numbers: Racial and Ethnic Categories in the Viceroyalty of Peru, 1532–1824." *Journal of Latin American Studies* 26, no. 2 (1994): 325–46.

Calhoun, Craig. *Nationalism*. Minneapolis: University of Minnesota Press, 1997.

Cardoso, Ciro F. S. "Historia económica del café en Centroamérica (siglo XIX): Estudio comparativa." *Estudios Sociales Centroamericanos*, no. 10 (January–April 1975): 9–55.

Casanova Fuertes, Rafael. "Hacia una nueva valorización de las luchas políticas del período de la Anarquía: El caso de los conflictos de 1845–1849." In *Encuentros con la historia*, ed. Margarita Vannini, 231–48. Managua: IHN-UCA and CEMCA, 1995.

———. "¿Héroes o bandidos? Los problemas de interpretación de los conflictos políticos y sociales entre 1845 y 1849 en Nicaragua." *Revista de Historia* (Nicaragua), no. 2 (1992): 13–26.

———. "Orden o anarquía: Los intentos de regulación protoestatal en Nicaragua. Década de 1840." In *Nicaragua en busca de su identidad*, ed. Frances Kinloch Tijerino, 277–94. Managua: IHN-UCA, 1995.

Cerutti, Franco. *Los Jesuitas en Nicaragua en el siglo XIX*. San José: Libro Libre, 1984.

Chamorro, Pedro Joaquín. *Máximo Jerez y sus contemporáneos (estudio histórico-crítico)*. Managua: Editorial "La Prensa," 1948.

Chamorro Zelaya, Pedro Joaquín. *Fruto Chamorro*. Managua: Editorial La Unión, 1960.

Charlip, Julie A. "Cultivating Coffee: Farmers, Land, and Money in Nicaragua, 1877–1930." PhD diss., University of California Los Angeles, 1995.

———. *Cultivating Coffee: The Farmers of Carazo, Nicaragua, 1880–1930.* Athens: Ohio University Press, 2003.

Chatterjee, Partha. *The Nation and Its Fragments.* Princeton: Princeton University Press, 1993.

Clayton, Lawrence A. "The Nicaragua Canal in the Nineteenth Century: Prelude to American Empire in the Caribbean." *Journal of Latin American Studies* 19 (1987): 323–52.

Cobo del Arco, Teresa. *Políticas de género durante el liberalismo: Nicaragua, 1893–1909.* Managua: UCA, 2000.

Collado H., María del Carmen. "Liberales y conservadores de Nicaragua: ¿Falsos estereotipos?" *Secuencia* 11 (1988): 65–76.

Comaroff, John L. "Of Totemism and Ethnicity: Consciousness, Practice, and the Signs of Inequality." In *Ethnography and the Historical Imagination*, 49–67. Boulder CO: Westview Press, 1992.

Comaroff, John L., and Jean Comaroff. "The Colonization of Consciousness." In *Ethnography and the Historical Imagination*, 235–63. Boulder CO: Westview Press, 1992.

———. "Ethnography and the Historical Imagination." In *Ethnography and the Historical Imagination*, 3–48. Boulder CO: Westview Press, 1992.

———. "Homemade Hegemony." In *Ethnography and the Historical Imagination*, 265–95. Boulder CO: Westview Press, 1992.

Cope, R. Douglas. *The Limits of Racial Domination: Plebeian Society in Colonial Mexico City, 1660–1720.* Madison: University of Wisconsin Press, 1994.

Coronel Urtecho, José. "Introducción a la Epoca de Anarquía en Nicaragua, 1821–1857." *Revista Conservadora del Pensamiento Centroamericano*, no. 134 (1971): 39–49.

———. *Reflexiones sobre la historia de Nicaragua (de Gainza a Somoza).* León: Editorial Hospicio, 1962.

Crowell, Jackson. "The United States and a Central American Canal, 1869–1877." *Hispanic American Historical Review* 49, no. 1 (1969): 27–52.

Cruz, Arturo J. *Nicaragua's Conservative Republic, 1858–93.* New York: Palgrave, 2002.

Cuadra, Pablo Antonio. *El nicaragüense.* Managua: Hispamer, 1993.

Cuadra Pasos, Carlos. *Obras.* 2 vols. Managua: Fondo de Promocion Cultural, Banco de America, 1976–77.

de Certeau, Michel. *The Practice of Everyday Life.* Trans. Steven F. Rendall. Berkeley: University of California Press, 1984.

Dengo de Vargas, María Eugenia. *Educación costarricense.* San José: Editorial Univerisdad Estatal a Distancia, 1995.

Dennis, Philip A., and Michael D. Olien. "Kingship among the Miskito." *American Ethnologist* II, no. 4 (1984): 718–37.

Deutsch, Karl W. *Nationalism and Social Communication.* Cambridge: MIT Press, 1966.

Díaz Lacayo, Aldo. *Gobernantes de Nicaragua (1821–1956): Guía para el estudio de sus biografías políticas.* Managua: Aldilá Editor, 1996.

Dore, Elizabeth. "Debt Peonage in Granada, Nicaragua, 1870–1930: Labor in a Non-capitalist Transition." *Hispanic American Historical Review* 83, no. 3 (2003): 521–59.

———. "Land Privatization and the Differentiation of the Peasantry: Nicaragua's Coffee Revolution, 1850–1920." *Journal of Historical Sociology* 8, no. 3 (1995): 303–26.

———. *Myths of Modernity: Peonage and Patriarchy in Nicaragua.* Durham NC: Duke University Press, 2006.

———. "One Step Forward, Two Steps Back: Gender and the State in the Long Nineteenth Century." In *Hidden Histories of Gender and the State in Latin America,* ed. Elizabeth Dore and Maxine Molyneux, 3–32. Durham NC: Duke University Press, 2000.

———. "Patriarchy from Above, Patriarchy from Below: Debt Peonage on Nicaraguan Coffee Estates, 1870–1930." In *The Global Coffee Economy in Africa, Asia and Latin America, 1500–1989,* ed. William Gervase Clarence-Smith and Steven Topik, 209–35. Cambridge: Cambridge University Press, 2003.

———. "La producción cafetalera nicaragüense, 1860–1960: Transformaciones estructurales." In *Tierra, café y sociedad: Ensayos sobre la historia agraria centroamericana,* ed. Mario Samper K. and Héctor Pérez Brignoli. San José: FLASCO, 1994.

———. "Property, Households and Public Regulation of Domestic Life: Diriomo, Nicaragua, 1840–1900." *Journal of Latin American Studies* 29, no. 3 (1997): 591–611.

Dospital, Michelle. *Siempre más allá . . . : El movimiento Sandinista en Nicaragua, 1927–1934.* Managua: Instituto de Historia de Nicaragua, 1996.

Dozier, Craig. *Nicaragua's Mosquito Coast: The Years of British and American Presence.* Tuscaloosa: University of Alabama Press, 1985.

Duara, Prasenjit. "Historicizing National Identity, or Who Images What and When." In *Becoming National: A Reader,* ed. Geoff Eley and Ronald Grigor Suny, 151–77. New York: Oxford University Press, 1996.

Dunkerley, James. *Power in the Isthmus: A Political History of Modern Central America.* London: Verso, 1988.

Dym, Jordana. "A Sovereign State of Every Village: City, State, and Nation in Central America, ca. 1760–1850." PhD diss., New York University, 2000.

Eagleton, Terry. "The Ideology of the Aesthetic." *Poetics Today* 9, no. 2 (1988): 327–38.

Edelman, Marc. *The Logic of the Latifundio: The Large Estates of Northwestern Costa Rica Since the Late Nineteenth Century.* Stanford: Stanford University Press, 1992.

Edelman, Marc, and Mitchell A. Seligson. "Land Inequality: A Comparison of Census Data and Property Records in Twentieth-Century Southern Costa Rica." *Hispanic American Historical Review* 74, no. 3 (1994): 445–91.

Enriquez, Laura J., and Marlen I. Llanes. "Back to the Land: The Political Dilemmas of Agrarian Reform in Nicaragua." *Social Problems* 40, no. 2 (1993): 250–65.

Fernández Molina, José Antonio. "Colouring the World in Blue: The Indigo Boom and the Central American Market, 1750–1810." PhD diss., University of Texas, 1992.

Folkman, David I. *The Nicaragua Route.* Salt Lake City: University of Utah Press, 1972.

Forbes, Jack. *Africans and Native Americans: The Language of Race and the Evolution of Red-Black Peoples.* Urbana: University of Illinois Press, 1992.

Frankenberg, Ruth. *White Women, Race Matters: The Social Construction of Whiteness.* Minneapolis: University of Minnesota Press, 1993.

Garrard-Burnett, Virginia. "Liberalism, Protestantism, and Indigenous Resistance in Guatemala, 1870–1920." *Latin American Perspectives* 24, no. 2 (1997): 35–55.

Geertz, Clifford. "After the Revolution: The Fate of Nationalism in the New States." In *The Interpretation of Cultures,* 234–54. New York: Basic Books, 1973.

———. "The Integrative Revolution: Primordial Sentiments and Civil Politics in the New States." In *The Interpretation of Cultures,* 255–310. New York: Basic Books, 1973.

Gellner, Ernst. *Nations and Nationalism.* Oxford: Basil Blackwell, 1983.

Gillis, John R. *A World of Their Own Making: Myth, Ritual, and the Quest for Family Values.* New York: Basic Books, 1996.

Gilroy, Paul. *The Black Atlantic: Modernity and Double Consciousness.* Cambridge: Harvard University Press, 1993.

———. *"There Ain't No Black in the Union Jack": The Cultural Politics of Race and Nation.* Chicago: University of Chicago Press, 1991.

Gobat, Michel. *Confronting the American Dream: Nicaragua under U.S. Imperial Rule.* Durham NC: Duke University Press, 2005.

González, Victoria. "From Feminism to Somocismo: Women's Rights and Right-Wing Politics in Nicaragua, 1821–1979." PhD diss., Indiana University, 2002.

Gootenberg, Paul. *Imagining Development: Economic Ideas in Peru's "Fictitious Prosperity" of Guano, 1840–1880.* Berkeley: University of California Press, 1993.

Gordon, Edmund T. *Disparate Diasporas: Identity and Politics in an African Nicaraguan Community*. Austin: University of Texas Press, 1998.

Gould, Jeffrey L. "El café, el trabajo y la comunidad indígena de Matagalpa, 1880–1925." In *El café en la historia de Centroamérica*, ed. Héctor Pérez Brignoli and Mario Samper K., 279–365. San José: FLASCO, 1993.

———. *El mito de "la Nicaragua mestiza" y la resistencia indígena, 1880–1980*. San José: Editorial de la Univerisdad de Costa Rica, 1997.

———. "La supresión de la comunidad indígena en Nicaragua, 1890–1940." In *Nicaragua en busca de su identidad*, ed. Frances Kinloch Tijerino, 459–80. Managua: IHN-UCA, 1995.

———. *To Die in This Way: Nicaraguan Indians and the Myth of Mestizaje, 1880–1965*. Durham NC: Duke University Press, 1998.

———. *To Lead as Equals: Rural Protest and Political Consciousness in Chinandega, Nicaragua, 1912–1979*. Chapel Hill: University of North Carolina Press, 1990.

———. "'¡Vana Ilusión!' The Highlands Indians and the Myth of Nicaragua Mestiza, 1880–1925." *Hispanic American Historical Review* 73, no. 3 (1993): 393–429.

Gould, Stephen Jay. *The Mismeasure of Man*. New York: Norton, 1981.

Grandin, Greg. *The Blood of Guatemala: A History of Race and Nation*. Durham NC: Duke University Press, 1999.

Grossman, Richard. "'*Hermanos en la Patria*': Nationalism, Honor, and Rebellion: Augusto Sandino and the Army in Defense of the National Sovereignty of Nicaragua, 1927–1934." PhD diss., University of Chicago, 1996.

Guardino, Peter F. *Peasants, Politics, and the Formation of Mexico's National State: Guerrero, 1800–1857*. Stanford: Stanford University Press, 1996.

Gudmundson, Lowell. *Costa Rica before Coffee: Society and Economy on the Eve of the Export Boom*. Baton Rouge: Louisiana State University Press, 1986.

Gudmundson, Lowell, and Héctor Lindo-Fuentes. *Central America, 1821–1871: Liberalism before Liberal Reform*. Tuscaloosa: University of Alabama Press, 1995.

Guerrero C., Julián N., and Lola Soriano. *Caciques heróicos de Centroamérica, rebelión indígena en 1881, y expulsión de los Jesuitas*. Managua: Librería Loaisiga, 1982.

———. *Carazo (monografía)*. Managua: n.p., 1964.

Gulden, Cristina María van der. *Vocabulario nicaragüense*. Managua: Editorial UCA, 1995.

Hale, Charles R. *Resistance and Contradiction: Miskitu Indians and the Nicaragua State, 1894–1987*. Stanford: Stanford University Press, 1994.

Helms, Mary W. "Of Kings and Contexts: Ethnohistorical Interpretations of Miskito Political Structure and Function." *American Ethnologist* 13, no. 3 (1986): 506–23.

———. "The Society and Its Environment." In *Nicaragua: A Country Study*, ed. James D. Rudolph, 61–101. Washington DC: Government Printing Office, 1982.

Herrera C., Miguel Angel. *Bongos, bogas, vapores y marinos: Historia de los "marineros" en el río San Juan, 1849–1855*. Managua: Centro Nicaragüense de Escritores, 1999.

———. "La hoja amarga en la hora de la nación." In *Nicaragua en busca de su identidad*, ed. Frances Kinloch Tijerino, 296–306. Managua: IHN-UCA, 1995.

Hirschman, Charles. "The Meaning and Measurement of Ethnicity in Malaysia: An Analysis of Census Classifications." *Journal of Asian Studies* 46, no. 3 (1987): 555–82.

Hobsbawm, Eric. "Introduction: Inventing Traditions." In *The Invention of Tradition*, ed. Eric Hobsbawm and Terence Ranger, 1–14. Cambridge: Cambridge University Press, 1983.

———. "Mass-Producing Traditions: Europe, 1870–1914." In *The Invention of Tradition*, ed. Eric Hobsbawm and Terence Ranger, 263–307. Cambridge: Cambridge University Press, 1983.

———. *Nations and Nationalism since 1780: Programme, Myth, Reality*. Cambridge: Cambridge University Press, 1990.

———. *Primitive Rebels: Studies in Archaic Forms of Social Movement in the Nineteenth and Twentieth Centuries*. Manchester: Manchester University Press, 1959.

Hobsbawm, Eric, and Terence Ranger, eds. *The Invention of Tradition*. Cambridge: Cambridge University Press, 1983.

Holt, Thomas C. "Marking: Race, Race-making, and the Writing of History." *American Historical Review* 100, no. 1 (1995): 1–20.

Juárez, Orient Bolívar, ed. *Por Nicaragua, por el partido liberal, por el general Zelaya: Polémica histórica/José Madriz, Adolfo Altamirano*. Managua: n.p., 1995.

Kaimowitz, David. "Nicaraguan Debates on Agrarian Structure and Their Implications for Agricultural Policy and the Rural Poor." *Journal of Peasant Studies* 14 (1986): 100–117.

Karnes, Thomas L. *The Failure of Union: Central America, 1824–1960*. Chapel Hill: University of North Carolina Press, 1961.

Kartunnen, Frances, and James Lockhart. *Nahuatl in the Middle Years: Language Contact Phenomena in Texts of the Colonial Period*. Berkeley: University of California Press, 1976.

Katzew, Ilona. "Casta Painting: Identity and Social Stratification in Colonial Mexico." In *New World Orders: Casta Painting and Colonial Latin America*, ed. Ilona Katzew and John A. Farmer, 8–29. New York: Americas Society, 1996.

Kinloch Tijerino, Frances. "El canal interoceánico en el imaginario nacional: Nicaragua siglo XIX." *Talleres de Historia* (Nicaragua), no. 6 (1994): 39–55.

———. "Civilización y barbarie: Mitos y símbolos en la formación de la idea nacional." In *Nicaragua en busca de su identidad*, ed. Frances Kinloch Tijerino, 257–76. Managua: IHN-UCA, 1995.

———. *Nicaragua: Identitidad y cultural política (1821–1858)*. Managua: Banco Central de Nicaragua, 1999.

Knight, Alan. "Racism, Revolution, and *Indigenismo*: Mexico, 1910–1940." In *The Idea of Race in Latin America, 1870–1940*, ed. Richard Graham, 71–113. Austin: University of Texas Press, 1990.

LaFeber, Walter. *Inevitable Revolutions: The United States in Central America*. New York: Norton, 1983.

Lancaster, Roger N. "Skin Color, Race, and Racism in Nicaragua." *Ethnology* 30, no. 4 (1991): 339–53.

Lanning, John Tate. *The Eighteenth-Century Enlightenment in the University of San Carlos de Guatemala*. Ithaca: Cornell University Press, 1956.

Lanuza, Alberto. "Estructuras socioeconómicas, poder y estado en Nicaragua, de 1821 a 1875." Tesis de grado, Facultad de Ciencias Sociales de la Univerisdad de Costa Rica, 1976.

———. "La formación del estado nacional en Nicaragua: Las bases económicas, comerciales y financieras entre 1821 y 1873." In *Economía y sociedad en la construcción del estado en Nicaragua*, ed. Alberto Lanuza, Juan Vázquez, Amaru Barahona, and Amalia Chamorro, 7–138. San José: Instituto Centroamericano de Administración Pública, 1983.

———. "Nicaragua, territorio y población (1821–1875)." *Revista del Pensamiento Centroamericano* 31, no. 151 (1976): 1–22.

Lauria-Santiago, Aldo. "Land, Community, and Revolt in Late-Nineteenth-Century Indian Izalco, El Salvador." *Hispanic American Historical Review* 79, no. 3 (1999): 495–534.

Lefebvre, Henri. *Critique of Everyday Life*. Trans. John Moore. Vol. 2. London: Verso, 2002.

Lévy, Pablo. *Notas geográficas y económicas de la república de Nicaragua*. Paris: Librería Española de E. Denné Schmitz, 1873.

———. "Notes ethnologiques et anthropologiques sur le Nicaragua." *Bulletin de la Société de Géographie* ser. 6, no. 2 (1871): 5–48.

Lindo-Fuentes, Héctor. *Weak Foundations: The Economy of El Salvador in the Nineteenth Century, 1821–1898*. Berkeley: University of California Press, 1991.

Little-Siebold, Todd. "'Where Have All the Spaniards Gone': Independent Identities, Ethnicities, Class, and the Emergent National State." *Journal of Latin American Anthropology* 6, no. 2 (2001): 106–33.

Lomnitz-Adler, Claudio. *Exits from the Labyrinth: Culture and Ideology in the Mexican National Space*. Berkeley: University of California Press, 1992.

Lopez, Francisco. "Notas sobre el proceso de acumulación originaria en Nicaragua (1862–1893)." *Revista Nicaragüense de Ciencias Sociales* 2, no. 3 (1987): 28–31.

Ludtke, Alf, ed. *The History of Everyday Life: Reconstructing Historical Experiences and Ways of Life*. Trans. William Templer. Princeton: Princeton University Press, 1995.

Lutz, Christopher H. *Santiago de Guatemala, 1541–1773: City, Caste, and the Colonial Experience*. Norman: University of Oklahoma Press, 1994.

MacLeod, Murdo J. *Spanish Central America: A Socioeconomic History, 1520–1720*. Berkeley: University of California Press, 1973.

Mahoney, James. *The Legacies of Liberalism: Path Dependence and Political Regimes in Central America*. Baltimore: Johns Hopkins University Press, 2001.

Mallon, Florencia E. *Peasant and Nation: The Making of Postcolonial Mexico and Peru*. Berkeley: University of California Press, 1994.

———. "The Promise and Dilemma of Subaltern Studies: Perspectives from Latin American History." *American Historical Review* 99 (1994): 1491–1515.

May, Robert E. *The Southern Dream of a Caribbean Empire, 1854–1861*. Baton Rouge: Louisiana State University Press, 1973.

———. "Young American Males and Filibustering in the Age of Manifest Destiny." *Journal of American History* 78, no. 3 (1991): 857–86.

McCreery, David. "Debt Servitude in Rural Guatemala, 1876–1936." *Hispanic American Historical Review* 63, no. 4 (1983): 735–59.

———. "An Odious Feudalism: *Mandamientos* and Commercial Agriculture in Guatemala, 1861–1920." *Latin American Perspectives* 13, no. 1 (1986): 99–117.

———. *Rural Guatemala, 1760–1940*. Stanford: Stanford University Press, 1994.

———. "State Power, Indigenous Communities, and Land in Nineteenth-Century Guatemala, 1820–1920." In *Guatemalan Indians and the State, 1540 to 1988*, ed. Carol A. Smith, 97–115. Austin: University of Texas Press, 1990.

Membreño Idiáquez, Marcos. *La estructura de las comunidades étnicas: Itinerario de una investigación teórica desde Nicaragua*. Managua: Editorial Envio, 1994.

Mörner, Magnus. *Race Mixture in the History of Latin America*. Boston: Little Brown, 1967.

Mory, Warren H. "Salvador Mendieta: Escritor y apóstol de la Unión Centroamericana." PhD diss., University of Alabama, 1968.

Nairn, Tom. *The Break-up of Britain: Crisis and Neo-Nationalism*. London: New Left Books, 1977.

Navarro-Genie, Marco Aurelio. *Augusto "Cesar" Sandino: Messiah of Light and Truth*. Syracuse: Syracuse University Press, 2002.

Naylor, Robert A. *Penny Ante Imperialism: The Mosquito Shore and the Bay of Honduras, 1600–1914.* Rutherford NJ: Fairleigh Dickinson University Press, 1989.

Newson, Linda A. "The Depopulation of Nicaragua in the Sixteenth Century." *Journal of Latin American Studies* 14, no. 2 (1982): 253–86.

———. *Indian Survival in Colonial Nicaragua.* Norman: University of Oklahoma Press, 1987.

Nobles, Melissa. *Shades of Citizenship: Race and the Census in Modern Politics.* Stanford: Stanford University Press, 2000.

Offen, Karl H. "The Geographical Imagination, Resource Economics, and Nicaraguan Incorporation of the Mosquitia, 1838–1909." In *Territories, Commodities, and Knowledges: Latin American Environmental History in the Nineteenth and Twentieth Centuries,* ed. Christian Brannstrom, 50–89. London: Institute of Latin American Studies, 2004.

———. "The Miskitu Kingdom: Landscape and the Emergence of a Miskitu Ethnic Identity, Northeastern Nicaragua and Honduras, 1600–1800." PhD diss., University of Texas at Austin, 1999.

———. "The Sambo and Tawira Miskitu: The Colonial Origins and Geography of Intra-Miskitu Differentiation in Eastern Nicaragua and Honduras." *Ethnohistory* 49, no. 2 (2002): 319–72.

Olien, Michael D. "Micro/Macro-Level Linkages: Regional Political Structures on the Mosquito Coast, 1845–1864." *Ethnohistory* 34, no. 3 (1987): 256–87.

Paige, Jeffery M. *Coffee and Power: Revolution and the Rise of Democracy in Central America.* Cambridge: Harvard University Press, 1997.

Palacios, Marcos. *Coffee in Colombia, 1850–1970: An Economic, Social, and Political History.* Cambridge: Cambridge University Press, 1980.

Palmer, Steven. "A Liberal Discipline: Inventing Nations in Guatemala and Costa Rica, 1870–1900." PhD diss., Columbia University, 1990.

Peña, Ligia, and Luisa Amelia Castillo. "Estado-iglesia y cofradías. Nicaragua, siglo XIX." In *Nicaragua en busca de su identidad,* ed. Frances Kinloch Tijerino, 481–94. Managua: IHN-UCA, 1995.

Pérez Estrada, Francisco. "Breve historia de la tenencia de la tierra en Nicaragua." In *Ensayos nicaragüenses,* 143–66. Managua: Vanguardia, 1992.

———. "Las comunidades indígenas en Nicaragua." In *Ensayos nicaragüenses,* 167–88. Managua: Vanguardia, 1992.

Pico, Fernando. "Coffee and the Rise of Commercial Agriculture in Puerto Rico's Highlands: The Occupation and Loss of Land in Guaonico and Roncador (Utuado), 1833–1900." In *Coffee, Society, and Power in Latin America,* ed. William Roseberry, Lowell Gudmundson and Mario Samper K., 94–111. Baltimore: John Hopkins University Press, 1995.

Pinto Soria, Julio C. *Centroamérica, de la colonia al estado nacional (1800–1840)*. Guatemala: Editorial Universitaria, 1986.

Raat, William D. "Leopoldo Zea and Mexican Positivism: A Reappraisal." *Hispanic American Historical Review* 48, no. 1 (1968): 1–18.

Radell, David R. "Historical Geography of Western Nicaragua: The Spheres of Influence of Leon, Granada, and Managua, 1519–1965." PhD diss., University of California Berkeley, 1969.

Ramírez, Sergio. "The Kid from Niquinohomo." *Latin American Perspectives* 16, no. 3 (1989): 48–82.

Rice, Michael D. "Nicaragua and the U.S.: Policy Confrontations and Cultural Interactions, 1893–1933." PhD diss., University of Houston, 1995.

Rodríguez, Jorge. *Elena Arellano, los salesianos en Centroamerica, y la Casa de Granada, Nicaragua*. Managua: MED, 1992.

Rodríguez, Mario. *The Cádiz Experiment in Central America, 1808–1826*. Berkeley: University of California Press, 1978.

———. *A Palmerstonian Diplomat in Central America: Frederick Chatfield, Esq.* Tucson: University of Arizona Press, 1964.

Rodríguez Rosales, Isolda. *La educación durante el liberalismo, Nicaragua: 1893–1909*. Managua: HISPAMER, 1998.

———. "Proyectos educativos en el período formativo del estado-nación, siglo XIX." In *Nicaragua en busca de su identidad*, ed. Frances Kinloch Tijerino, 381–401. Managua: IHN-UCA, 1995.

Roediger, David R. *The Wages of Whiteness: Race and the Making of the American Working Class*. Rev. ed. New York: Verso, 1999.

Rojas, Margarita, Margarita Tórrez, and José Antonio Fernández. "Acceso a la tierra y actividades económicas en cinco comunidades del occidente nicaragüense, el censo de 1883." *Revista de Historia* (Nicaragua), nos. 3–4 (1994): 21–31.

Romero Vargas, Germán. *Las estructuras sociales de Nicaragua en el siglo XVIII*. Managua: Vanguardia, 1988.

———. "La presencia africana en el Pacífico y el Centro de Nicaragua." *Revista Wani* 13 (1992): 20–34.

———. *Las sociedades del Atlántico en Nicaragua en los siglos XVII y XVIII*. Managua: Fondo de Promoción Cultural–BANIC, 1995.

Romero Vargas, Germán, Flor de Oro Solórzano, Mario Rizo Zeledón, Marcos Membreño Idiáquez, Alessandra Castegnaro de Foletti, Jeanette Avilés C., and Betty Muñoz. *Persistencia indígena en Nicaragua*. Managua: CIDCA-UCA, 1992.

Roseberry, William. "Beyond the Agrarian Question in Latin America." In *Confronting Historical Paradigms: Peasant, Labor, and the Capitalist World System in Africa and Latin America*, ed. Frederick Cooper, Allen F. Isaacman, Florencia E. Mallon, William Roseberry and Steven J. Stern, 318–70. Madison: University of Wisconsin Press, 1993.

Sahlins, Peter. *Boundaries: The Making of France and Spain in the Pyrenes.* Berkeley: University of California Press, 1989.

Salvatierra, Sofonías. *Máximo Jerez inmortal, comentario polémico.* Managua: Tip. Progreso, 1950.

Schoonover, Thomas D. *The United States in Central America: Episodes of Social Imperialism and Imperial Rivalry in the World System.* Durham NC: Duke University Press, 1991.

Schoonover, Thomas D., and Ebba Schoonover. "Statistics for an Understanding of Foreign Intrusions into Central America from the 1820s to 1930: Part III." *Anuario de Estudios Centroamericanos* 17, no. 2 (1991): 77–119.

Schroeder, Michael J. "Horse Thieves to Rebels to Dogs: Political Gang Violence and the State in the Western Segovias, Nicaragua, in the Time of Sandino, 1926–1934." *Journal of Latin American Studies* 28 (1996): 383–434.

———. "'To Defend Our Nation's Honor': Toward a Social and Cultural History of the Sandino Rebellion in Nicaragua, 1927–1934." PhD diss., University of Michigan, 1993.

Scott, James. *Weapons of the Weak: Everyday Forms of Peasant Resistance.* New Haven: Yale University Press, 1985.

Scott, Joan Wallach. "A Statistical Representation of Work: *La statistique de l'industrie à Paris, 1847–1848.*" In *Gender and the Politics of History,* 113–38. New York: Columbia University Press, 1988.

Scroggs, William O. *Filibusters and Financiers: The Story of William Walker and His Associates.* New York: Macmillan, 1916.

Seed, Patricia. "The Social Dimensions of Race: Mexico City, 1753." *Hispanic American Historical Review* 62, no. 4 (1982): 569–606.

Smith, Anthony D. *The Ethnic Origins of Nations.* Oxford: Basil Blackwell, 1986.

———. "The Origins of Nations." *Ethnic and Racial Studies* 12 (1989): 349–56.

———. *Theories of Nationalism.* 2nd ed. New York: Holmes & Meier, 1983.

Smith, Carol A., ed. *Guatemalan Indians and the State, 1540 to 1988.* Austin: University of Texas Press, 1990.

Stansifer, Charles L. "José Santos Zelaya: A New Look at Nicaragua's 'Liberal' Dictator." *Revista/Review Interamericana* 7 (1977): 468–85.

Stepan, Nancy. *The Hour of Eugenics: Race, Gender, and Nation in Latin America.* Ithaca: Cornell University Press, 1991.

Stevens, Donald F. *Origins of Instability in Early Republican Mexico.* Durham NC: Duke University Press, 1991.

Stoetzer, O. Carlos. *Karl Christian Friedrich Krause and His Influence in the Hispanic World*. Koln: Böhlau Verlag, 1998.

Stone, Samuel Z. *The Heritage of the Conquistadors: Ruling Classes in Central America from the Conquest to the Sandinistas*. Lincoln: University of Nebraska Press, 1990.

Stutzman, Ronald. "*El Mestizaje*: An All-Inclusive Ideology of Exclusion." In *Cultural Transformations and Ethnicity in Modern Ecuador*, ed. Norman E. Whitten Jr., 45–93. Urbana: University of Illinois Press, 1981.

Sullivan-González, Douglass. *Piety, Power, and Politics: Religion and Nation Formation in Guatemala, 1821–1871*. Pittsburgh: University of Pittsburgh Press, 1998.

Taracena Arriola, Arturo. "El vocabulo 'Ladino' en Guatemala (S. XVI–XIX)." In *Historia y antropología de Guatemala: Ensayos en honor de J. Daniel Contreras R.*, ed. Jorge Luján Muñoz, 89–104. Guatemala: Universidad de San Carlos, 1982.

Téllez Argüello, Dora María. *¡Muera la gobierna! Colonización en Matagalpa y Jinotega (1820–1890)*. Managua: Universidad de las Regiones Autómas de la Costa Caribe Nicaragüense, 1999.

Teplitz, Benjamin I. "Political and Economic Foundations of Modernization in Nicaragua: The Administration of José Santos Zelaya, 1893–1909." PhD diss., Howard University, 1973.

Thurner, Mark. *From Two Republics to One Divided: Contradictions of Postcolonial Nationmaking in Andean Peru*. Durham NC: Duke University Press, 1997.

Tilly, Charles. *Coercion, Capital, and European States, AD 990–1992*. Cambridge MA.: Blackwell Press, 1992.

———. "War Making and State Making as Organized Crime." In *Bringing the State Back In*, ed. Peter Evans, Dietrich Reschemeyer, and Theda Skocpol, 169–91. Boulder CO: Westview Press, 1985.

Tompson, Douglas A. "Frontiers of Identity: The Atlantic Coast and the Formation of Honduras and Nicaragua, 1786–1894." PhD diss., University of Florida, 2001.

Torres-Rivas, Edelberto. *History and Society in Central America*. Trans. Douglass Sullivan-González. Austin: University of Texas Press, 1993.

Troy, Floyd. *The Anglo-Spanish Struggle for Mosquitia*. Albuquerque: University of New Mexico Press, 1967.

Tutino, John. "Family Economies in Agrarian Mexico, 1750–1910." *Journal of Family History* 10, no. 3 (1985): 258–71.

Twinam, Ann. "The Negotiation of Honor: Elites, Sexuality, and Illegitimacy in Eighteenth-Century Spanish America." In *The Faces of Honor: Sex, Shame, and Violence in Colonial Latin America*, ed. Lyman L. Johnson and Sonya Lipsett-Rivera, 68–102. Albuquerque: University of New Mexico Press, 1998.

Urban, Greg, and Joel Sherzer, eds. *Nation-States and Indians in Latin America*. Austin: University of Texas Press, 1991.

Valle, Alfonso. *Los Somoza y la estirpe sangrienta*. Managua: Editorial La Hora, 1959.

Van Cott, Donna Lee. "A Political Analysis of Legal Pluralism in Bolivia and Colombia." *Journal of Latin American Studies* 32, no. 1 (2000): 207–34.

Vargas, Oscar-René. *Floreció al filo de la espada: El movimiento de Sandino, 1926–1939*. Managua: Centro de Estudios de la Realidad Nacional, 1995.

———. *La revolución que inició el progreso: Nicaragua (1893–1909)*. Managua: Centro de Investigación y Desarrollo ECOTEXTURA, 1990.

Velázquez, José Luis. *La formación del estado en Nicaragua*. Managua: Fondo Editorial Banco Central de Nicaragua, 1992.

Vijil, Francisco. *El Padre Vijil: Su vida*. Granada: El Centro-Americano, 1930.

Vilas, Carlos M. "Family Affairs: Class, Lineage, and Politics in Contemporary Nicaragua." *Journal of Latin American Studies* 24, no. 2 (1992): 309–41.

———. "El sujeto social de la insurrección popular: La Revolución Sandinista." *Latin American Research Review* 20, no. 1 (1985): 119–47.

Wade, Peter. *Blackness and Race Mixture: The Dynamics of Racial Identity in Colombia*. Baltimore: Johns Hopkins University Press, 1993.

———. *Race and Ethnicity in Latin America*. London: Pluto Press, 1997.

Walter, Knut. *The Regime of Anastasio Somoza*. Chapel Hill: University of North Carolina Press, 1993.

Warren, Kay B. *Indigenous Movements and Their Critics: Pan-Maya Activism in Guatemala*. Princeton: Princeton University Press, 1998.

———. *The Symbolism of Subordination: Indian Identity in a Guatemalan Town*. Austin: University of Texas Press, 1978.

Watanabe, John M. "Enduring Yet Ineffable Community in the Western Periphery of Guatemala." In *Guatemalan Indians and the State, 1540 to 1988*, ed. Carol A. Smith, 183–204. Austin: University of Texas Press, 1990.

Weber, Eugen. *Peasants into Frenchmen: The Modernization of Rural France*. London: Chatto and Windus, 1977.

Wheelock Román, Jaime. *Imperialismo y dictadura: Crisis de una formación social*. México: Siglo XXI, 1979.

———. *Raíces indígenas de la lucha anticolonialista en Nicaragua*. México: Siglo XXI, 1976.

Williams, Brackette F. "A Class Act: Anthropology and the Race to Nation across Ethnic Terrain." *Annual Review of Anthropology* 18 (1989): 401–44.

———. *Stains on My Name, War in My Veins: Guyana and the Politics of Cultural Struggle.* Durham NC: Duke University Press, 1991.

Williams, Robert G. *States and Social Evolution: Coffee and the Rise of National Governments in Central America.* Chapel Hill: University of North Carolina Press, 1994.

Wolf, Eric R. "Closed Corporate Communities in Mesoamerica and Central Java." *Southwestern Journal of Anthropology* 13 (1957): 1–18.

Wolfe, Justin. "Rising from the Ashes: Community, Ethnicity, and Nation-State Formation in Nineteenth-Century Nicaragua." PhD diss., University of California, Los Angeles, 1999.

———. "Those That Live by the Work of Their Hands: Labour, Ethnicity, and Nation-State Formation in Nicaragua, 1850–1900." *Journal of Latin American Studies* 36, no. 1 (2004): 57–83.

Woodward, Ralph Lee, Jr. *Central America: A Nation Divided.* Oxford: Oxford University Press, 1985.

———, ed. *Positivism in Latin America, 1850–1900.* Lexington MA: Heath, 1971.

Wortman, Miles. *Government and Society in Central America, 1680–1840.* New York: Columbia University Press, 1982.

———. "Government Revenue and Economic Trends in Central America, 1787–1819." *Hispanic American Historical Review* 55, no. 2 (1975): 251–86.

Wünderich, Volker. *Sandino: Una biografía política.* Managua: Editorial Nueva Nicaragua, 1995.

Zea, Leopoldo. *Apogeo y decadencia del positivismo en México.* México: El Colegio de México, 1944.

———. *El positivismo en México.* México: El Colegio de México, 1943.

Zelaya G., Chester J. *Nicaragua en la independencia.* San José: Editorial Universitaria Centroamericana, 1971.

Zúñiga C., Edgar. *Historia eclesiástica de Nicaragua.* Managua: Editorial Union, 1981.

Index